Applied Child Study

A Developmental Approach

Applied Child Study

A Developmental Approach

3rd Edition

Anthony D. Pellegrini
University of Minnesota

David F. Bjorklund
Florida Atlantic University

LAWRENCE ERLBAUM ASSOCIATES, PUBLISHERS
1998   Mahwah, New Jersey   London

Lawrence Erlbaum Associates, Inc., Publishers
10 Industrial Avenue
Mahwah, NJ 07430

Cover design by Kathryn Houghtaling Lacey

Library of Congress Cataloging-in-Publication Data

Pellegrini, Anthony D.
Applied child study : a developmental approach / Anthony D. Pellegrini, David F. Bjorklund. — 3rd ed.
p. cm.
Includes bibliographical references and indexes.
ISBN 0-8058-2756-0 (hardcover : alk. paper). — ISBN 0-8058-2757-9 (pbk. : alk. paper)
1. Child psychology.   2. Child psychology—Methodology.
3. Child development.   I. Bjorklund, David F., 1949–   .   II. Title.
BF721.P366   1998
305.231—dc21   98-11806
                                                            CIP

Books published by Lawrence Erlbaum Associates are printed on acid-free paper, and their bindings are chosen for strength and durability.

Printed in the United States of America
10 9 8 7 6 5 4 3 2 1

Contents

Acknowledgments

This book is now in its third edition, something I clearly did not anticipate when I began the project many years ago. As in most developmental processes, much has changed in each of the volumes. For one thing, this edition has two authors. Each of us brings to the volume complementary strengths, yet we each share the view that children are unique developmental beings and that good practice with children should be guided by sound theory and research.

This edition, as past editions, has been improved by comments of students and colleagues who have used the book in undergraduate and graduate child study courses. Most notably, the following people have either read chapters or extended our understanding of issues discussed in this book: John Evans, Lee Galda, David Lancy, Peter Smith, Brian Sutton-Smith. They, of course, are not responsible for limitations in this work.

Our work on this book has been supported by the Institute for Behavioral Research (University of Georgia), the School of Education of the University of Cardiff, and a grant from the W T Grant Foundation.

Applied Child Study

A Developmental Approach

1

Applied Child Study:
An Introduction

This book is meant to serve as a source for the varied group of professionals who work with children. This group includes researchers, parents, educators, pediatricians, nurses, social workers, and child psychologists. In short, the book is written for those interested in examining and describing children as well as those interested in creating educational environments for children. As such, this book outlines different ways in which children can be viewed.

Child study is a very complex field; human beings, and children, specifically, are very complex. Consequently, simple answers and solutions to problems are very often too simple. A short example helps make the point. Most of us have had the unfortunate experience of having problems with our car. We take the car to the mechanic and explain the problem. The mechanic diagnoses the problem and attempts to solve it. We get the car back, and very often the problem is still there! Why is this all-too-familiar example relevant? The reason is, compared to children, cars are VERY SIMPLE! If well-trained professionals have difficulty with this relatively simple entity, think of the difficulty involved in "figuring out" children, who are vastly more complex than even the most complex car.

Our best hope for gaining insight into children and their worlds is through the systematic study of the varied contexts in which they live and function. This is best accomplished through training in a variety of methods following the scientific method. After a phenomenon is recognized, we should generate hypotheses, or educated hunches, that we think might be causing or related to the phenomenon. These hunches should then be tested, systematically, until we arrive at a satisfactory answer. Furthermore, seemingly similar phenomena may have different causes and consequences with different children, thus the process should be repeated under slightly varying conditions.

Our message, in short, is that there are very few simple answers and solutions to working with children. Indeed, we are skeptical of such simple answers. Your best guide in the venture of working with children is an understanding of theory and methods in child study. This book provides that basis.

Our underlying belief is that sound theory and empirical research are needed to guide effective work with children. Consequently, this book is organized such that different theories and methods for studying children are presented. Our aim is provide students with a repertoire of theoretical and research skills that will be useful in their work. Students should view the theories and methods as a "tool kit" that can be applied to various situations.

Another underlying basis of this book is its "developmental orientation," which assumes that children are qualitatively different from adults: They see the world in ways different from adults. Some of the best, and most common, examples of this qualitative difference between children and adults come from Piaget. For example, children have difficulty looking at a problem from a number of perspectives. So when we ask a question about which two arrays of sticks is greater in number, spatial arrangement of those items affects children's answers more directly than answers given by adults.

Correspondingly, we do not assume that these developmental differences between children and adults are deficits. We assume that these characteristics have evolved in direct response to the demands of childhood. In other words, there is good reason for children to be as they are: They are not merely imperfect adults. The notion of development is explicitly addressed in the next chapter.

In writing each chapter we tried to stress the skills necessary to describe children and ways in which different situations, or contexts, affect children and the theories underlying all this. An assumption of this book is that we need both objective ways of studying children and good theories of child development to make sense of our observations. Such theoretical descriptions, in turn, are necessary before we can design environments and programs that will optimally facilitate children's development. Thus, description, theory, and application are seen as interdependent processes necessary to study and work with children.

This book is organized to reflect this orientation. We discuss a number of current theories of child development and learning as well as a number of different methods of studying children, because there are currently several feasible theories to explain children's behavior and thinking in any given domain. The observer should examine each theory critically and decide what is the most relevant for his or her purposes. Too often textbooks adhere to only one theory, either implicitly or explicitly. This leaves the naive reader with the assumption that the theory being discussed is not a theory but truth. The history of science generally (Kuhn, 1962), and the history of child psychology specifically, indicates that theories wax and wane no matter how entrenched they may be at any one time.

Readers of this text will, hopefully, see the relative merits of different theories and support the theories in light of their observations of children's behavior. An important test of a theory, of course, is its ability to account for what children do; that is, do children act the way a theory predicts? Additionally, students with an interest in applied issues have an additional requirement for a theory: the extent to which the theory can be used to change children's and caretakers' behavior and thinking in applied settings. In short, theories are needed to help us explain the phenomena we study and to apply that knowledge.

The interdependence of theory as part of the "basic" scientific venture of studying children cannot, from our perspective, be divorced from the contexts they inhabit. That is, children's behaviors probably evolved in response to and in order to affect the contexts in which they live. As is discussed in more detail in chapter 3, this interdependence between context and behavior necessitates that we consider them in concert. This orientation is basic to certain constructs such as "adaptation" and "everyday cognition."

Such an "everyday" approach to child study is useful, then, because it helps us understand the ways in which children *do* develop and grow to the extent that children are embedded in multiple contexts. Knowledge gained from the study of children who develop optimally in different contexts can then be used to design specific programs.

A *number* of different methodologies are also reviewed. We also stress "number" here because we are convinced that there is no one best method by which to study children. As noted earlier, the venture is much too complex to be adequately addressed by one method, so different methods are used to answer different questions. Questions, in turn, are determined by our theories. Thus, unity is necessary to correctly study children: Specific theories assume specific questions and methods; again, however, the choice of a method and corresponding theory should be grounded in the ability of the theory to explain children in their everyday contexts.

An important point to be made here is that different methods have different theoretical assumptions. Our assumptions of children and the worlds in which they live should be made explicit through theoretical statements, which should then guide our study of children to the extent that our methods of studying children and designing environments for them are consistent with our assumptions.

As the reader can infer, there are no "quick fixes" in child study. It is a laborious process with no quick or certain answers. Answers are only as meaningful as the theories and data collection methods that are used to answer the questions; as such, this book does not provide answers to questions such as:

How do I discipline and teach my children? It does provide answers relevant to questions about studying children's behaviors and learning. The reader will then have to apply his or her preferred theory to the observations to tests those answers. Answers to specific questions, such as discipline methods, therefore, are provided only after the student observes children, generates hypotheses, and then tests the hypotheses. The student trying to answer such practical questions uses similar procedures to those employed by a researcher studying children. The reason we have chosen this analytic approach to child study is really very simple. Children and the contexts they live in are very complex and often unique. No one writing a book can reasonably provide answers for discipline or learning problems that he or she knows little or nothing about. Further, professionals working with children, such as teachers, clinicians, nurses, and physicians, should and can be given the opportunity to design programs they feel are best for their group of children. This goal can be accomplished only through systematic child study. In short, this book should help you engage in the enterprise of the scientific study of children in applied settings. The theories and methods presented should be judged useful to the extent that they explain children's behavior in your specific situation.

The book should be used as a source that outlines, in an objective way, different theories of development/learning and different methodologies; the decision on how to collect and interpret data will be left to the reader. Thus, the dichotomy between research and practice should be replaced by an orientation of using research to solve everyday, or practical, problems.

WHAT IS CHILD STUDY?

Child study starts with working with children. First we try to understand the ways in which they develop, grow, and learn in their everyday habitats. This knowledge is then used to design environments for children. Various theories attempt to explain the meaning of children's behavior and development, provide different methods of collecting child data, and show how intervening in children's lives can facilitate optimal development. By its very nature, therefore, child study is interdisciplinary. In this volume we draw from theory and research in fields ranging, literally, from anthropology to zoology.

This interdisciplinary approach to child study makes the field stronger because children are viewed from many different perspectives. Indeed, an interdisciplinary approach is necessary to understand the complex behavior of children. For example, we need the zoologist's orientation to understand the ontogenetic phylogenetic histories of children.

All of these disciplines attempt to draw pictures of children at different levels of specificity. Some psychologists attempt to describe the normative behavior of children. The best example of such a normative description of behavior can be found in Piaget's (1970) stage theory. These stages are said to describe children independent of their cultural histories. Thus, this is a universalistic description of behavior. Such an approach to child study also assumes specific methods by which children can be studied. Typically, psychologists have a specific theory about children and they design tests or experiments to elicit behaviors relevant to the theory. Observed behaviors are used as the data for inferences about children's competence. More recently, however, such normative descriptions have often embedded children in various contexts that affect development (e.g., Bronfenbrenner, 1979; Laboratory of Comparative Human Cognition [LCHC], 1983).

Anthropologists and ethologists are more concerned with cultural and environmental effects on behavior. That is, they believe that the environments and the people who live in them are interdependent; they affect each other. As such, children from different environments will behave differently. Such researchers typically spend a great deal of time describing the contexts in which children are being studied because it is those contexts, they believe, that elicit children's behaviors. The method of child study followed by this group of researchers is often naturalistic to the extent to which children are studied in their everyday environments.

In short, the question "What is child study?" can be answered thus: Child study describes children and the various contexts in which they interact.

FUNCTIONS OF CHILD STUDY

Why should we study children?

At the most general level, child study serves the function of describing children in various situations. Child study can provide normative pictures of children at different ages and in different situations and how they develop, grow, and learn. General pictures can be drawn of different groups of children by their responses to test items and their behavior in different environments. Child psychologists and developmental psychologists often engage in this type of child study, as they are most interested in objectively describing children. They are minimally interested, however, in the applications of the descriptions. Educational psychologists and educators are most interested in making practical applications of child study. Applications of child study are often related to designing environments that facilitate children's learning/development. To engage in this venture, however, we must first objectively describe children in the target environments. This description phase is critical in order to understand the aspects of behavior to be studied and to form hypotheses, or theories, about what causes what, and such hypotheses should then be tested. Only after the hypotheses have been tested and supported can we apply our knowledge of children to the actual designing of facilitative environments.

Child study can be used in applied settings as an important part of the school curriculum or program implementation cycle. A basic assumption is that knowledge of children should provide the basis on which programs are developed. A program, or curriculum, is a plan of actions and environments to which children are exposed in order to bring about desired changes in them. For example, a preschool language program might outline student and teacher activities designed to stimulate children's communicative competence. The program implementation cycle involves the following stages: diagnosis of children's need, program design, program implementation, and evaluation of program. Child study is a necessary part of each of the components of this cycle. The first, or diagnostic, phase consists of the analysis and description of the current state of the children in the program. If we are interested in children's ability to use language as a communicative tool (i.e., communicative competence), we must determine children's level of expertise with this tool. This can be accomplished through a number of child study techniques: diagnostic testing, observations, and interviews. This phase of the program implementation cycle therefore, provides baseline, or beginning, data on the children. Again, we should make sure that the diagnostic procedures used are appropriate for the children that are being studied. For example, is the procedure part of the way in which they are expected to use language at home? Are the stimulus materials, examiners, and examination room familiar to the child?

The second phase, program design, involves testing of an intervention process that will affect children's behaviors. Theory becomes particularly important at this stage, because theories of language development suggest ways in which children's communicative competence can be facilitated. The researcher should design an experimental environment following a particular theory in order to facilitate communicative competence. The particular environment chosen should also be relevant to the particular type of children in the program, such as Native Americans. As noted earlier our job is to establish a bridge from the children's everyday context to intervention contexts such as schools or clinics. After programs are tested systematically and shown to be effective they may be implemented.

Implementation of a program, the third phase, also uses child study techniques. Very often the program implemented is very different from the actual program designed. As a result, child study techniques such as observation are necessary to determine the extent to which the program guidelines are being followed.

The last phase is the evaluation of the program's effectiveness in the specific context. This phase of the cycle answers the question: Did the program have its intended effects? The intended effects often are indicated in terms of improved test scores, behavioral changes, or both. We should take care, however, to ensure that the changes do indeed occur in the contexts in which they were intended and are maintained. For example, does a nutrition program for children affect their choice of snacks in the cafeteria? Are these food preferences maintained after the program is completed? Child study is certainly germane to this stage. In short, child study can help us improve the environments in which children live; it can help us help them realize their potential.

ETHICAL CONSIDERATIONS IN CHILD STUDY

When we engage in the enterprise of child study we must consider the ethical implications of our work. The American Psychological Association has long been concerned with the ethical problems in psychology. This concern has resulted in a document entitled "Ethical Principles of Psychologists." Although this document was written for psychologists, it is relevant for all of us working with children. For that reason, we highlight some of its relevant points. Principles that should be followed are:

1. *Responsibility:* Professionals should take responsibility for the consequences of their actions; their services should be used appropriately.
2. *Competence:* Professionals should recognize their area of competence and their limitations.
3. *Moral and legal standards:* Professionals should be sensitive to community and professional standards of behavior.
4. *Public statements:* Statements about one's work should be made to help the public make informed choices and judgments.
5. *Confidentiality:* Information acquired in the course of one's work should be kept confidential unless the consent of the involved parties is obtained.
6. *Welfare of the consumer:* Professionals should protect the people with whom they work.
7. *Professional relationships:* Professionals should respect the needs and competence of other professionals.
8. *Assessment techniques:* Professionals should promote the welfare and children and families by guarding against the misuse of assessment results.
9. *Research with human participants:* Participants, their parents, or both should be well informed as to the intent of a research project.

An example of a consent form is given in Fig. 1.1.

ORGANIZATION OF THE BOOK

The book is organized to guide the reader through our most basic assumptions first.

In chapter 2 we address the construct of "development" and the ways in which it is crucial to our understanding of children. In chapter 3, we outline the interdependence between behavior and context. As noted earlier, we believe that behavior must be studied in the context in which it occurs in order to gain the most thorough understanding.

Chapters 4 through 7 all address methods for studying children. In chapters 4 and 5 methods that "elicit" information from children by placing them in contrived, or analog, situations (tests and experiments, respectively) are discussed. In chapters 6 and 7 more naturalistic methods (direct observation and ethology and interpretive methods, respectively) are outlined. The positive and negative dimensions of each method are presented so that you can decide the usefulness of the appropriateness of each method. We stress the fact that each method is used to address specific issues. A method is not good or bad; it is more or less appropriate for answering a specific question in a specific setting.

I give consent for my child, _____, to partici-pate in the research entitled Children's Vigorous Play and Social Development being conducted by Dr. A. D. Pellegrini. I understand that this participation is entirely voluntary; I or my child can withdraw consent at any time and have the results of this participation returned to be, removed from the experimental records, or destroyed.

The following points have been explained to me and my child:

1. The reason for research is: to describe the development of children's play and how it relates to their social development.
2. The procedure is as follows: Children will be observed monthly while they play at recess. They will, twice yearly, fill out friendship nomination forms. Each year teachers will rate children's social behavior in class.
3. No discomfort or stress is involved.
4. There will be no risks to the children. They will always be supervised.
5. The results of the participation will be confidential and will not be released in any individually identifiable form without prior consent unless required by law.
6. The investigator will answer any further questions about the research, either now or during the course of the project.

_____   _____

Signature of Investigator   Signature of Parent(s) or
                                                               Guardian(s)

_____

Date

PLEASE SIGN BOTH COPIES. KEEP ONE AND RETURN THE OTHER TO THE INVESTIGATOR.

FIG. 1.1.   Sample consent form.

In chapters 8 through 11 we discuss specific domains of children's development. In chapters 8 and 9, respectively, children's cognitive and linguistic processes are discussed. The discussions in each chapter focus not only on the development of these processes but also on children's cognitive and linguistic functioning in school. In chapter 10 social competence is discussed. Both basic and applied aspects of social competence are addressed, and we stress the ways in which children's social competence is crucial in their school experience. Finally, in chapter 11 children's play is discussed. A separate chapter is dedicated to play because it is the quintessential childhood behavior. In order to understand children we must understand their play.

2

What is *Developmental*?

The orientation of this book is *developmental*, a term used in many different ways by those of us interested in children. Most basically, the term applied has its origins in biology. Recall that Piaget was, first, a biologist. The construct *development* is also of interest to those of us interested in human development, psychology, and education. Even at the level of statewide educational policy, the notion of development is evoked: Some states have developmental kindergartens, classrooms for children not promoted to first grade from kindergarten.

Development is also used in terms of curricula and evaluation procedures for children as being "developmentally appropriate" (National Association for the Education of Young Children [NAEYC],1988). Here development means that curriculum and evaluation procedures should be congruent with the children's level of competence. For example, in the area of evaluation, because preschool and kindergarten children's test-taking motivation is highly variable (e.g., affected by the gender, race, or both of the tester) more naturalistic approaches of evaluation (e.g., observation of behavior) are developmentally appropriate for this period.

It should be clear that the term *developmental* has broad and disparate uses. In this chapter we discuss development as it applies to children. We begin our discussion with two very different models of development. The first, and probably more familiar, considers the child an unfinished or incomplete adult. This view is represented in the theories of Piaget and Vygotsky. The second view considers each developmental period to be valuable for that specific time. "Childish" behaviors are not considered to be imperfect, but important responses to the niche of childhood. This view is represented in the theories of Bateson and Kagan. These different views of development have obvious implications for the ways in which we interact with children and the parameters specified in this discussion, we hope, should be used to guide our interactions with children.

VIEWS OF DEVELOPMENT

There are at least two views of development. Each of these views presents the child in very different lights in terms of their competence and what is expected of them. For these reasons, each of these views has very important implications for the ways in which we interact with children.

Development as a Continuous Process Toward the Finished Product of Adulthood

Probably the more common view of development for those of us working with children is that presented by theorists such as Vygotsky and Piaget. In each of these theories, development is considered to be a continuous path toward the outcome of adulthood. Most developmental theories under this heading consider the existence the an extended period of childhood in terms of training for adulthood (Bruner, 1972). Thus children's behavior is understood in terms of adult behavior. The child behaviors are usually framed in terms of their deficiency vis-à-vis adults (e.g., preoperational thought is deficient relative to formal operational thought) behaviors and how early behaviorists contribute to more mature behaviors (children's behaviors become "transformed" into mature behaviors).

In Piaget's terms, the end point is formal operational thought. The thought of preschool children is thus considered to be a "less developed" than formal operational thought or merely a means to the end of operational thought. It is the job of the developmentalist to chart the course from infancy and early childhood through adolescence to adulthood. Typically, and as exemplified by Piaget's model, one developmental pathway is specified.

The educational implications of this view are that we present children with materials and activities at their "developmentally appropriate" levels, but the importance of these tasks is considered in terms of the ways in which they contribute to operational thought. Further, we often consider the specified pathways as the only ways in which children can reach desired outcomes. For example, we may think that all children must engage in symbolic play if they are to develop into competent adults. Alternative pathways to competence are not typically considered.

Related to the notion of continuous progress toward adulthood is the stress on early experiences. If development is continuous, the argument goes, disturbances in the early processes should have important, and sometimes irreversible, effects. It is these early experiences on which subsequent development is based.

Viewing of infancy and early childhood as "critical periods" (to be discussed here later) is an example of this perspective.

Development in the Niche of Childhood

Alternatively, developmental processes can be viewed as responses to the specific demands of specific niches in development, such as childhood. Thus specific behaviors such as egocentric responses and pretend play are not viewed as immature versions of adult behavior but as adaptive responses to the special needs of the niche of childhood. Take the example of very young children's limited locomotor capabilities. These could be viewed in immature, unfinished terms or it could be viewed as adaptive in that this limited mobility results in children staying closer to their caregivers (D. F. Bjorklund & Green, 1992).

Educationally, this stance also stresses the need for "developmentally appropriate" practice, but emphasis is placed on the role of these activities for the specific needs of childhood, rather than as preparation for adulthood.

This view of development also has implications for our views on the continuity of developmental pathways. Accordingly, this view suggests that individual children may take many different pathways to developmental competence in different periods (Kagan, 1980). There is no one royal road to competence. The road taken is a result of children's individual differences and a result of different niches. We discuss implications of this view for "critical periods" later. Suffice it to say for now that we have two views of development: one stressing the child as an incomplete version adults, the other viewing childhood as having its own integrity. Correspondingly, the behaviors and cognitions characteristic of childhood have value for that period. Because of the importance of our conceptions of development in working with children, we further discuss some crucial dimensions of development. First we want to dispel some common misconceptions of development.

"Outmoded" Concepts in Development

In order to more clearly understand what development is, first we should consider what it isn't. That some of these misconceptions are still held require that we dispel them. If we do not there is danger that practice may be based on such incorrect assumptions. These outmoded concepts of development, as specified by (Gottlieb, 1983), have not been able to withstand the scrutiny of specific inquiry. The first, and probably most often encountered is the notion that ontogeny (or within-species development) recapitulates phylogeny (or across-species development or evolution) This concept, popularized by Hall (1916), suggests that the development of human beings (i.e., ontogeny) repeats the evolutionary path of *homo sapiens* (phylogeny): "Ontogeny recapitulates ontogeny."

For example, the presence of gills in human embryos is considered a repetition of part of our phylogenetic history when animals lived in water. Similarly, the tree climbing and war play of preschool children was said to be a recapitulation of our primate and hunter/gatherer histories, respectively. There is some value in this outmoded theory, however. It points out the fact that humans do seem to develop through a series of stages in a specific order (a topic to be addressed under Basic Concepts) and that stages are *qualitatively* different from each other

The logic of Hall (1916) and his intellectual forebear Haechel (cited in Gottlieb, 1983), needs to be inverted, however. That is, phylogeny seems to be affected by ontogeny to the extent that developmental changes within the individual may affect evolution (Gottlieb, 1983). The ways in which individuals develop, successfully or unsuccessfully, will have an impact on the way in which individuals in the future develop: Individuals utilizing successful practices will pass those on (through their genes and through their practices) to future generations.

The second outmoded concept is that nature (or a genetic endowment) and nurture (or the environment in which we live) have independent affects on behavior and learning. For example, common knowledge may hold that height is determined by nature (or one's genetic endowment),whereas social skills are determined by environment, or nurture. In truth, nature and nurture are inextricably linked. In the case of the aforementioned examples, height is affected by environmental factors, such as the mother's diet during pregnancy whereas social skills can have a biological component (as in the case of children's temperament).

Although a dichotomy between nature and nurture is simplistic it is useful to recognize that children's behaviors can be placed in a continuum from those that are environmentally stable (implying a strong genetic component, such as infant's crying when in pain) to those that are more labile (implying an environmental affect, such as ability to read; Hinde, 1983). As such, we should recognize that all behavior has environmental and genetic components. One's genetic endowment seems to set possible limits on development. The realization of the endowment interacts with the environment.

Thus, it is more accurate to think of nature and nurture as influencing each other. Individuals with certain biological traits (which, we stress, are malleable) seek out and construct specific environments, or niches. In this way individuals affect their environments. Relatedly, the specific dimensions of an environment also affect individuals. Take the example of a physically active child. We know that physical activity, like other dimensions of temperament, has a biological component, yet its expression is limited or facilitated by the environment. This active child chooses play environments, usually ones that enable him (active children are more typically boys than girls) to run around and make noise. In the course of things, he changes the environment by moving and rearranging equipment and possibly by convincing an adult to let him do certain things.

Additionally, this environment's enforced rules and availability of props and space affect his behavior.

A good example of the way in which biological and environmental influences on behavior have been artificially, and simplistically dichotomized can be drawn for current discussions of attention deficit hyperactivity disorder (ADHD). ADHD has been defined, albeit inconsistently, as being composed of two constructs: hyperactivity and inattention. Currently many children, most of whom are boys, are diagnosed as suffering from these problems and these children generally do very poorly in school (A. D. Pellegrini & Horvat, 1995). The syndrome "appears" when children enter formal schooling. It is considered to have a biological origin (it was originally labeled minimal brain disfunction) and is treated organically, with drugs.

As noted earlier, physical activity does have a biological, and heritable, component. But the extent to which children are functional or dysfunctional is also related to the context in which they are expected to function. Is it accidental that active children—again, usually boys—are considered a problem when they enter an institution dominated by those who value sedentary behavior? Would these children be less attentive or active if they were in a classroom that had them interacting with peers and moving around the class to learning centers? Again, human behavior is much too complicated to proffer simplistic solutions.

A third, and related, outmoded concept of development is that of the maturation versus experience dichotomy. Maturation is typically applied to processes that are unaffected by environmental, or experiential, factors and are stable across time (Hinde, 1983). Stability, however, can be and usually is due to both maturational and experiential factors. For example, intelligence has both maturational and experiential components. Intelligence obviously depends on the maturation of the brain and the nervous system. These systems, of course, develop in the content of some experiential context. Thus the stability of intelligence will be a function of both maturation processes as well as stability of the environment. Both of these factors influence stability and stable environments result in stable behaviors.

Thus, like the nature–nurture discussion, it is incorrect, and much too simplistic, to dichotomize maturation and experience. Current views of development present the individual and the environment as *transactional*; that is, organism and environment influence each other.

Current Views of Development

Now that we know what development is not, it is time to consider what we think it is. These principals are drawn, primarily, from current research in developmental psychology (Gottlieb, 1983) and ethology (Hinde, 1983).

The first concept of development is that of *forward reference* or the preadapted quality of newborns (Gottlieb, 1983). That is, some behaviors of newborns, such as the sucking or grasping reflex, are present prenatally so as to maximize the probability of early survival. Sucking is necessary for feeding and grasping for maintaining proximity to caregivers. These behaviors are present prenatally and continue during the neonatal period to maximize survival. In short, this principle describes the continuity across the perinatal period.

A second current concept of development is that of *differentiation and hierarchical organization.* This concept states that organs and organisms undergo differentiation as they move from homogeneous (i.e., relatively undifferentiated and simple states) to heterogeneous (i.e., differentiated and more complex) states. The concept can be and has been applied to the development at the organ level (e.g., reproductive organs) and at the organism level. At the latter level children's motor skills, such as the ability to use one's fingers, become more differentiated with age (see Connolly & Elliot, 1972), as does their interaction with the environment; for example, children initially will explore new environments only in the presence of mothers, and later they explore new environments, albeit cautiously, independently

The third concept is that of *optimum stage* or *critical/sensitive periods.* This concept, in its strong form (i.e., critical period), holds that there are certain periods in development that are critical to development of specific behaviors. For example, there seems to be an optimal period to learn language (see chapter 9). The evidence here shows that children and prepubescent youngsters learn language quite easily. Not only is language learning more difficult after this time, but the brain is less capable of using alternative structures in language learning after puberty. Thus if language is to be learned it must be done during this time. Similarly, languages can be most effectively taught to children beginning at a young age.

An equally familiar example of the critical period hypothesis comes from the attachment literature. Early theory held that if infants did not securely attach to the mothers they would suffer from subsequent personality anomalies (see Bowlby, 1969, for a thorough review). The critical period hypothesis was based on Lorenz's (1935, cited in Hinde, 1983) imprinting experiments with birds, wherein young birds would learn to respond to a moving object as they would a parent within the first hours of life. This process was thought to be irreversible; thus the notion of critical stage.

Subsequent research has shown that adverse conditions encountered during those critical periods were indeed reversible; thus the notion of sensitive, rather than critical, period. For example, the effects of maternal deprivation during a critical period can be remediated in later life through exposure to younger peers (Suomi & Harlow, 1972). The sensitive hypothesis can, and has, been applied to an important aspect of child study—infant day care. Currently, there is debate over the long-term effects of day care on children while they are infants. The sensitive period hypothesis holds that a sensitive period for attachment exists; this attachment is hypothesized to be the basis for subsequent social competence.

The fourth concept of development involves *individual differences*. This concept suggests that individual variations exist within a species. These differences in children, especially those in emotionality and mood, are often considered in terms of "temperament" Campos, Barrett, Lamb, Goldsmith, & Stenberg, 1983). For example, some boys may be physically active whereas others may be more sedentary. Individual differences are often thought to have biological components (e.g., they are related to certain hormones) and are stable across the life span. For example, a child's level of activity may be affected by prenatal factors, such as mother's level of tobacco and alcohol consumption, and factors within the child, such as the nature of the individual child's limbic system. The expression of these differences, however, is mediated by the environments in which children are raised. Differences will be exacerbated if children are encouraged to be active (e g, children reared in spacious and enriched environments) or limited if high levels of activity are not supported by the environment (e.g., children are reared under crowded and dangerous conditions).

As we discuss in later chapters, the notion of individuals' contributions to development also relate to natural selection. This sort of genetic variation is basic to natural selection. Certain gene and environment combinations result in organisms adaptation. Further, evolutionary psychologists suggest that we must consider individuals' contributions to development if we are to conceptualize "culture" as being creative rather than reproductive, or mere copying of preceding culture.

The fifth concept, sequence of behavior stages, suggests a regularity despite individual differences. Regularity relates to the specific sequence, or order, in which behaviors appear. As noted earlier, this proposition is part of the bias suggesting that development is continuous. This well-known concept is best illustrated in Piaget's (1970) theory of cognitive development wherein children progress from sensorimotor to preoperational to operational levels of intelligence. Although the ages may vary for each stage, they appear in the specified order. This stage sequence concept further incorporates the idea that stages are qualitatively different from each other. That is, experiences and concepts at Stage I are qualitatively different than similar phenomena at Stage 2. For example, a preoperational child's concept of the number five is different from that of a formal operational child to the extent that for the former this array (1 1 1 1 1) may be greater than this array (11111); they would be equal for the older child.

The sixth developmental concept relates to functional considerations (Hinde, 1983); that is, the use of specific behavior. Function can be considered at the level of reproductive fitness or in terms of beneficial consequences. Beneficial consequences are those outcomes of a specific behavior that are positive. For example, a beneficial consequence of an infant's smile might be that an adult approaches him.

Beneficial consequences of a behavior can be either immediate to the developmental period during which it is observed or deferred to a later period. Take the example of locomotor play during childhood. Immediate benefits of this activity could be muscle and cardiovascular fitness for that period. Alternatively, deferred benefits of locomotor play could be considered in terms of later skeletal development (Fagen, 1981).

The idea that a behavior, such as play, has immediate rather than deferred benefits is consistent with the view that development is an adaptation to the specific demands of a niche, such as childhood. The important point to stress here is that behavior may serve different functions at different periods of development. To use Hinde's (1983) simple but cogent example, caterpillars are superb leaf eaters, but not very good flyers; as butterflies, however, they become superb flyers. The lesson here is that we should not consider the function of a behavior in childhood in terms of adult status. The deferred benefits argument is consistent with the idea that childhood is a period of preparation for adulthood and those skills learned there will be useful for their functioning as adults.

The seventh and final developmental concept relates to discontinuity/continuity in development. Like developmental concepts five and six, this concept explores the extent to which behavior, traits, or skills are continuous, or stable, or discontinuous, or instable, across the life span; for example, is intelligence or temperament stable from infancy through childhood? This concept, in conjunction with the earlier concepts, is particularly important from an applied perspective to the extent that it informs us as to the relative importance of specific behavior/skills at specific periods. In this section we address this concept in detail because of its importance. This section is based on Kagan's (1971) discussion of the issue.

Although the aforementioned distinction is relevant to factors affecting development, the following discussion is relevant to aspects of development that are continuous or discontinuous. Continuity, or stability, in behavior may be endogenous (i. e., an internal process); for example, stable intelligence in a preschool child is responsible for the stability of his or her verbal ability across the preschool and primary school periods. Stability may also be exogenous, or external. For example, the aforementioned stability in verbal ability may be due primarily to a stable home environment rather than internal processes. Of course, we should keep in mind that such dichotomies between internal and external and nature and nurture are outmoded. The point to be made here, however, is that stability in development is affected by internal and external forces, probably working in conjunction.

In some cases continuity of very similar behaviors is observed across time, for example, a child may be very active during the infancy and preschool years.

In this *homotypic continuity,* we have very similar response modes across time, such as locomotion. Heterotypic continuity is more difficult to gauge to the extent that it involves the interrelation of different response modes across time. Although in different modes, heterotypic continuity can be established when the behaviors are theoretically related. For example, the ability to engage in make-believe play at 3 years of age is related to word reading at 5 years of age (Galda, Pellegrini, & Cox, 1989). In this case, make-believe play and word reading involve different response modes but are theoretically related to the extent that both involve the manipulation of symbolic representations.

Heterotypic continuity has rightfully been labeled "cryptic" by Kagan (1971)to the extent that discovering relations between *dissimilar* phenomena is akin to solving a puzzle or mystery. This is, however, the essence of "being developmental" in that there are qualitative changes, via transformations, across the life span. Our job is to try and chart them. Our map in this journey must be good developmental theory, only through which can we explain the relation between seemingly different sets of behaviors.

There are situations that provide clues to the solution of this mystery. Kagan (1971) listed principles that can be applied to detecting continuity or discontinuity. First, homotypic continuity is less common during the first 10 years of life than later. Specifically, there are two critical junctures during this period where heterotypic continuity is most likely to occur: 18 and 24 months of age and 5 to 7 years of age. During the first period, children's interactions with objects become dominated by their talking about them. In short, children move from concern with sensorimotor coordination to symbolic concern. The second period, 5 to 7 years of age, is marked by a qualitative change in children's cognitive functioning whereby children become more able to inhibit irrelevant acts and select appropriate ones, maintain a problem-solving set, and appreciate the requirements of a problem. In short, children become more reflective.

To conclude this section I have shown that a developmental approach involves conceptualizing children as qualitatively different from each other at different periods. They are certainly different from adults. In the applied realm, this translates into identifying those behaviors and skills that are typical for a particular stage or period. Again, in making the choice we should be aware that the criteria for such a choice is that it should be relevant for that period, *not* adulthood. The next step in our applied endeavor involves making the theoretical connection of behaviors and skills from one stage or period to another.

DEVELOPMENTAL CHILD STUDY

Developmental study generally takes one of two directions. First, there is the normative/descriptive type of work in which we describe children's behaviors and skills at various stages of continuity and discontinuity. That is, to what extent is Behavior A at Time 1 related to Behavior A (continuous development) or Behavior B (discontinuous development) at Time 2? Alternatively, to what degree are the benefits of a specific behavior unique to a period? Further, these studies often take place in children's natural environments—such as schools, hospitals, and homes—and are longitudinal; that is, they study the same children across time. They are not cross-sectional, and thus do not study different children at different ages. The second type of developmental study is experimental, not naturalistic. The motivation behind experimental studies of development is a search for *causality*. Causality, as it is discussed in the chapter on experiments, can be inferred by systematic manipulation and control of variables. For example, to address the critical/sensitive period issue discussed earlier, experimental studies have been used to determine the extent to which monkeys isolated from their mothers during infancy could later be rehabilitated (Suomi & Harlow, 1972). In this case exposure to mothers is manipulated.

Although such experimental manipulation allows us to begin to make causal inferences about specific relations, serious concerns have been raised about the experimental approach from the area of "basic" and "applied" studies of child development. One of the most influential critiques of the laboratory experimental approach has come from Bronfenbrenner (1979), who has described the current state of experimental child development as descriptions of strange environmental factors on one behavior of a child in an artificial situation. In other words, experiments may study isolated factors (such as specific toys) affecting individual behavior (such as sharing behaviors) on children in a laboratory playroom. The results of such experimental manipulations indicate that children's behaviors *can or cannot* be changed in the predicted direction. The more interesting question is to what extent these factors actually *do* affect behavior (McCall, 1977). The experimental results may tell us by exposing children to specific toys their play can be changed in predictable directions. It may be however, that in the real world these children do not play with these toys and, as such, their play behavior in the experimental are different from the child's play in the "real world." In short, the experimental results may not provide insight into the ways in which children develop naturally.

We should not throw out the baby with the bathwater, however. Experiments are important in child development to identify possible causes; however they can be ecologically valid (Bronfenbrenner, 1979). Such experiments should be analogues of children's real-world environments and the fact that we compare such experimental results with naturalistic results, such as the same or similar children playing with the same toys in their preschool classroom. Following these guidelines we can test the ecological validity of an experiment (see A. D. Pellegrini & Perlmutter, 1989, for an example of such an experiment). For example, in designing an ecologically valid experiment to study the effects of specific toys on children's play we should use toys actually found in the children's environment, such as dolls and dress-up clothes, and form social groups similar to those found in that environment, such as same-gender dyads. Further, the demands placed on children in the experiments should be similar to those at school; for instance, if children are required to interact with specific materials in their school, we could also manipulate their exposure to toys in an experiment.

Developmental Studies Should Also Be Longitudinal

If we are interested in understanding development, or changes within individuals across time, we should study them across time. Although cross-sectional studies can be used initially, they are not the final word in developmental study. An example should make the point. If we are interested in the developmental relations between mothers reading books to toddlers and children's subsequent kindergarten literacy we could begin by examining the relations between mother–child behaviors and measures of reading with two separate age groups of children. Results from such an investigation would give us insight into *age differences* in mothers' reading styles and relations between these styles and children's reading. Longitudinal research is needed to determine the ways in which mothers' and children's behaviors change from the toddler to the kindergarten period. Further, to determine the extent to which book-reading behaviors predict reading, the antecedent–subsequent dimensions of a longitudinal design are necessary. Finally, longitudinal research enables us to document the ways in which individual differences in children influence and are influenced by the developmental process.

DEVELOPMENT AS A BASIS FOR WORKING WITH CHILDREN

In this final section we present an outline of the ways in which notions of development have been used by professions that work with children. Probably the most influential group here is the National Association for the Education of Young Children. In the criteria listed for appropriate practices for infants through school-age children, NAEYC explicitly noted that the criteria for each age group, but especially, for the infant-through-3-year-old group, are not mere distillations of skills and practices appropriate for older youngsters. They recognize that children, especially the very young ones, have unique needs.

Although we might argue with the empirical reality of some of the NAEYC claims, we still think it is important that they be considered in full, if for no other reason than their widespread use, and in some cases, acceptance. Of course, the orientation we advocate in this volume is one where practices and policies are based on the empirical record. An important next step in our advocacy of developmental approaches for working with young children is to examine the degree to which the NAEYC criteria are indeed empirically true.

3

Behavior in Context

This chapter examines the relations between context and behavior. Generally, context is defined as being composed of environmental and personal variables, such as room size and the psychological aspects of those being studied, respectively. For example, personal variables for kindergarten children may include their age and gender. Environmental variables are those aspects of the physical and social environment in which the children and adults interact. For example, children may interact in different areas (e.g., block or book corners) within their kindergarten classroom.

As we stressed in the chapter on development, our conceptualization of context is one in which people and context influence each other in a transactional way. Any change in one set of variables, by definition, affects the others. For example, take the case of children playing with a set of blocks (an aspect of the physical environment). Children certainly affect the blocks by moving and arranging them in different ways. Further, children of different ages and in different peer groups will play in different ways. Similarly, the blocks affect children by limiting, to a degree, the themes of their play.

In this chapter we stress, as we do throughout the book, this interrelationship between context and behavior. In order to understand behavior one must consider the child and his or her environment as one constellation of interdependent variables. Viewing behavior, or any data set, as an interdependent totality in context has been labeled a field (Einstein, 1933; Kohler, 1925; Lewin, 1954). The realization that behavior and context affect each other is necessary to child study. Investigators must try to identify the factors (contextual and biological) affecting children's behavior if they are to understand the behavior.

As such, the function of this chapter is to familiarize the student of child study with various models of contextual and behavior.

The two models reviewed in this chapter are very different. In one case, context is viewed as *coercive*, or as having a direct effect on behavior. The other model is more consistent with our transactional view of people and context. In the first case, Barker and Wright's (1955) model of context, ecological observation, describes children's behavior as a function of more immediate context: the setting (e.g., a reading lesson); behavioral objects (e.g., specific texts used); and the behavior episode (or the specific behaviors in that context). As such, this is useful for investigators interested in the extreme cases where children's behavior is restricted in specific contexts.

Bronfenbrenner's (1979) system, on the other hand, expands the Wright and Barker model in that it defines contexts in a more differentiated fashion by talking about microsystems (Interactions at specific face-to-face levels) and macrosystems (at the level of culture). Children's behavior in a specific microsystem (e.g., talking with a specific teacher or with mother) also is affected by and affects macrosystem level variables (such as the ways in which a cultural groups interact among themselves). The bidirectional relationship of people and context is a hallmark of this system and clearly separates it from the Barker and Wright model.

ECOLOGICAL OBSERVATION

The system of ecological observation and ecological psychology was developed by Barker and Wright (1955). Like Lewin's model, it is useful to the extent that it helps the observer analyze children's behavior in context. Barker and Wright, who earlier collaborated with Lewin, outlined a three-tier system of defining behavior in context: the behavior setting, the behavior object, and the behavior episode. This system developed out of their study and book, *Midwest and Its Children*. Generally, the theory states that individuals in specific environments act in ways consistent with the demands characteristic of that environment. Barker (Barker & Wright, 1955) made the analogy that participants in a behavior setting are like atoms are to molecules; they are controlled by an overriding structure. Consequently, one's actions (behavior/episodes) in a context (behavior setting) form natural behavioral units. The actions of different people are thus similar in a specific context. To use Gump's (1989) term, settings can be "coercive" (p. 35). Similarly, the fewer the inhabitants in a context the more potent the effects of the environment on each inhabitant.

This effect was illustrated in a study of large and small schools. Children in small schools received more "deviation-countering" influences than students in the larger school (Williams, 1965). As such, their model is unidirectional: Environments affect people. The particulars are discussed in the following.

The Behavior Setting

The behavior setting, or the community unit, was characterized as having the following distinguishable features. First, a behavior setting has a set of expected behaviors that are somewhat independent of participants in the setting. This is called the *standing pattern of behavior*. For example, the standing pattern of behavior of Catholic church worship is independent of individual church users, in that the behavior pattern of worship goes on in a consistent way, independent of individuals who participate in the service. Similarly, in most American classrooms the behavior setting of saluting the American flag before the start of school in the morning probably varies very little across schools.

Next, the standing pattern of behavior must be *synomorphic* with a specific environment. A synomorphic relationship indicates that the behavior and the environment go together. The relationship also has a spatial–temporal component. For example, people worship in a school gym on Sunday at 10 a.m. Worshiping and church on Sunday at 10 a.m. are thus in a synomorphic relationship with each other; playing basketball at that time and in that place would not be compatible. Basketball and cheering would be synomorphic for Friday night at 7 p.m.

That the environment exists independently of the standing pattern of behavior is another characteristic of the behavior setting. That is, the environment itself exerts an influence of its own. For example, a church may elicit reverent behavior at times other than Sunday morning.

Finally, the environment surrounds the standing pattern of behavior in a spatial–temporal sense. More specifically, certain behaviors are expected at certain times and places within the environment. For example, different behaviors are elicited in the church on Saturday afternoon (e.g., confessions) than on Sunday morning. In a school gym on Saturday morning children may play in a community basketball league and use language and behavior that would not match with a school physical education period during the week in that same space.

BRONFENBRENNER'S ECOLOGICAL THEORY

Bronfenbrenner's model is an extension of Lewin's (1954) field theory of psychology. By way of introduction we briefly discuss it.

Lewin's Theory

Lewin saw behavior (B) as being a function (F) of the person (P) and his or her environment (E): $B = F(P,E)$. Further, Lewin suggested that the person and his or her environment must be considered as one constellation, or field, of interdependent variables. The totality of these factors was labeled one's *life space* (LSp). Thus, the previously noted equation could be expanded to include life space, such that B = F(PE) = (LSp). In order to explain behavior in this model one must be able to thoroughly describe life space and determine the ways in which behavior is related to life space, or field. This interdependence of person and situation affects Lewin's attempts to interface psychology and ecology. That is, situations affect behavior (as in adaptation) while, simultaneously, situations are affected by its inhabitants (as in stereotype).

In order to describe the field accurately, the observer must attempt to describe it as the target or as the subject views that field. For example, if we are observing a child in a hospital ward, we must attempt to describe the ward from the child's perspective, not from an adult's. Thus, Lewin's model implies that individuals, particularly individuals at different ages, perceive field differently. An example of the differential perception of field for different age groups is when 3-year-old and 5-year-old girls interact in same-age groups with male-preferred toys, such as blocks. The older girls perceive these toys as male-preferred and something inappropriate for them to interact with; consequently, their behavior, in comparison with the younger girls, is less sophisticated (A. D. Pellegrini & Perlmutter, 1989). With age, therefore, situations are differentially defined by children.

In describing the field, it should be noted that social and physical aspects of a situation ought to be described. For example, children behave differently with different toys, but the addition of more adults, children, or both to a physical context will, in turn, further affect children's behavior (A. D. Pellegrini, 1984a). As noted earlier, however, children define these situations differently with age.

In describing the field, one must also determine specific psychological factors affecting participants such as goals, stimuli, and social relations. In addition, general psychological factors of the field, such as an atmosphere, should be considered; for example, is the atmosphere friendly?

As can be seen from these criteria of field, both psychological and physical variables comprise the concept of field. In analyzing behavior (or the psychology of a field) these factors should be considered as interdependent. These factors determine the psychological field of the person being analyzed.

The Ecology of Human Development

In his book *The Ecology of Human Development*, Bronfenbrenner (1979) outlined ways in which people and contexts interact and the ways in which his work is built on that of Kurt Lewin. Like Lewin, Bronfenbrenner believes that children's behavior can only be explained in context and that these contextual experiences, in turn, affect children's subsequent development.

Bronfenbrenner, unlike Lewin, examined contexts on varying degrees of specificity: from microsystems through mesosystems, exosystems, and macrosystems. He was concerned with the dynamics within each of these contexts and transitions between these contexts. These levels of context are discussed in this section. Further, relations between participants and contexts are transactional to the extent that they affect each other. To best understand Bronfenbrenner's model we should consider his metaphor for the model, Russian dolls, which are nested in a series wherein the largest doll contains all subsequent dolls. Contexts, too, are embedded in larger contexts. The microsystem is embedded in the mesosystem, which is embedded in the exosystem.

The Microsystem.   Bronfenbrenner defined a microsystem, as "a pattern of activities, roles, and interpersonal relations experienced over time by the developing person in a given setting with particular physical and material characteristics" (Bronfenbrenner & Crouter, 1983, p. 380). Further, a setting is a place where people engage in face-to-face interactions; for example, a schoolroom, a restaurant, a workplace, and so on. These elements interact with each other to affect behavior directly and indirectly.

Bronfenbrenner made the point that children make transitions between different microsystems and within microsystems. For example, a transition between microsystems may have a child going from home to day-care center. A within-system transition may have a child getting a new brother or sister and, as a result, having a new role in the family setting. Each of these changes makes demands on children's behavior.

It is the ability to negotiate changes within and across microsytems that determines development in this model: Developmental changes should be described in terms of behavioral changes in more than one microsystem. Children should exhibit more advanced attitudes or actions across places and time in order for the changes to be considered a developmental change. Only those analyses that meet this criterion are said to be developmentally valid. For example, children may be trained in a laboratory to use a certain social skill. The children must use this skill in the laboratory and at home if the study is to have developmental validity. Only by examining in detail the composition of microsystems and how children's behaviors vary in different microsystems can we hope to understand behavior.

The Mesosystem.   Mesosystem comparisons involve comparisons across at least two microsystems. Again, the procedure used attempts to determine the extent to which the behavior being observed is idiosyncratic to one setting or is a consistent part of a child's behavioral repertoire. A behavior is a consistent part of a repertoire when it occurs in more than one setting.

One of the most common mesosystem analyses involves comparisons between children's behavior with adults in home and other environments. For example, the ways in which children and parents use and talk about print varies greatly. In some families the practice bears close resemblance to the practices in school, whereas in others there is little commonality (Heath, 1983). The match or mismatch between the design features of the home and school microsystems is a powerful predictor of school success.

The Exosystem. The exosystem is represented by external forces such as school board policies toward certain educational practices, such as bilingualism in classrooms, as well as parental occupation. School policy has a direct effect on children in classrooms. Correspondingly, children and their families can influence policy and classroom practice. Specifically, school policy determines what is valued and discouraged in classrooms. At the preschool and kindergarten levels, policy toward the role of play, for example, has an important impact on teachers and children's face-to-face interaction. For elementary schools, policy toward different conceptions of literacy and numeracy, for example, is an important concern. Specifically, culturally different children have different literacy and numeracy experiences at home than in traditional school curricula. The extent to which the school incorporates the former experiences has an impact on microsystem interactions (A. D. Pellegrini, Perlmutter, Galda, & Brody, 1990; Resnick, 1987; Saxe, Guberman, & Gearhart, 1987).

What does parental occupation have to do with children's school performance, beyond the simple effect of salary? Research has shown that fathers who have jobs that require compliance to authority tended to stress obedience in their children (Bronfenbrenner & Crouter, 1983). Other aspects of the exosystem that affect children's and parents' behaviors include parents' social networks. The existence of parental support systems is related to parental and child behaviors. For example, parents who are experiencing economic difficulty but have a large social support system are more competent; that is, they are less likely to abuse their children compared to those with less support. Similarly, where parents have help with child care and housekeeping tasks, they are more supportive and less abusive parents.

The point of the exosystem level of analysis, therefore, is that parents' and children's behaviors are affected by a number of not-so-immediate variables such as occupational demands, extrafamilial support systems, and peer groups.

Using the Ecological Model of Human Development in Applied Child Study.
This model defines context most inclusively, from the exosystem to the microsystem. The clearest example involves studying children in schools. We use high school children for illustrative purposes. First, at the exosystem level we must consider school policy; for example, a policy toward bilingualism. In this case, the school policy is to discourage use of languages other than English in schools. Next we should determine the ways in which this policy effects interactions at various microsystems. Regarding teacher–student interaction, nonnative speakers of English may be viewed by

teachers as more bothersome than native speakers because they cannot communicate, according to policy. This will have predicted effects on students; for example, they will be less likely to succeed in school than native speakers. Consequently, there will not be a smooth transition from the microsystem of the home to the microsystem of school. At the mesosystem level, the failure of nonnative speakers of English in school may be inferred from the mismatch between these two microsystems. In short, using this approach involves examining children at different levels of specificity.

THE SCHOOL AS CONTEXT

Schools exert profound influence on children and their families. For this reason, we discuss school as a specific context. Our reason for dedicating a chapter to a single context is straightforward enough: Schools are such important institutions in our society that most children are expected to be exposed to school until they are at least 16 years old. Consequently, schools may have lasting effects on children's future. It seems imperative, therefore, to examine closely this social filter through which children are expected to pass.

In this section we examine the school context at many different levels. First, we examine the philosophical bases of schools. Most social scientists would agree that good educational practice should be based on a good idea or theory. Without such a theory we have no guide for instructional actions. Second, different educational philosophies have correspondingly different psychological and educational practices. In the third section of this chapter we attempt to outline the components of a very important aspect of schooling, the curriculum. In the fourth section we examine within the effects of classroom variables on preschool and elementary school children. Following the organization of Minuchin and Shapiro (1983), classroom variables are conceptualized in terms of educational theory and physical settings.

Philosophical Bases of School Practice

In their important paper "Development as an Aim of Education," Kohlberg and Mayer (1972) suggested that the most important issue confronting educators is the choice of the ends, or goals of the educational practice. By ends, they mean a goal, or the bases on which students will be evaluated. They argued that the only rational way to choose educational goals is to base the goals on valid psychological theories and noted that a number of philosophies of human development and learning have been translated into psychological theories. These psychological theories, in turn, have been translated into corresponding theories of pedagogy. By using this orientation, educators can specify educational outcomes as well as the processes by which they can reach them. As such, different philosophies have different ends of education as well as different processes to reach those ends. The ways in which children are taught and evaluated, obviously, is part of the context of school: Children are treated differently according to different theories.

Some schools, most of which are at the preschool level, have their philosophical roots in Romanticism and the work of its main proponent, the 18th-century French philosopher Jean-Jacques Rousseau. Rousseau, who outlined his theory of education in his famous book *Emile*, believed that children were naturally good. As such, children should be allowed to explore their world with minimal adult obstruction, so as to allow their natural goodness to unfold. Through this self-exploration they could harness or purge any inner evil that existed. The Romantics viewed children in terms of a biological metaphor; their mental and physical health were synonymous. Children's environments, if natural and not corruptive, provide the necessary nourishment for this growth. The film *L'Enfant Sauvage* by François Truffaut, is an interesting portrayal of this approach as applied to a "wild child" found and educated in France in the late 18th century.

The psychological movement associated with Romanticism has a maturational orientation. Children's social and cognitive development is viewed by those psychologists as basically an innate program, minimally affected by the environment. The theories of G. Stanley Hall and Sigmund Freud are indicative of this group.

Given the innate basis of the Romantics, their view of schooling is fairly laissez-faire. That is, they recommend that children should not be prevented from exploring their environments. The goal of Romantic education is children's awareness of their inner selves. They understand themselves only by exploring their environments. As children come to understand themselves they can learn to understand others. Children's social-emotional development, as well as dimensions of achievement, are of concern for this group. The best example of a Romantic educational orientation is Neil's (1960) Summerhill. Summerhill is a school in England noted for its permissive policies that allow children to explore their inner selves. More restrictive policies, Neil suggested, inhibit this self-awareness. Further, restrictive environments may result in children's repressing their unexpressed thoughts and feelings. Such repression, following a Freudian orientation, will result in maladjusted children.

At the opposite end of the philosophical continuum and probably much more representative of schooling in most industrialized societies is what Kohlberg and Mayer (1972) labeled *cultural transmission philosophy*. Here the goal of education is to transmit an existent body of knowledge to children. This theory implies that knowledge exists outside of children and that children internalize this knowledge through explicit instruction. Whereas the Romantic philosophy was child-centered (the child must become aware of inner self), the cultural transmission philosophy is society-centered: Children must learn a body of knowledge in order to fit into modern technological society.

The psychological theory corresponding to cultural transmission philosophy is learning theory in its various forms, such as the operant conditioning model of B. F. Skinner. In this model of behaviorism children come to learn an existent body of knowledge by approximating a predetermined goal. The task is broken into its component parts and presented to children as discrete bits to be learned. Children are motivated to learn because principles of reinforcement have been applied.

Further, this discrete knowledge transmission approach, reflects the nondevelopmental orientation of this group: Young children are different from adults only in terms of the amount of information they possess and the amounts they can be taught; they are not seen as qualitatively different from adults. Thus children are presented with mature concepts, simplified quantitatively by being offered in small bits. The concept is defined as the sum of the discrete parts.

The last philosophical orientation is represented by the Pragmatic philosophy of Dewey (1938), who believed that development, not only learning, should be the goal of education. By development he meant that children are qualitatively different from adults to the extent that they see the world differently. Children come to understand their world by interacting and conflicting with different aspects of society. Whereas the cultural transmission group stresses children's conformity to an existent set of knowledge, *progressivism* has children constructing their own concepts of the world. They are motivated to do so not by positive reinforcement, but by the desire to resolve conflicting bodies of information.

The psychological work of Piaget and Vygotsky, as well as other developmentalists, correspond to some of the tenets of this philosophy. As is well known, Piagetian and Vygotskian theories state that children develop in a stage-like manner, wherein children construct their views of the world through the process of conceptual conflict and resolution. The quest for equilibration motivates development.

Educational interpretations of Piagetian and Vygotskian theories are fairly common. Piagetian notions such as active involvement, physical manipulation, self-direction, discovery learning, and stage-appropriate instruction are represented in a number of preschool programs (e.g., Forman & Kuscher, 1977; Kamii & DeVries, 1978). Vygotskian pedagogy is most readily represented in the zone of proximal development where children's development is a result of their participating in various tasks with a more competent tutor.

To conclude, good educational practice should be rooted in theory, despite the theory one chooses. Such theoretical consistency is necessary because specific educational goals and practices must go together. Further, the theory and the pedagogy should match the form and content of evaluation. We stress

the direction from theory to practice to evaluations. Evaluation should not
determine what is taught; instead, this should be determined by theory, and that
should determine evaluation. We now address the specifics of the way in which
material is taught.

The School Curriculum

This section examines more specifically the components of the school curriculum. The individual theories discussed previously each utilize these same
components but they differ in the ways in which they flesh them out. These
components are outlined in Table 3.1 (E. Evans, 1982).

Theoretical Foundation

Theoretical orientation, as discussed earlier should determine the "goals" of
what children "should" be like as a result of their experience with a particular
education program. For example, the Romantic group has self-realization as its
goal for the children. The cultural transmission group, on the other hand,
advocates the mastery of specific culturally relevant facts. The contexts in each
of these schools will differ systematically in terms of the ways in which children
interact with peers, adults, and materials.

The way in which these goals are realized is determined by the administrative
policies of those in charge of educational programs (E. Evans, 1982). The
administrative policy, or the specific way in which the program is implemented,
is determined by school personnel (both staff and children), the physical setting
of the school, and the way in which the effectiveness of the educational program
will be evaluated.

Characteristics of children and families in educational programs and the
staff used to implement them are important to consider. Characteristics typically examined here are age of children, parents' levels of income and
education and cultural background, and children's health status. Knowledge
of these characteristics is useful to the extent that state and federal guidelines
for a number of educational programs require this information. For example,
in Head Start programs, children's age and parents' income must be recorded
as part of the program's compliance with legal guidelines. With high school
children, Rutter, Maughan, Mortimore, and Ouston (1979) found that student
background is an important factor. Schools with a predominance of economi-
cally deprived children have high rates of delinquency.

TABLE 3.1
Components of School Curriculum

Theoretical Foundations	Administrative Policies	Curriculum Content
a. Goals	a. School personnel	a. What is taught
	b. Physical setting	b. How it is taught

Knowledge of pupil and family characteristics is also important in terms of trying to implement the program goals. For example, program goals for children's language development must take into account children's native language and culture. Different goals should be established for different types of children and families. This dimension of the curriculum attempts to document a mesosystem relationship between the two microsystems of the classroom and the family.

Regarding the program staff (e.g., administrators, teachers, and aides), a staff must have a certain level of expertise in child development and education in order to implement certain program goals. For example, more expertise is required to implement a curriculum that attempts to individualize instruction than to implement a standardized curriculum. In the former case, teachers must analyze children's level of competence and design methods and materials to teach specific subject matter. In the case of standardized curricula, some teachers merely read the bold-print instructions in teachers' manuals.

Other important dimensions of staffing include teachers' level of experience, teachers' planning habits, and degree of centrality of planning. Regarding experience, high school teachers with more experience are more effective classroom managers than their less experienced counterparts (Rutter et al., 1979). Teachers' level of engagement in joint planning with other teachers is related to students' higher achievement and attendance patterns. High schools where planning is centralized in the hands of senior colleagues have higher achievement among students than less centralized schools. This effect, however, is mediated by the fact that the senior personnel in effective schools consider the opinions of individual teachers.

Physical setting consists of the physical characteristics of the school and classroom. To begin our discussion of physical settings, it must be noted that little research has been on the effects of physical settings has been conducted outside the preschool. Where it has been conducted in elementary schools, it has been related, for the most part, to comparisons of "open" and traditional room arrangements. At the high school level, Rutter et al's work suggests that aspects of physical setting, such as building age, school size, social density, and staff to student ratio, have minimal effects on children's school behavior, achievement, attendance, and delinquency.

Crowding. The extent to which human beings are crowded in with other human beings and objects has clear effects on their behavior. McGrew (1972b) and P. K. Smith and Connolly (1980) examined the effects of crowding on preschool children and teachers' behavior. They defined crowding along two dimensions: social density and spatial density. Social density was defined as an increase in the number of people within a set physical space. For example, given a 25' x 35' classroom with 20 children, an increase in social density would require an addition of children; a decrease in social density would require a decrease in children. Spatial density, on the other hand, keeps the number of people constant but increases or decreases the available space. For example, spatial density could be increased or decreased by the use of room partitions.

Research suggests that children engage in less large motor activities when their space is decreased (McGrew, 1972a, b). In some cases, increased spatial density has resulted in increased children's aggression (P. K. Smith & Connolly, 1980). When children have more space, they engage in less social interaction with their peers. Teachers generally prefer to have children in less crowded conditions because it cuts down on noise and aggressive acts.

The teacher to child ratio also affects children's behaviors. This is a particularly relevant issue in light of the ongoing debate on the possible negative effects of large classroom size. P. K. Smith and Connolly (1980) examined the effects of teacher to child ratio on child–child interaction and communication between children and teachers. Their results suggest that as the number of children increased or the number of staff decreased (i.e., a "worsening ratio"), children's interactional groups became larger. Under such conditions, children talked more frequently to teachers but they were less likely to elicit a teacher's response. Further, teacher use of prohibitive communications also increased with the peer ratios. Under these poor circumstances, children had less of an opportunity to interact positively with their teachers. This may be related to the fact that children in larger, compared to smaller, classrooms have lower academic achievement (Blatchford & Mortimer, in press).

The specific materials that children play with also has an effect on their behavior (see Phyffe-Perkins, 1980; P. K. Smith & Connolly, 1980, for reviews). Generally, research suggests that different types of materials have very specific effects on social-cognitive aspects of children's behavior. For example, children's sustained activity is affected by materials (Phyffe-Perkins, 1980). More open-ended materials (i.e., material and vague functions, such as clay and blocks) result in more sustained activity than more explicitly defined materials (e.g., puzzles). Further, complex materials are also related to children's sustained activity. More complex materials (i.e., number of different subparts to materials) result in more sustained activity.

A. D. Pellegrini (1982a; A. D. Pellegrini & Perlmutter, 1989) conducted two studies to examine the effects of play materials on social-cognitive aspects of preschool children's behavior. The social-cognitive aspects of behavior were defined in terms of the Smilansky–Parten play matrix (see chap. 11, this volume, for a discussion of the matrix). Results generally indicated that children's behavior varied according to where they played. They tended to elicit solitary-constructive behavior in constructive activities (such as art centers) and social-dramatic behavior in housekeeping blocks centers.

Program evaluation is an important part of curriculum. As we discuss more fully in the final chapter, program evaluation criteria should correspond very closely with instructional objectives. That is, we should evaluate only what we taught; the evaluation should have content validity.

Content. Curriculum content covers what is taught and how it is presented (E. Evans, 1982). Evans suggested that the basic consideration of what should be taught often involves choosing among cognitive/intellectual growth, social/affective growth, or mastery of specific factual material. The different orientations, again, reflect different philosophical orientations and are translated into different contexts for children and school personnel. For example, primary concern with affective growth was advocated by the Romantics, whereas primary concern with mastery of specific skills is advocated by the cultural transmission group.

Categorization of content is also important as it specifies the scope, priority, and structure of the curriculum. *Scope* refers to the variety of content within a curriculum. For example, the notion of an integrated curriculum advocates the integration of specific content across a number of different subject areas; curriculum content for the geography of Europe can be dealt with in reading, arithmetic, social studies, and science. More recently, "whole language" approaches to literacy instruction advocate similar levels of integration.

Priority refers to the amount of time given to specific content. Obviously, higher priority content is allocated more time in which to be conveyed.

Structure relates to the sequencing of content. Theories suggest that children learn in hierarchic fashion (see e.g., Gagne, 1978; Piaget, 1970). There is little agreement across theories, however, in the specifics of learning hierarchies. The hierarchy one chooses should follow one's preferred theory of learning or development.

The ways in which curriculum is conveyed—the method of teaching (instruction)—also varies according to specific theoretical bases. Behavioristic models suggest that instruction of a content area should proceed through successive approximation. That is, the curriculum content is broken down into ordered discrete units and children are given positive reinforcement as they approximate the goal. Teachers motivate children to learn in this model by their selective use of reinforcement. An assumption is that children should be rewarded, or reinforced, for doing the "right" thing and not reinforced for other responses. Generally, children do better on numerous measures when they are rewarded. They do worse when they are punished (Rutter et al., 1979).

Piagetian educators believe that children construct knowledge by interacting with physical materials and peers. As such, instruction in this model involves providing materials and social situations that will raise conceptual conflict within and between children. Development occurs through the processes of assimilation, accommodation, and equilibration.

Vygotskian instruction is based on the zone of proximal development, where the goal of the instructor is to maximize the student's participation in the task. This is accomplished by the tutor first gauging the student's level of task competence. For low-competence children, the instructor uses low-demand, highly structured strategies, such as pointing to a word or letter and asking the student to label it. For highly competent children, the tutor is more demanding and provides less support; the teacher may simply assign a book to be read by the student.

CONCLUSION

In this chapter we have examined the role of context in children's development generally and in their school lives specifically. Although different theories of context were presented, we concluded that those theories which specified the transaction between contexts and persons were most accurate. We also examined more closely the school context, from the level of theory guiding school practice to the specifics of within-classroom variation, and attempted to describe the ways in which school practices (curriculum) should be consistent with the philosophical and psychological theories behind them.

4

Tests and Performance-Based Assessment

Child study, as we noted in earlier chapters, involves making inferences, or educated guesses, about children's behavior and development. There are a number of different tools available to help us make these inferences. Testing is commonly used by teachers, clinicians, and other practitioners. Increasingly, tests are used as indicators of numerous outcomes, such as teacher effectiveness, entrance/exit requirements for students, and in other "high-stakes" areas. By high stakes we mean areas where the outcomes of the tests have important, often life-effecting implications for those taking the tests.

From preschool onward testing is probably the dominant mode of child assessment. Indeed, national testing proposals are circulating as part of the battle for "educational effectiveness" (Morison, 1992); testing is often seen as the common denominator in this battle. Consequently it is imperative for us to understand what tests are, how they work, and how to construct them. Only with this knowledge can we use tests wisely and guard against their inappropriate use. In this chapter, we recommend that tests be used as part of a larger and more complete battery of assessment procedures. Tests, when constructed and used appropriately, can provide useful information. This information, however, represents only a part of what we can know about children. The other methods we discuss help complete the puzzle.

THE APPEAL OF TESTS AND THE DETRACTORS

This widespread use and appeal of testing probably resides in the fact that tests have an aura of objectivity as a result of their yielding numerical values.

Numbers, we assume, provide objective, scientific indicators of that which we are measuring. We further assume that test scores can provide comparisons across individuals who have taken the test. For example, we assume that two children scoring in the 95th percentile of a test are equally competent. This, as we see here later, is a problematic assumption. When policy makers and politicians present test scores as evidence it is typically done with an aura of objectivity, and an almost, "How can you argue with this? The numbers tells all!" attitude. An example of this was presented in President Clinton's 1997 State of the Union address: Education must be improved and tests scores provide the evidence for improvement or failure. As shown later, a number of factors, some of which are extraneous to that which is being assessed, influence those scores.

Another possible attraction of tests is that they can be used to improve instruction. That is, they can be given to identify students' strengths and weaknesses. Teachers can then use this information to design curricula. Of course, tests can be used for this purpose when the time lag between test administration and test scoring is minimal. As such, tests that must be sent out of the school or school district for scoring are less useful than other sorts of tests, such as teacher-made tests, which typically provide immediate feedback. Additionally, tests can be used to improve instruction only when there is match between the content of the test and the content of the the curriculum. In many cases, the match is minimal, thus the validity of the test results are also minimal. Of course the directionality between test content and curriculum should be such that curriculum is chosen first and then an appropriate test is constructed or found. "Teaching the test" presents the wrong directionality where the content of the test determines what's taught.

The Detractors

Testing as a mode of assessment is not without its justified critics. Tests are criticized along dimensions. The most simple criticism relates to what has been labeled "test pollution," or the fact that testing takes up an increasing portion of available instructional time. Relatedly, the importance and abuse of testing is reflected in the fact that schools sometimes "teach the test" as well as manipulate test administration procedures by, for example, using the same tests year after year and reviewing test items before the actual test administration to raise test scores.

Although these problems are associated with the "ethics" of tests and teaching, there are also some basic problems associated with testing even when these ethical issues are no longer a concern. These are addressed by Miller-Jones (1989). First, the structure of the knowledge domain being tested must be adequately understood so as to allow test items to be generated which measure that domain. Specifically, when we ask a child a question, such as to recognize a written word, we should recognize the domain from which that question is sampled. Is the word a common word? Is it a word in which there is regular (compared to irregular) letter–sound correspondence? To remediate this problem, tests would sample a wide variety of items within a domain and across different domains.

Second, we must understand the mental processes underlying each knowledge domain such that we can make adequate inferences about differential performance on test items. That is, when we ask a question of a child, what are the mental processes that he or she must go through in order to answer that question? For example, does asking a child to read a specific word require that the child know general or specific letter–sound correspondence rules? Teachers should therefore understand what mental processes they are expecting of children when they choose or construct specific test items.

Third, test items should not be biased such that they favor a particular cultural or age group over another. Such biased tests are those with a systematic influence of extraneous factors, such as gender or ethnic group membership, on test performance. Certain testing procedures, especially group-administered, standardized tests are biased against young children. In most "standardized" situations, test administrator are told not to probe the child, encourage alternate responses, or provide feedback to the child as to the adequacy of his or her responses (Miller-Jones, 1989). Such practices are recommended so that all children will be treated uniformly. These procedures, however, typically minimize children's exhibition of competence to the extent that by not receiving feedback on the adequacy of answers children may not know what counts as appropriate responses to particular questions. This problem is compounded when children's understanding, or definition, of the task is different from that of the test administrator.

To remediate this test administrators should be allowed, even encouraged, to probe children's understanding. For those concerned about "standardization" (and that certainly is not an unreasonable concern, especially in norm-referenced measurement), a wide range of standardized probes could be available. Indeed the sorts of probes used by testers could be useful in understanding children more fully. As is noted in chapter 8, the Vygotskian notion of the zone of proximal development suggests that we can make inferences about a children's competence based on the sorts of probes we use with them. If less structured and demanding probes engage a child, he or she is probably more competent in that area than a child for whom more structured and less demanding probes are necessary for engagement.

Mismatches in understanding are particularly common when we are dealing with young children and children from different cultures. For example, Lee Galda and I (Galda, Pellegrini, & Cox, 1989) had a group of preschoolers, ranging in age from 2½ years to 5 years, tell "stories" about different arrays of toys. We thought that our instructions to the children to "tell a story about these things" was sufficiently clear to be understood by even the youngest children. Our unexpected finding in this study was that children did indeed understand the word "story," but for the youngest group, "story" meant "describe," not tell a narrative; thus, children and experimenter had different task definitions even though they used the same words. It was not that the youngest children were incompetent storytellers, they simply had different meanings for the task than did the experimenter. To minimize such problems, testers should be certain that they and their children are talking about the same things and that they have shared meanings for them. Without such agreement, the information yielded by tests, or indeed any assessment procedure, is less than meaningful.

Children's cultural group membership also affects their test performance. Standardized tests, like IQ tests and the SAT, are often criticized as being biased against certain cultural groups, like African-Americans. There are at least three explanations for the relatively low performance of these groups on such tests. The first is that these groups are intellectually inferior and the test scores accurately reflect this. This position should be disregarded outright for reasons given earlier, such as differing task definition.

The second explanation expands on the differing task definition argument by suggesting that culturally different children may perform poorly on standardized tests vis-à-vis mainstream culture children but equally well when tasks are "equated" for cultural differences. For example, one body of research on mother–child book reading behavior suggests that lower socioeconomic status mothers are less competent teachers of their children than are middle-class mothers. In these studies lower class and middle-class mothers and their children are observed interacting around traditional (middle-class) children's books. These early literacy events are thought to be similar to school-based literacy events and, consequently, responsible for differential class performance in school. The format found in children's books often read to middle-class children often is similar in form to a multiple choice test item.

It is a well-established fact that lower class families have fewer of these books in their homes than do middle-class families; consequently, this assessment format is unfamiliar to the former group. When book-reading tasks are familiar to culturally different families, however, such as using comic strips and toy advertisements instead of narrative and expository trade books, respectively, these parents appear as competent as their mainstream culture counterparts (A. D. Pellegrini et al., 1990). It should be noted, however, that the establishment of task equivalence is extremely difficult.

The third explanation for cultural differences on test performance is the social ecological position, stating that cultural differences on tests reflect the usefulness of the information contained in the test for specific groups (Miller-Jones, 1989; Ogbu, 1988). More specifically, mainstream-culture children do better on standardized tests than do non-mainstream-culture children because the information contained in the test is useful, or adaptive, for the former but not the latter group.

The second and third explanations should be taken into account when we test non-mainstream-culture children. There should be little doubt that our institutions, like school, reflect specific cultural biases. The values of elementary schools are, for the most part, middle-class, white, and female. If we doubt this, a make a quick survey of the teachers in a local elementary school or the students in most teacher preparation classes.

In this chapter we show that tests can be a useful form of measurement when used appropriately. However, they are only one of the many forms of assessment available. As noted earlier, they are most useful when they are integrated into a larger, diverse assessment program. In the remainder of this chapter the following is discussed: types of tests (norm-referenced and criterion-referenced, which include teacher-made tests), conditions for testing, and technical and practical considerations.

TYPES OF TESTS

Generally, there are three types of tests or assessment: norm-referenced, criterion-referenced, and performance-based. Each is discussed in this section. Norm-referenced tests (NRT) usually measure general, rather than specific, knowledge and have scores derived from comparisons with norming groups. Thus, NRTs provide information about a student's relative standing (i.e., relative to the students in the norming group), not about the amount or type of information a student possesses; more specific knowledge assessment can be obtained with criterion-referenced tests (CRT) and performance-based assessment. Because of this property, NRTs are useful for grouping children and evaluating program impact.

Norm-Referenced Tests

Because the meaning of NRT scores is dependent on comparisons with a norming sample, conditions of test administration are standardized. That is, all children are read the same instruction, given the same amount of time to complete the test, and provided with the same materials. The familiar example of high school students all being read the same instructions for the SAT on the same Saturday at the same time is an example of standardized administration procedures. The rationale for this is clear: If the scores give information about relative standing, then all children should take the test under reasonable similar conditions.

Another important issue related to test content is the extent to which the items on the test reflect the content of your educational program. If they are not, the test will not be (content) valid.

Similarity between your children and those who comprised the test's norming sample is also relevant to NRTs. Given the comparative nature of the scores, it is important that there be a match between your children and those on which the test was normed. For example, if you are a principal in rural Georgia you would want a test with a similar norming group, not one with a group predominantly drawn from West Coast cities. Information about norming samples is typically found in the technical manuals of the tests. Preliminary examination of this information is time well spent because the scores derived from an NRT are only as meaningful as the norming groups are similar.

The scores yielded by NRTs reflect their comparative nature: percentiles, z-scores, t-scores, grade equivalent scores, and stanines. Briefly, percentile scores tell us the students' relative standing, on a 1–100 scale; for example, a score in the 85th percentile means that the student or the class has scored higher than 85% of the students in the norming sample. Although percentile scores are intuitively easy to understand, they have the disadvantage of being unequal units; for example, the 10 percentile units from the 40th to the 50th are much smaller than the 10 units from the 80th to the 90th. Consequently, percentiles should not be used in mathematical calculations.

Z-scores, on the other hand, are equal-interval units. At the mean, or arithmetic average, of the distribution a z-score of 0 would be observed; scores below the mean have negative values whereas those above the mean have positive values. In both cases the scores range from 0 to 4 and tell us the extent to which the scores deviate from the mean.

To the extent that they are standardized, equal-interval-unit scores, t-scores are similar to z-scores. Further, t-scores, unlike z-scores, are normalized; that is, when the t-scores are plotted in a graph they are normally distributed. The other difference, and also advantage, of the t-score is that there are no negative and fraction scores. Scores range from 0 to 100, with a mean of 50. A final advantage of the t-score is that mean t-scores on different tests will be the same. Consequently, students' performance on different tests can be compared. For example, if we are interested in using standardized test scores to determine admission into a teacher training program but not all students took the same test, we could convert the different test scores to t-scores and thereby have a common metric.

Grade equivalent scores are another commonly used NRT score. Although these scores are intuitively appealing they are very problematical. For example, a third grader scoring at the 3.0 level at the beginning of the school year indicates that he is "on grade level," meaning that the child has scored at the mean for his group at the time of the test. Scores above or below grade level are deviations from this mean. For example, if our mythical third grader scored 2.5 this would mean that he scored a certain level below the mean for his grade. It *does not* mean that a second grader took the test and scored at that level. The same holds true for the typically sought-after above-grade scores. Another problem with grade equivalent scores is in their assumed uniform growth rate across the year. That is, it is assumed that the academic year can be divided into 10 equal-interval units. The reason for this is that tests norms are generally established by yearly test administrations at each grade; for example, the average for the beginning of third grade may be a raw score of 45 and the raw score at the beginning of fourth grade is 55. Consequently, monthly growth would be estimated by a raw score of one. (This is derived by dividing the difference in scores by 10). Teachers know this is an unrealistic assumption to the extent that children's learning is not uniform across the school year. Children, for example, do not learn as much from September to October as they do from March to April. Additionally, some children actually "lose ground" during the summer to the extent that their scores on a test are higher at the end of the previous year than at the beginning of the next year. In short, grade equivalent scores seem to be of little use. Their appeal is deceptive.

Stanine scores are the last type of scores typically given in NRTs. Stanines are equal-interval units ranging from 1 to 9, with a mean of 5. The top 4% of the test scores are assigned to the 9th stanine; the next 7% go into the 8th stanine; the next 12% go into the 7th; the next 17% go into the 6th; the next 20% into the 5th; etc. The major problem with stanines is that they are large units; for example, two children may be in the same stanine but at widely different levels. For precision we need two-digit units.

That the meaning of NRT scores are relative (to others that took the test) necessitates that test administration procedures be standardized. Consequently, NRTs are also standardized tests. Such standardized procedures, as noted earlier, often underestimate children's competence because there may not be correspondence between children's and adults' interpretations of the event. This is a result of not allowing test administrators to provide feedback to children.

Types of Norm-Referenced Tests

There are a number of different types of NRTs but we will only discuss a few of the more commonly used types: aptitude, intelligence, and achievement.

First, we examine aptitude tests, which typically measure children's scholastic aptitude, or school-oriented learning. Aptitude tests and intelligence tests are similar to the extent that they both measure one's capacity to learn; indeed, intelligence tests are a form of aptitude test. Perhaps the most well-known aptitude tests are the Scholastic Aptitude Test (SAT) and the Graduate Record Examination (GRE). These tests measure the extent to which students are capable of learning and, as such, are used as predictors; for example, the SAT is used as a predictor of college grade point average. Consequently, predictive validity is particularly important for aptitude tests. (Validity is discussed later in this chapter).

Second, and most controversial, are intelligence tests. The concepts of intelligence, IQ, and intelligence testing are controversial, as noted earlier. For example, intelligence can be conceptualized as a general factor or as a number of different intelligences. Where intelligence tests are accepted it is assumed that they measure general ability. Intelligence tests scores are typically expressed via the ubiquitous IQ.

Both intelligence and aptitude test scores are influenced by both one's ability to learn, which seems to have a genetic component, and one's environment. In short, the environmental and genetic components of IQ are inextricable. The meaning of intelligence tests scores should be interpreted, in light of the constant controversy surrounding the issue, as the specific score yielded by the IQ test. This sounds a bit circular, at best, but we encounter problems when we try to make inferences about the meaning of IQ test scores into other areas, such as being used as a measure of preschool program effectiveness. (See Zigler and Trickett, 1978, for a discussion of this issue.)

Many scholars have suggested that the use of IQ tests with young children should be replaced with broader measures of children's functioning, such as social competence, or the extent to which children have adapted to their environments. This issue is discussed in a subsequent chapter on social competence (see chapter 10). This seems a reasonable alternative to the extent that intelligence tests possess construct validity if they measure children's ability to function in their environments.

Whereas aptitude tests attempt to predict future status, achievement tests attempt to measure children's current status. For example, a math achievement test will tell us how much math a child knows in reference to the norming group. Consequently, content validity is particularly relevant to achievement tests. Aptitude and achievements are both, however, sensitive to children's educational experiences. Indeed, aptitude, intelligence, and achievement tests for children tend to be interrelated. That is, scores on each tend to be similar. The content of that which is assessed on achievement tests, however, is much more specific than that which is measured on either aptitude on intelligence tests. For this reason, it is imperative that the content of achievement tests and the content of an instructional program be closely matched. The extent to which there is a mismatch between what is tested and what is taught should be of principle concern in the choice of a standardized achievement test, along with norming group similarities.

Criterion-Referenced Tests

Whereas NRT achievement tests measure skills more specific than aptitude and intelligence tests, criterion-referenced tests (CRT) measure yet more specific skills. CRTs are measures of very specific instructional performance criteria, typically instructional objectives. As such, children are not compared against a norming group, as they are with NRTs, but against a performance criterion; for example, that the child can recognize all the letters of the alphabet. The passing of the criterion denotes that the child has mastered the content tested.

The tricky aspect of CRTs, however, is in the establishment of the appropriate criterion level. For example, should children identify the letters of the alphabet with 100%, 90%, 80%, or 70% accuracy? Such decisions are often arbitrary and not based on empirical research. Cutoff or criterion scores should be based on research that establishes the importance of a specific scores. For example, a specific criterion might indicate children's subsequent success in an area; scores below that level might indicate that children are likely to fail.

The educational practices that are explicitly tied to CRTs are mastery learning and minimum competency testing, as used by a number of states to determine children's grade-to-grade promotion, teacher certification, and other high-stakes decisions. The problem of the arbitrariness of the criterion level, added to another problem, the arbitrariness of the difficulty level of the tests items—that is, most test items assess lower level, not higher level skills—suggest that CRTs should be used cautiously and in conjunction with other measures, especially when making important decisions like grade promotions and retentions.

Although the most common use of CRTs is in the form of teacher-made tests, a number of commercially prepared CRTs exist. These measures are often diagnostic in nature in that they test very specific skills and provide educators with information on students' strengths and weaknesses.

These tests are from the areas of math and reading, reflective of their importance in school curricula. The use of these, and similar tests, should be based on the specific objectives tested and their relation to one's own curriculum and the specific information generated by the tests.

Teacher-Made Tests

Probably the most commonly used and most influential form of CRT is the teacher-made test. When all is said and done they are the measure by which children are evaluated in their daily classroom life. In this section of the chapter we discuss a number of commonly used teacher-made assessment formats: multiple-choice tests, true–false tests, short-answer tests, and matching tests. For each of these procedures we discuss uses and test construction. Finally, test item analysis is discussed.

Multiple-choice tests are commonly used by teachers and often preferred by psychometricians. Multiple-choice tests can be used to measure a variety of skills and processes, from the simple to the complex. The major advantage in using this format is that it requires children to discriminate among alternate responses and it can be scored accurately and easily. They typically involve a test item stem, in which the problem is stated, and a list of alternatives. The alternatives should be labeled alphabetically; for example, 5 + 5 = (A)3 (B)10 (C)0 (D)8.

In constructing a multiple-choice test, or any other teacher-made test, we should start with instructional objectives. These objectives may be stated in a variety of formats. One of the more common formats for instructional objectives is D. Bloom's (1956) Taxonomy of Educational Objectives: Cognitive Domain.

This scheme, although not actually hierarchical along the six levels (Pellegrini & Galda, 1982) does reflect a low level—that is, knowledge—and high level. The model is useful for the construction of test questions measuring different levels of knowledge. This point is particularly important in light of the often-leveled criticism that teacher-made tests and standardized tests alike only measure low-level knowledge. The items should measure the specific instructional objectives of the classroom teacher, of course. Thus, teachers should begin the test-construction process by drafting a number of different items for the instructional objectives covered. More items should be written for the more important material. More instructional time is spent on important material than on less important material.

Specific suggestions for constructing multiple-choice tests have been outlined by Hopkins and Stanley (1981):

1. The stem should contain the main question fully. For example, "The major difference between preoperational and operational children is that _____."
2. Each item should be as short as possible.
3. Avoid using negative items, but when they are used, use them carefully.
4. Ask for the "best" or most appropriate answer.
5. Where omissions are used, as in item 1, the omission should be at the end of the stem.
6. The reading level of the questions should be low.
7. List distractor in logical order, if possible. For example:
   10 + 5 = (A)12 (B)15 (C)18 (D)20.
8. Avoid patterns of correct responses.
9. Distractors should be reasonable.
10. Alternatives should be of similar grammatical structure and length.
11. Have three to five alternates for each item.
12. Avoid items with verbatim textbook or lecture language and order.
13. Avoid alternatives that reveal answers to other items.
14. Avoid determiners such as "never" and "always."
15. The following alternatives should be used: "None of the above," "All of the above," "More than one of the above."
16. Use numerals for the items and letters for the alternatives.

The next format is true–false questions. These questions should be absolutely true or false, not sometimes; thus the use of specific determiners is important. Like multiple-choice items, these questions can be used to measure low and high skills. A major advantage of true–false questions, in relation to multiple-choice items, is that they take less time for students to complete and, consequently, more material can be assessed during limited time slots. Similar procedures should be followed in constructing a true–false test regarding the use of instructional objectives. Specific suggestions for this format have also been provided by Hopkins and Stanley (1981):

1. Avoid using determiners that could serve as clues. "Strong" words, such as "all," "never," "always," are often used in false questions.
2. Avoid patterns of correct answers, such as too many true or false answers or alternating patterns of true–false.
3. Avoid questions taked verbatim from texts or lectures.
4. Each statement should test only one proposition.
5. Avoid negative and complex words and phrases.
6. Use true–false items in conjunction with other item formats.

The next format involves the use of short answers. Often taking the form of fill-in-the-blank questions, this format can be used to measure who, what, why, and when knowledge as well as vocabulary. The question, like multiple-choice items, should have the response slot at the end of the statement. The short answer format is qualitatively different from the other formats discussed thus far to the extent that the students must supply the required information rather than respond to the teacher's statements. This has the advantage that students are more likely to remember their answers to this sort of question than to the multiple-choice and true–false formats (Gay, 1980; cited in Hopkins & Stanley, 1981). Again, specific guidelines for the preparation of short answer items comes form Hopkins and Stanley:

1. Direct questions are preferable to statements.
2. Required responses should be brief.
3. Avoid textbook or lecture wording.
4. Avoid indefinite statements.

The final format to be discussed is matching. Matching items assess children's associative knowledge, not higher forms, using a format where the question stems are usually numbered and the alternatives are usually alphabetized. For example:

1.	Wisconsin	A.	Providence
2.	Ohio	B.	Cincinnati
3.	Minnesota	C.	Columbus
4.	Rhode Island	D.	Madison
5.	Maine	E.	St. Paul
		F.	Minneapolis
		G.	Augusta

Suggestions for the construction of matching items include:

1. Include homogeneous material in each list; for example, only measure states and their capitals in a list not that plus states and their natural resources.
2. Place all items on a single page.
3. Limit the number of items to 10 to 15.

Item Difficulty and Discrimination. Item difficulty is typically conceptualized as the percent of the group that answered the item correctly, whereas item discrimination is the extent to which the item discriminates those who did well on the test from those who did not.

Test items are answered correctly or incorrectly for at least two reasons. The first is related to the children, such as their knowledge, extraneous factors, and so forth, and the second is related the teacher who constructs the test. It is this second area that is discussed here. Teachers should make sure the test has content validity; that is, the test should measure what was taught. As noted earlier, the best way to achieve this goal is to write test items directly from the instructional objectives. The most important objectives, that is, those on which most time was spent, should be given greater attention and thus reflected in more test items.

When we construct tests for children we want tests to discriminate. In such cases, the items should differentiate those who know the material from those who do not. The logical consequence of this position is that not all students will get all items correct or all items incorrect; such items do not discriminate. The reasoning for this is straightforward, although some may question the proposition that a good test does not have all students answering all items correctly. After all, isn't this just a reflection of good instruction? Simply put, no. Good instruction and good testing involves presenting students with material that is challenging; challenging material is more difficult than less challenging material to the extent that the former typically involves low-level skills whereas the latter involves higher level skills. It is probably the case that a test on which all students answer items correctly is most likely a test that measures low-level skills, skills that students already possessed before instruction, or both. Although such a test may serve a motivation function for students, it tells us nothing about the effectiveness of the instruction or what children have learned. Further, such tests shortchange students in that neither the more capable nor the less capable students are probably not being challenged.

Test item discrimination can be established with a simple mathematical procedure. First, all tests should be scored and ordered from the highest to the lowest score. Second, the top and bottom third of the test should be identified. Third, the following formula can be applied to each item to determine its level of discrimination.

$$D = U - L$$
$$N$$

D is equal to the item's discriminating power, L is equal to the number in the lower one third who got the item correct, and U is equal to the number in the upper one third who got the item correct. A score of .20 or less indicates low discrimination; scores above this point to .40 are discriminating; scores greater than .40 are very discriminating. Obviously, positive, not negative, values are desired. For example, in a class of 15 children, 5 in the upper one third got the item correct, whereas 2 in the lower one third got it correct:

$$D = 5 - 2 = 3$$
$$15 \quad = .2$$

This item is not discriminating and probably should be omitted or used on motivation exercises.

Conditions for Testing

In this section we discuss the conditions under which tests should be administered. The conditions to be recommended are relevant for standardized and teacher-made tests, but recommendations specific to standardized tests are addressed first.

As noted earlier, standardized tests are administered under standardized, or uniform, conditions. The reasoning behind this process is straightforward to the extent that the test scores derived from these tests are scores of relative standing; that is, the scores on a test tell us how the test taker(s) performed relative to those in the norming sample. For this reason three specific aspects of standardized testing conditions are important: the norming sample, the empirical norming dates, and machine scorable answer sheets. Alhough we briefly discussed the importance of a match between the norming sample and the students to be tested, its importance merits restatement. Test users should take great care in examining the technical manuals of tests to assure demographic similarity. Some tests actually provide norming information for the specific schools being tested, in addition to regional and national norming formation. This seems to be the best-case scenario.

Empirical norming dates are the actual dates on which the test publisher administered the tests to their norming sample. In some cases a discrepancy exists between this date and the dates given in the score conversion tables. For example, the empirical date for a test might have been in October and the score conversion tables list Fall and Spring norms. It would be wise to administer the test as close to the empirical date as possible to the extent that deviations from that date affect scores systematically; a test administered in September would suppress scores in that students had one less month of instruction than the norming group, whereas a test administered in November would inflate test scores. Generally, tests should be administered within 2 weeks of the empirical norming dates.

Analogous to staying close to the empirical norming dates is following the recommended time limits. Using more time than specified inflates scores, whereas using less time suppresses scores.

The use of machine-scorable answer sheets is common with standardized tests. Test takers, especially children, seem to have difficulty with them, however. Studies indicate that children in fourth grade and below score lower on tests when they used separate answer sheets than when they marked answers on the test booklets. It seems that when separate answer sheets are used with children on tests at least two separate things are being measured: The content in the test and the ability to use answer sheets. Unless use of answer sheets is an instructional objective we should try to minimize the influence of this factor on test performance. We have at least two options: First, and probably the wisest, is to choose a test that does not use separate answer sheets; second, children should be given plenty of practice using such sheets before the actual testing time.

These recommendations should help us maximize the extent to which the test scores inform us on the content that is being tested, not on the content plus extraneous variables. There are other recommendations that are relevant to both standardized and teacher-made tests that help us maximize children's exhibition of competence in this situation. Clear instructions are very important. Additionally, teachers should read the instructions aloud, and they should be followed by the execution of a number of practice items. Teachers should ask students to go through the actual procedures in answering the sample questions. This procedure will hopefully minimize children's misunderstanding of the task. Such misunderstanding typically results in the incorrect entering of answers or in students interrupting the testing session to ask for clarification.

Other forms of distractions can also be minimized. "TESTING" signs on classroom doors can eliminate unnecessary interruptions, as can notices sent to the school custodians. Classroom windows being washed or grass being cut beneath the classroom windows have a disruptive effect.

Allowing adequate time for the test to be completed is another important factor. Tests should be constructed such that all children have adequate time to complete them. Such "power" tests, compared to speed tests, are preferred in most areas, with the notable exceptions being in fields where speed is an important performance factor, such as reading.

The time of day and the day of the week may influence children's test performance. Try to avoid giving tests directly after or before exciting or disruptive events, like recess, lunch, a holiday, or a weekend. If we have difficulty working on a Friday afternoon or on the day after a vacation, think of the difficulty children have!

The intent of this section is to make suggestions that maximize children's performance on tests. Again, we should be interested in measuring the content of the test, not the content plus extraneous variables. Goodwin and Goodwin (1997) offered further recommendations that should be used. For example, in assessing children's math competence, more than one teacher-made test should be used in conjunction with each other and with NRTs. In all cases, the measures used should be content-valid, or measure the instructional objectives taught.

Second, tests should measure a range of difficulty. As noted earlier, one of the more frequent, and justified, criticisms of the use of tests is that they measure low-level concepts. Time should be taken to assure a variety of levels of concepts are tested. The use of taxonomies such as B. Bloom's (1956) is helpful in this regard.

Third, the testing environment should be comfortable and not anxiety-producing. Students' anxiety can be reduced when they are told what is expected of them, provided with clear direction, and minimal interruptions, are familiar with test administrators, and have their progress on the test monitored. In the cases of standardized tests, the recommended administration procedures should be followed.

Fourth, test data should be recorded and stored systematically. Data-recording procedures should be uniform across all students and individual files should be made for each student. For example, a teacher may choose to have a file for each student wherein test data, work samples, homework samples, and behavioral observations are stored. The form and content of the file should be such that they can be easily shared with parents and other professionals. It should be remembered that parents have both the legal—as stated by the Buckley Amendment of 1974—and moral rights to their children's assessment data. All forms of assessment should be collected, stored, and used with these rights in mind. Indeed, particularly valuable use of the assessment data stored in students' files can be made during discussion at parent–teacher conferences.

Performance-Based Assessment

Testing is but one form of assessment. Although they yield important information, there are complementary modes of assessment that are also important, and the multimethod approach we have discussed throughout the book should be taken in this area.

Performance-based, or authentic, assessment (PBA) is one of the more current innovations in student achievement (Baker, O'Neil, & Linn, 1993). Its development has been, in many ways, in direct response to the inadequacies and misuses associated with more traditional forms of assessment. Indeed, this reactive nature has lead to PBA being defined in terms of what it is not. Specifically, it is not true–false or multiple-choice questioning and it is not norm-referenced (Baker et al., 1993). H. Gardner (1993) suggested that we should be concerned with children's "understanding," not the mere production of answers that show the teachers have covered the material. Productions indicative of understanding are assembled in PFA or portfolios.

The following six characteristics have been proffered as defining attributes of PBA (Baker et al., 1993):

1. Open-ended tasks.
2. Requires higher level skills.
3. Utilized context sensitive strategies.
4. Uses complex problems requiring several types of performance.
5. Uses either group or individual performance.
6. Significant degree of student choice.

Open ended typically means that children can produce a number of different products as evidence of understanding. For example, it would be acceptable for children to generate a drawing, a poem, or a dramatic reenactment as evidence of story comprehension

That PBA requires complex cognition is one of the more important attributes. H. Gardner (1993) talked about organizing instruction and subsequent instruction around "gritty central questions" that have provoked scholars of all ages. A sample of these issues includes: my place in the world (e.g., Where do I live and how did I get there?), relations with others (How should you treat other people?), and the biological world (e.g., What about other creatures?). Clearly in order to address these questions higher cognitive skills are demanded, as there are really no clear answers!

Regarding context sensitivity, the tasks on which children are assessed should be taken from their own worlds. Math problems might relate to local problems, such as those relevant to an agricultural community. An important dimensions of context sensitivity is that assumption that local topics are motivating to children and they should exhibit high levels of competence in responding.

Complex problems require that children utilize a number of different performance indicators and that they present projects at various stages of completion. For example, a child might draw a picture, write a poem, and make a model of an ecosystem. By presenting the project at different stages, he or she will reflect on the process of completing a project. Further, this iterative process (which in many ways resembles the scientific method) is a realistic approximation of the ways in which "real problems" get solved. Ideas get generated, tested, presented, and revised. The more proximal levels of presentation and assessment are probably also more reinforcing (positive!) than final, and one-off, assessments.

That PBA assessments are often group-oriented reflects the current belief that knowledge is socially constructed. Further, this sort of presentation again more typically resembles the ways in which problems get solved in the work place and in society, more generally. Groups are responsible for solving problems. It is often the case that individuals are given parts of the problem to solve in which they display expertise. In this way, individuals see how their specific skills fit into larger processes.

This sort of division of labor may be particularly important for children who ordinarily may have difficulty with schoolwork. If they are given a task on which they are expert, they can benefit from knowing that they can solve a problem. This self-efficacy should then generalize to more spheres.

Finally, the idea of student choice relates, again, to motivation. Given a wide variety of "gritty questions," students should have the opportunity to chose those of interest. High levels of interest should again relate to children's exhibition of high levels of comptence.

With this description of PBA in mind, educators should be aware of a number of issues associated with its use. First, we should ask ourselves about the relative importance of performances and products (Messick, 1994). Performances are probably important to assess in those circumstances where the actual procedure for doing something is taught, such as the scientific method. Products as outcomes of assessments are probably more relevant to cases where instruction is concerned with outcomes, not processes, especially in cases where multiple processes can be used to reach a desired outcome.

Additionally, in choosing authentic assessment, educators should ask what it is authentic to: to other tasks in the classroom? To the work place? If so, which one? To the community? If so, which one? (Messick, 1994).

As in other forms of assessment, validity is important (Messick, 1994). The content of the assessment should relate to the construct being assessed and to the purpose of the assessment (construct validity). Further, validity relates to the degree to which the performance or product is the focus of the assessment or if the assessment is to be used as an indicator of more general skills. By way of guidance, educators should have in mind the construct being taught and design multiple assessment guided by that construct.

TECHNICAL AND PRACTICAL CONSIDERATIONS IN TESTING AND ASSESSMENT

Technical Considerations: Reliability

Now that we have discussed the ways in which tests can and should be used in meaningful ways, it is time to comtemplate two final issues: reliability and validity, and the practical considerations related to test usability.

Reliability of tests and other forms of assessment typically refers to the consistency of scores obtained by individuals when reexamined with the same instrument on different occasions (test–retest reliability), with different types of equivalent items (alternate form or split-half reliability), or with consistency of the scoring of the instrument (scorer reliability). Each of these forms is discussed in turn.

Test–retest reliability is determined by the same assessment being given on different occasions. For example, an achievement test can be given on Monday and Friday. The reliability, typically expressed as a correlation coefficient or as a percent, is the extent to which the two test scores are similar. This form of reliability gives insight into the stability of the test scores across time and situations. The higher the coefficient or percent, the more stable the test. Test–retest reliability coefficients are notoriously low for young children.

This state of affairs is probably the results of children being particularly vulnerable to extraneous factors affecting their performance. Indeed, a number of commercial tests for preschool and primary school children do not have test–retest reliability data reported in their technical manuals! This should tell us something about the overreliance on this sort of test with young children. What confidence should be put in a test that tells us one thing about a child on Monday and a different thing on Friday? For this reason, among others, a test must be reliable in order to be valid, or truthful. Hopefully, what is truthful on Monday will also be truthful on Friday!

Alternate form reliability is a way in which different forms of the same tests can be compared. For example, many achievement tests have separate forms to measure the same content; these different forms are often used as separate pre- and posttests. The extent to which alternate forms are related can be expressed like other reliability statistics, with percent scores or correlation coefficients. Alternate form reliability statistics reflect a test's temporal stability, similar to test–retest reliability, as well as a test's consistency of responses to different items that measure similar content.

Split-half reliability measures the extent to which a test is homogeneous. This form of reliability is typically determined by splitting the test responses into two categories, responses to the odd items and responses to the even items. The split-half reliability statistic, again expressed as a percent or correlation coefficient, tells us the degree to which these two sets of scores are similar.

Scorer reliability compares the ways in which different scorers make quality judgements about performance. For example, given a 25-item math test, what is the scorer agreement in marking the items right or wrong? On objective tests, the agreement should be perfect, or close to it. Scorer reliability is only a problem when the criteria to be scored are not clear; for example, there should be less agreement on grades given on an essay test than on a multiple-choice test because the grade on the former is influenced by extraneous factors, like handwriting and neatness, whereas the latter is not. Criteria for performance should therefore be clearly and explicitly presented so that all scorers are clear on what counts and what does not.

Technical Considerations: Validity

As most students will recognize, reliability is necessary but not sufficient for validity. That is, a test must be reliable to be valid, but reliability is not enough. For example, if the instructor in a child study course was to administer a test of single-digit addition as a midterm examination for that course, the test would be reliable along all of the dimensions noted earlier. It certainly would not be a valid test of the material covered in a child study course, however. Validity of an assessment instrument is related to what is measured and how well it is measured. In short, the validity of a test is its truth value. In this section we discuss construct, content, and criterion-related validity.

Construct validity has traditionally been defined in terms of the test or instrument measuring a psychological construct, trait, or ability. Examples of constructs are intelligence, creativity, ability, aptitude, dominance, and so forth. Messick (1983) made the point that all tests should provide construct valid information regarding what is and what is not measured. For example, a math achievement test should measure math achievement but not reading achievement. Construct validity is usually established by relating, through the use of correlation coefficients, the test of interest with other tests that have been shown to measure that construct. Further, the test of interest should not be related to tests that measure other constructs.

More recently, the definition of construct validity has been broaden to include the social interpretation and policy repercussions of test scores or assessment outcomes (Messick, 1995; Moss, 1992). This is related to the use, and abuse, of tests in high-stakes decisions. Thus, a test used for promotion or retention decisions should have construct validity data relevant to those sorts of decisions.

Content validity tells us the extent to which tests measure what was taught. As noted earlier, content validity is import for both teacher-made and standardized tests. The content validity of a test can be examined or established (in the case of teacher-made tests) using a relatively simple procedure. First, the instructional objectives for the period to be tested should be listed on separate lines across the top of a sheet of paper.

Next, with each test being examined, each of the test items should be categorized as belonging to a specific objective or not belong to the objectives. In the latter case the item should be placed in the "No objective" column. This process determines the extent to which the instructional objectives are being assessed. Obviously it is desirable for most of the objectives to be covered by the test. Further, the objectives that are the most important should account for most of the test items. For example, if most of the course content revolves around

Objectives 5 and 6, then most of the test items should be categorized under these objectives. If more than one test is being reviewed for content validity, the test that most closely measures the program content should be chosen. Similarly, when constructing a test, test items should correspond to their stress in the content of the program.

Criterion-related validity has two components—concurrent and predictive validity. Concurrent validity indicates the interrelation between two measures at the same period in time. For example, we would be interested in the concurrent validity of a student behavioral checklist and students' actual behavioral problems on the playground. The extent to which these two measures concur is the extent to which they have concurrent validity. Again, concurrent validity is usually expressed with correlation coefficients.

Predictive validity is the extent to which one measure predicts another. Whereas concurrent validity was the relation between measures at the same time, predictive validity is the interrelation of measures across time. Using the example given earlier, to what extent does the student behavioral checklist in Grade 1 predict behavior problems in Grade 2? A more common example of predictive validity is the relation between SAT scores and college grade point average. Predictive validity is typically expressed with correlation coefficients.

The predictive validity of tests for young children are difficult to the extent that scores from one period may not predict performance at a future point. The reasons for this are many; for example, young children are very susceptible to the effects of extraneous factors and they undergo significant development change. These specific developmental issues were addressed in chapter 2.

The reliability and validity of tests are very important considerations. Baldly stated, tests that do not have these quantities are meaningless. Those making decisions for the choice of tests and for the construction of tests should keep this in the foreground. Other factors, what we will call usability factors should also be considered when choosing and constructing tests.

CONCLUSIONS

In this chapter we have discussed the use of tests and performance-based assessment with children. Today tests are the target of much criticism, although they are being used in an increasing number of areas, resulting in abuses and the subsequent rise in PBA techniques. We have suggested that there is nothing inherent in any form of assessment that leads to abuse; any form of assessment can be misused.

Abuse can be minimized if we are guided by concerns of construct validity and if tests and PBA are used in conjunction with these other data sources. It is particularly important to use varied modes of assessment when making important decisions, such as grade promotions, retentions, or assignment to special classes. In all, tests are probably most useful as a means to improve instruction and, consequently, should be used that way.

5

Experimental Methods

THE EXPERIMENTAL APPROACH

In this chapter we discuss experimental methods, which approach child study in a way similar to those methods used in testing situations. In both cases, the researchers try to elicit information from children by putting them in a contrived, or analogue, situation. Typically the conditions under which these methods are used are controlled.

These methods are easily contrasted with the more naturalistic approaches to be discussed in the next chapter. In naturalistic approaches to child study, children are observed in their natural habits, not controlled situations. Although each set of methods has positive and negative dimensions, the ultimate choice for a method of child study should be guided by one's question and the most effective method to answer that question should dictate choice. Ultimately, however, we think that the complexity of children's lives cannot be understood with only one method. Consequently, a multiple method approach to the study of children is probably most fruitful and the experimental method should represent one of many strategies used.

Despite this commonsense approach, there seems to be a "paradigm war" (Gage, 1989) raging between experimentalists and interpretive, naturalistic researchers, especially in the area of educational research. Although polemics are helpful at the beginning of major disagreements between groups so that they can each define themselves clearly, at this point we should recognize that there is no one "silver bullet" or crystal ball that will provide all the answers. We should draw what we can from each approach to help us better understand the complexities of childhood.

SOME BASIC PREMISES OF EXPERIMENTAL METHODS

Whereas naturalistic approaches attempt to study children in the everyday environment, the experimental approach attempts to create an experimental, often contrived, environment in which to examine children. Aspects of the environment thought to affect children's behavior are manipulated and controlled. Through manipulation and control researchers can make causal inferences about these manipulations.

Experimental environments can be real classrooms, as in the cases of field experiments of curriculum and design (P. K. Smith & Connolly, 1980), laboratories, where children are taken from their natural habitats and studied (Pellegrini & Perlmutter, 1989), or hybrid designs where parts of classrooms are experimentally controlled and manipulated (I. Jones & A. D. Pellegrini, 1996). These terms *manipulate* and *control* are crucial to the experimental method, and are discussed in greater depth later because they help us make causal inferences about sets of variables.

Generally, experiments are conducted in order to isolate specific cause–effect relationships. That is, experimenters attempt to identify the effects of certain independent variables (e.g., crowding) on behavior, or dependent variables (e.g., children's aggression). The independent variables are manipulated to examine their effect on the dependent measure. Other, extraneous, variables are controlled so that they do not influence the relation between independent and dependent variables, and thus cloud the causal picture. Experiments that give us insight into the effects of an independent variable on a dependent variable, without confounding effects of extraneous variables, are said to be *internally valid*.

Experiments are thus most beneficial where the investigator is interested in identifying such cause–effect relationships. Further, experiments can be conducted only in situations where investigators are free to manipulate and control aspects of the children's environment. For example, to investigate the cause–effect relationhip between certain styles of teachers' reading books to children and children's literacy, the investigator must be free to vary, or manipulate, different reading environments.

Two types of experiments are relevant. True experiments are defined as those in which participants and conditions are randomly assigned to groups and data collection schedules are standardized, whereas quasi-experiments do not have the benefit of randomization or standardized data collection schedules (Campbell & Stanley, 1963). True experiments are difficult to conduct in most applied settings because one cannot usually randomly assign children and manipulate environments at will; quasi-experiments, however, can be implemented in many applied settings.

This chapter is intended to familiarize the reader with the process of conducting experiments. In this way, the reader can intelligibly consume the experimental literature that addresses issues in child study. In addition, the chapter serves as a general guide to conducting an experiment and outlines some basic assumptions about the experimental approach. First we discuss the experimental approach as an extension of the scientific method. In the next two sections, we discuss laboratory and field experiments. Then we discuss research design, outlining the basic premises involved in designing experiments, and examine important concepts related to research design: internal, external, and ecological validity. Generally these concepts refer to the truthfulness of the results obtained (internal validity), the extent to which these experimental results are interpretable in the world outside of the laboratory (external validity), and the extent to which demands of the experimental laboratory match the demands of the situation to which results will be generalized. We also discuss ecological validity of experiments, or judging experiments in terms of their approximations of the actual worlds that children inhabit.

Most experimenters examine their results through a variety of statistical techniques. Although we do not outline specific statistical procedures here, the reader is referred to a number of excellent introductory books that discuss experiments and appropriate statistical analyses of experimental results (Kerlinger, 1973, 1980; McCall, 1980). We discuss some of the underlying principles, however, that should be applied to experiments in order to apply certain statistical analyses. In the final section we discuss the advantages and disadvantages of the experimental approach in comparison with the naturalistic approach.

BEHAVIORAL RESEARCH AS "SCIENCE"

A common aim of scientific inquiry is to know about a phenomenon, and an assumption behind many different forms of enquiry is that truth can be uncovered, or is knowable. A general rule of thumb for using scientific enquiry to know involves the elimination of false ideas. First, however, the idea must be put in terms that allow it to be tested for "falsifiability." A common example involves discussions over the origins of man. The creationist view that man was created by God in the Garden of Eden, for example, cannot be subjected to test of falsifiability. An alternative idea, natural selection, can be tested, and evaluated in terms of the consistency of the evidence with the theory. The methods used to expose falsehood are indeed varied. Different modes of inquiry typically include observing naturally occurring behavior, asking others questions, or both. We then make inferences about the meaning of those behaviors as part of our quest to know.

Another approach to knowing is the experiment. Experimental methods originated in the physical sciences and were adapted by the behavioral sciences. A basic assumption behind the experimental approach is that we have a theory, or explanation, for the way in which something works. For example, following massed versus distributed practice theory, we might posit that providing children with a recess break after prolonged periods of classroom works to improve their performance on those tasks. We could design an experiment where children's attention to classroom tasks is measured before and after recess. We then manipulate the duration of time before recesses are provided. It may be that on certain days recess is every 2 hours and on other days it is every 3.5 hours. Our idea, or hypothesis, would be supported if children in the 2-hour group were more attentive than the other group. This procedure, however, also affords the possibility of not having our hypothesis supported (falsified). Consequently, the extent to which theories and their data are capable of tests that deem them true or false is, *the* hallmark of science.

Experimenters manipulate aspects of situations in order to produce their predicted effects. Extraneous variables, or those not of interest, must be controlled, or made to not influence the results. An example of manipulation and control may help clarify the point. Researchers have a theory that recess, and other types of breaks, maximizes children's attention to tasks and possibly learning (A. D. Pellegrini & D. F. Bjorklund, 1997). The prediction is that the frequent, compared to infrequent, breaks should result in increased attention. In order to test this experimentally we would have to manipulate, or systematically vary, subjects' exposure to the independent variable—different recess timing regimens—or the dependent variable—attention to classroom tasks. Different groups, or the same groups at different times, would experience different recess regimens. Extraneous variables, which could effect results, should be controlled. For example, different teachers or different types of tasks may influence children's attention; thus teachers and tasks musts be controlled. Extraneous variables are not directly relevant to our theory but could influence results. For example, one can easily imagine cases that teachers who allow more frequent recesses might have other attributes that relate to children's attention. Similarly, there are clearly some tasks that are more interesting to children than others. Thus we should control tasks and teachers so that their effects do not "confound" or contaminate the effects of recess timing on attention.

Aside from manipulation, another feature of experimental inquiry is objectivity (Kerlinger, 1980). Indeed, naturalistic, psychometric, and experimental approaches all aspire to obtain objective data. By objective we mean two things: First, an observation or datum is objective if it can be observed by more than one observer; second, results are objective if they can be replicated by other researchers. The importance of replication is the reason for the elaborately described Methods sections of most experimental reports (see the section in this chapter describing the experimental report). For example, descriptions of the exact age of the children involved in a study, as well as the number and types of toys that children play with in an experimental setting, are necessary for replication attempts.

Replication is also important in making policies that affect children. We as researchers should be clear that our programs can be replicated before the lives of children, parents, and teachers are affected. Relatedly, programs that are implemented before they have been replicated have a negative effect on the likelihood that other innovative programs might be adopted. Why should policy makers and taxpayers, the reasonable person might ask, support adoption of a program that has uncertain effects?

The third hallmark of behavioral science is the reliance on evidence or data (Kerlinger, 1980). Again, reliance on data is not only advocated by experimentalists, but by all empirical researchers. Reliance on data simply means that interpretations and conclusions should be based on the data obtained from objective observations, experiments, or both. Again, the data should guide policy and implementation of programs.

CAUSALITY

Most researchers would agree that the hallmark of experimental research is the ability to infer cause–effect relationships. Causal inferences can be made when our experimental manipulations result in predicted outcomes. Of course, they must be embedded in a theory to the extent that experiments are designed to test theories. In short, causal inferences are only as good as our theories. Experimental manipulations and predicted results are not, however, unequivocal.

Although we may conduct an experiment and the results might support or hypotheses, there may be room for discussion about the meaning of the results. First and foremost, we should recognize the fact that just because kids do something in an experiment, or in any other situation where we choose to study them, does not mean that they will also do it in other situations. It may be, as Robert McCall (1977), noted 20 years ago, that experiments tell us what children can do; they may not tell us what they actually do in their lives. Relatedly, it may be that the observed experimental effects only explain a portion, albeit it a statistically significant portion, of our results. There is the real possibility that other children in other situation reach those same outcomes through very different means. Thus, an experimental treatment may result in a child learning a certain strategy; this result does not preclude the possibility that other treatments may have similar results.

We offer these qualifiers as a prologue to our discussion on causality. Human being are very complex beings and defy simple explanation. We should remain equivocal in our examination of evidence. This stance should not, however, result in nihilistic responses that there is no meaning anywhere. We should continue to try and find out what works for certain children in certain situations, recognizing that we always have more to learn, remaining open to alternative explanation, and testing those explanations.

Of course, poorly designed experiments tell us little if anything about the veracity of ideas. For example, suppose we found in an experiment that children exposed to sugar were more hyperactive than the children in a sugar-free group. Our causal inference regarding the effects of sugar may be inaccurate. The differences in children's behaviors may have been due to the food that the sugar was put on, not to the sugar itself; thus the food confounded the effects of the sugar.

Correlations between variables are often confused with causal relations. Rather, they show the extent to which they are interrelated (in a linear way) with each other. Thus there is usually a positive correlation between the amount of time children spend studying and their achievement scores; the more one studies, the higher the score. A common negative correlation involves the relation between aggression and popularity: The more aggressive a child is, the less popular he or she is (usually). Correlations, however, do not show causality. It may be, for example, that children are aggressive because they are disliked, not vice versa. Only through experimentation do we know that aggression does cause children to be disliked.

A necessary, but not sufficient, condition for causality is the existence of an antecedent–consequence relationship. That is, one variable, the antecedent, must precede the outcome, or consequence, in time. Thus aggression must precede rejection within a specific peer group. Obviously, these antecedent–consequence relations can be observed outside of the laboratory, and longitudinal research design, or studying children across a time span, is one excellent way to accomplish this.

Causality involves more than antecedent–consequence relations, however. Causality can be established only when extraneous variables are controlled and theoretically relevant variables are manipulated. Although these conditions can be met with naturalistic studies utilizing a form of statistical testing, or *structural models* (see A. D. Pellegrini, Galda, & Flor, 1997, for an example involving peer group, oral language, and early literacy), they are usually accomplished through laboratory or field experimentation.

LABORATORY EXPERIMENTS

An experiment attempts to construct a controlled, analogue model of the world inside of the laboratory. The environment is constructed such that the researcher is manipulating aspects of the environment relevant to the hypothesis being tested. For example, a researcher may be interested in the effects of specific museum exhibits on children's social behavior; an experiment would thus be designed to approximate a museum. The specific exhibits (or independent variable) are experimentally manipulated to determine their causal effects on certain social behaviors (the dependent variable). The children may be exposed to dinosaurs and then to prisms. Inferences regarding the effect of these exhibits on behavior are based on the observations of children interacting with each exhibit. As such, the first purpose of laboratory experiments is to discover relations between variables under "uncontaminated" conditions (Kerlinger, 1973). In the experimental museum exhibit example, children's free choice of exhibits is controlled, and thus it does not contaminate the effect of the exhibit. Exposure to specific exhibits is manipulated and we can judge their effects on behavior, without the contaminating effects of children's self-selection into exhibits. Self-selection must be controlled because it would probably affect behavior. That is, there probably are real differences in children who choose to go to museum and those who choose not to go; similarly there are probably differences between children who choose to interact with different exhibits within a museum, and these differences probably affect behavior.

By controlling extraneous variables and manipulating relevant variables we can make reasonable, although cautious, inferences about the effects of the independent variables on the dependent variables.

Laboratory Experiments: Strengths and Weaknesses

A real strength of experiments is the ability to make causal inferences. We can manipulate and assign in many different ways; quasi-experiments exist when we cannot randomly choose and assign subjects. As such, they are probably a more realistic choice for most applied settings, and we can thus make precise tests of theories. We can be more sure that our results are due to our manipulations than we could if we utilized other research approaches.

The main weakness of the experimental approach is equally as obvious as its strengths. The artificiality of the experimental situation may mean that the subjects behave differently in the laboratory than they do in "real world" situations (Bronfenbrenner, 1979). Indeed, we might argue that the more controlled the experiment, the further it is from an approximation of a real world situation. Children may act one way in a laboratory playroom but very differently in their classroom. Recall McCall's warning: Laboratory experiments tell us what children can do, not what they actually do.

Taking a point repeatedly made in cross-cultural psychology theorizing (e.g., Cole, 1988; Rogoff & Morelli, 1989; Wertsch, 1985), the specific context in which children development affects their development. By examining children in different contexts we become aware of possible causal mechanisms in development. In order to design such different experimental contexts, however, we must be aware that such differences exist and design experiments that are appropriate for the question under consideration. An example will clarify. We are interested in what causes some infants to walk earlier than others. In order to study this, we be aware of the different ways in which infants' sensorimotor development is treated in cultures that have different walking onset periods. Differences are typically due to specific context differences; in cultures with early onset, infants' sitting and walking are encouraged, crawling is not. In short, the choice of the context that we think will elicit behavior is all important.

Probably more relevant to studying children in laboratory experiments is the fact that young children are extremely vulnerable to the effects of strange situations. As we noted in our discussion of testing, when children are put into a strange situation, they become anxious. Anxiety, in turn, relates to children exhibiting low, rather than high, levels of competence.

So what to do? Simply, make the experimental environment as familiar as possible. The discussion on ecological validity to follow will be most helpful here. Children should be observed in experimental settings on numerous occasions or, if that is not a possibility, observe them for a prolonged period. For example, if we are interested in the differential effects of toys on children's play behaviors, we should observe a child repeatedly in each of the toy settings. A useful rule of thumb has been presented by Wachs (1985). He suggested that if we observe one occasion it should be for 90 minutes; two occasions should be 45 minutes each. Repeated or prolonged exposure to the experimental setting will make it less strange and anxiety-producing to the child.

Of course, experimentally manipulating dimensions of those contexts that children usually inhabit, such as schools or clubs—field experiments—is a preferred option.

FIELD EXPERIMENTS

In the previous section on laboratory (true) experiments, we noted that all aspects of the environment had to be randomized and controlled in order to make causal inferences about our treatments. To say the least, randomization and control are very difficult to achieve in applied settings. We offer field experiments as a compromise in that they are more realistically achieved in applied settings.

Field experiments are experiments that take place in real situations. The researcher, however, manipulates these environments. Some of the best examples of field experiments involve research in preschool settings. The work of Johnson and his colleagues (e.g., J. Johnson & Ershler, 1981), Lawton (e.g., Lawton & Fowler, 1989), and P. K. Smith and Connolly (1980) with preschoolers is illustrative of excellent field experiments where the differential effects of curriculum was studied. In other cases with primary schools, researchers have manipulated children's exposure to different recess timing regimens to determine their effect on children's attention to seat work (Pellegrini, 1995). In one Johnson study, for example, preschool curriculum (traditional–didactic vs. open–exploratory) was systematically manipulated in each classroom to determine the effect of each on children's play behaviors (Johnson & Ershler, 1981). Lawton and Fowler (1989) compared Piagetian and Ausubelian programs on teachers' and children's language. In the P. K. Smith and

Connolly (1980) study, classrooms that differed on aspects of social and spatial density as well as types of toys were designed. Pellegrini and colleagues compared the effects of long versus short periods during which children were deprived of recess.

A major advantage of field experiments over those in a laboratory is that the children are being observed in a realistic and familiar setting. As a result, the conclusions made about children's observed behavior also are likely to be supported by observations in similar, nonmanipulated, settings.

The field experiment also has its disadvantages. Experimenters typically exercise control on an external institution, like the classroom, as they can in an experimental situation. For example, teachers in a field experiment, because they were often hired for reasons other than their ability to act as experimenters, may not be consistent in their use of a particular experimental technique. As a result, the actual experimental treatment may not be consistent with the ideal treatment. Experimenters who are trained and retrained to implement a specific procedure may be more reliable.

"NATURAL" EXPERIMENTS

Moving down the ladder of control from true laboratory experiments we come to the interesting case of "natural" experiments. Natural experiments exist when important natural events occur which may have an effect on children's behavior. Examples of such events include: a family moving from one neighborhood to another, a fetus' in utero experience, or a group witnessing a traumatic event. We then gauge the effect of these events (considered independent, or predictor, variables) on theoretically relevant behavior. Take the case (reviewed in Rutter, 1985) of a child who is having behavior problems in one school. His parents move house and he attends another school, one with fewer boys having behavior problems. The boy's problems then decline. We conclude that if we statistically control the effect of extraneous variables, such as income, the move and school change contributed to the decline.

Another case: A mother is having pregnancy difficulties and her physician prescribes hormones (androgens). These male hormones represent a "treatment" on the fetus' development and they typically result in girls exhibiting more male-typical behaviors than comparisons.

These cases are interesting because they involve manipulation that researchers either could not or would not execute. Given the "natural" occurrence of the interventions, however, they becoming interesting cases. Of course a number of other variables, other than those listed as "treatments," may also be influencing the dependent variable. In the boy moving example, it might be the case that more affluent, compared to less affluent, parents tend to move out of areas where there are "problems" in schools. Parents' SES and their desire to "move up" probably have added effects on children's problem behaviors. In the hormones cases, mother may be aware of the relation between male hormones and children's behavior and thus treat their daughters differently.

Practioners and researchers alike should take advantage of natural experiments as a way of studying something that otherwise would be impossible to study. However, because of the probable influence of numerous other variables, various explanations should be systematically explored and rejected where appropriate.

RESEARCH DESIGN

Research design is the procedure by which experiments are designed and actually implemented. They are most relevant to both laboratory and field experiments, and less relevant to natural experiments, as we do not design them. Issues of design are relevant here, however, to the extent that they inform us as to the multitude of forces that affect the dependent measure.

Experimental designs are blueprint-like plans describing the plan of the research. The concepts of internal and external validity determine different types of research designs. Experiments should be designed such that they are internally, externally, and ecologically valid.

Internal Validity

Experiments should be designed such that threats to the internal validity of the experiment are minimized. Internally valid experiments are those in which the stated experimental manipulations (or independent variables) are the main factors causing variation on that which is being measured (dependent variable). In other words, internally valid experiments control the effects of extraneous (of nonmanipulated) variables on the dependent measures. In the example previously outlined about the effects of sugar on hyperactivity, we noted a scenario wherein the causes of hyperactivity may have been due to the food on which the sugar was applied. The food, therefore, was not controlled and, as a result, confounded the effect of the sugar. In this case the food was an extraneous variable. In order to control this extraneous variable we should have used exactly the same food for both groups, adding sugar to food of one group.

Campbell and Stanley (1963), in their classic monograph on experimental design, outlined eight extraneous factors that could affect the internal validity of experiments. They are listed in Table 5.1.

History, or specific events occurring between two measurement points, can have an extraneous effect. For example, in the case where students are given an experimental science curriculum to improve their achievement, inclusion of their regular science curriculum may be an extraneous variable affecting achievement. In order to prevent history from affecting results, or controlling history, we should have members of all experimental groups be exposed to virtually the same experiences over time. Following the sugar example pre-

TABLE 5.1
Threats to the Internal Validity of Experiments

1. History	5. Instrumentation
2. Maturation	6. Differential selection
3. Testing	7. Experimental mortality
4. Statistical regression	8. Selection–maturation interaction

viously given, children in both groups should be exposed to the same curriculum so that they have equal experiences that might elicit hyperactivity. The groups should differ only in the experimental treatments they receive.

Maturation is the effects of passing time on subjects. For example, children may be more tired at the end of an experiment than at the beginning. As a result, fatigue has an extraneous effect. Maturation can be controlled in a way similar to history. Have all students in all conditions experienced the same time span and events between the data collection points?

Testing is where students' exposure to a pretest affects their performance on a posttest. For example, students may show improvement from one test to the other simply because they remember test questions. This knowledge of the test has an extraneous effect on their measured growth. Testing can be controlled by extending the time span between the pre- and posttest.

Statistical regression occurs when students score very low or very high on the pretest. They tend to "regress toward the mean" (or score more near the average) on the posttest. As a result, differences between pre- and posttest scores may be due to regression, not the treatment. Regression to the mean can be controlled by administering pre- and posttests to all groups in the experiment.

Instrumentation is when changes occur between pre- and posttest due to a change in measurement instruments. For example, for the pretest a student may have been given a test using machine-scorable answer sheets; the posttest may have used interviews. Differences between these scores are probably due to the different procedures used. Instrumentation can be controlled by administering the same, or parallel, form of a test for pre- and posttesting purposes.

Differential selection means that between-group differences may be due to the procedures used to select and assign children to different groups in the experiments. Differential selection can be controlled by randomly selecting the sample and then randomly selecting assigning the selected subjects to different experimental groups.

Experimental mortality, or attrition, is when subjects leave the experiment before it is over. If they leave for reasons related to the experiment itself (for example, "Treatment A" may be too difficult), then between-group differences may be affected by persons leaving the experiment. For example, because only the slower students left the experiment, "Treatment A" has more bright students left in it than the other groups. Between-group differences may be due to group differences, not treatment differences. Mortality can be controlled by checking to see if the subjects who have left the experiment are significantly different from those who remained in the study.

Selection–maturation interaction means that certain types of students (selection) may be more prone to the maturation effect. For example, hyperactive children are more likely than nonhyperactive children to experience fatigue during a treatment. Selection–maturation can be controlled by random selection and assignment and by equalizing the amount of time of each group's treatment.

Examples of Research Designs

In this section we examine two specific research designs. The purpose of this section is to illustrate the way in which certain designs control for or fail to control for threats to internal validity. Campbell and Stanley (1963) provided a very thorough discussion of the threats to the internal validity of 12 research designs. The reader interested in this topic is referred to that source. The second example given in this chapter should serve as a guide in conducting an experiment.

The first example, the one-group pretest–posttest design is an example with many threats to internal validity. The design of the study involves, first, a group of children being selected and assigned, not randomly, to one experimental group. The group is then given a pretest (O). The pretest is given to provide information on the group before the experimental treatment is administered. Next, the group receives the treatment (X). Following the treatment a posttest (O) is administered to determine children's status after the treatment. This research design can be graphically represented, following Campbell and Stanley (1963), as O X O.

With this design, however, there are a number of extraneous factors that could be responsible for pre- and posttest score differences. We examine this experiment in terms of each of the eight threats to internal validity. First, history could be affecting results. Many events, other than the treatment, occurring between the pre- and posttest could have been responsible for differences in scores. If the pretest was given on a Tuesday and the posttest on a Friday, differences in scores may have been due to children's eagerly anticipating enjoying the weekend; as a result, they were not attentive on the posttest. Similarly, maturation, such as boredom with the task over the experimental period, could affect performance.

Regarding testing and regression, simultaneously, changes in pre- and posttest scores may have been due to either children becoming "test-wise" after the pretest (testing) or regressing toward the mean on the posttest. That is, if they scored at an extreme on the pretest, they would have scored closer to the mean on the posttest. The regression effects are less clear in this design than the testing effects, however.

Instrumentation may affect results because the way in which children are measured may change from pre- to posttest. For example, observer fatigue during the second observation may cause inaccurate scoring of the posttest.

Selection and morality are not problems. Regarding selection, because there is only one group, differential assignment to groups cannot affect results. Similarly, with mortality, because there is only one group, mortality cannot affect one group differently than another.

This brief discussion of the one-group pretest–posttest design should point out the weaknesses of such an approach. Results obtained with this design actually raise more questions than they answer; because of this, we question using such an approach.

In the next experimental design to be discussed, the pretest–posttest control group design, we can eliminate all threats to internal validity by adding two procedures to the inadequate one-group pretest–posttest design: random assignment to groups and two different experimental groups. In this design all children are randomly (R) assigned to one of two groups. This means that all subjects have an equal chance to be in either group. All subjects are given both pre- and posttest (O) but only one group receives an experimental treatment (X). The other group is the control group. That is, it has all the same experiences as the experimental groups except for the experimental treatment. Thus, an important first step in conducting an experiment is the random assignment of subjects to conditions. This design has been graphically represented by Campbell and Stanley (1963) as:

R O X O

R O O

In this design, neither history, maturation, nor testing differentially affects results: Both groups should have equally mature students and the passage of time should affect them equally. In addition, children in both groups experience the same pre- and posttest. Instrumentation is controlled when we control intrasession, or within session, history, particularly when students respond to standardized written tests or observers are randomly assigned to make posttest observations.

Regression is not a problem with this design because both groups experience both pre- and posttest; thus, regression should affect them equally. As a result, no between-group differences due to regression should occur.

Selection is controlled because students are randomly assigned to groups. Different types of students (e.g., motivated vs. not motivated) should be equally distributed between groups because of the randomization.

Mortality should be checked. When students leave the experiment, the researcher should check to see if more students leave one group (e.g., the treatment group) than the other. In addition, the type of students leaving should be checked. Is one particular type of student (e.g., bright) leaving?

This brief discussion of two experimental designs should make clear the importance of both randomization and control groups. By incorporating these two procedures into a weak design, we made it much stronger.

External Validity

Experimenters are typically most concerned with the internal validity of experiments (Campbell & Stanley, 1963). A premium is placed on knowing that results are due to specified experimental manipulations, not extraneous factors. The concern with external validity is often given less prominence. External validity is concerned with the extent to which the experimental results can be "generalized" outside of the experimental setting (Bracht & Glass, 1968; Campbell & Stanley, 1963). For example, can an experiment involving middle-class children attending a university preschool be generalized to a group of lower socioeconomic status (LESS) Head Start children?

Campbell and Stanley (1963) discussed four possible threats to the external validity of experiments. The reactive or interactive effect of testing poses a threat to external validity. That is, occurrence of a pretest may sensitize subjects to the upcoming experimental treatment. As such, the pretest may make the subject more or less susceptible to the experimental treatment. The use of the pretest with the experimental group may mean that the results of the treatment are not generalizable (or applicable) to the unpretested population at large.

Selection biases interacting with experimental treatments also effect external validity. This means that certain types of subjects chosen for an experiment may be more or less susceptible to an experimental treatment than others. For example, in a study (Saltz, Dixon, & Johnson, 1977) where preschool children were trained to engage in thematic-fantasy play (see this volume's chap. 11, on play, for a discussion), it was found that the training was more effective with brighter preschoolers than it was with less bright children. This result suggests that the type of subjects chosen often affects results. These results can only be generalized to a population similar to the population used in the experiment.

Reactive effects to experimental arrangements is a threat to external validity. In short, people, especially children, behave differently in an experimental laboratory than in a more familiar, less contrived settings (e.g., Eisenberg, 1983). Indeed, the mere presence of an observer in a familiar setting causes children to act differently than if they were not being observed (Brody, Stoneman, & Wheatley, 1984). The best example is probably from the infancy literature. It is well known that infants' exploratory behavior decreases when they are put in a strange situation (Ainsworth, 1971). As a result, children may behave one way during an experiment but very differently when the same treatment is used in a more familiar context.

The last threat to external validity discussed by Campbell and Stanley (1963) is interference due to multiple treatments. This means that if experiments are designed in which children are given more than one treatment, the effects of the previous treatments may be maintained. As a result, we can only generalize to those groups having the same series of multiple treatments.

Generalizability, or the extent to which we can generalize results from one experiment to the population we have sampled from, is an important aspect of the external validity of experiments. Bracht and Glass (1968) discussed two general categories related to the generalizability of experimental results. They are population validity and ecological validity. Population validity is concerned with the ability to generalize from the experimental subjects (kindergartners in Clarke County, GA) to the population at large (all kindergarten-age children in the Western world!). Ecological validity (not defined the same as Bronfenbrenner, 1979) is concerned with the extent to which experimental results can be generalized to other environmental conditions.

Bracht and Glass (1968) have expanded Campbell and Stanley's (1963) threats to external validity by adding:

1. Explicit description of the experimental treatment is necessary so that others can try to replicate the results in similar and different conditions.
2. Novelty and disruptive effects suggests that changes in behavior may be merely due to a change in routine (e.g., having a different color reading book) rather than to the content of the experimental treatment (e.g., a new reading series).
3. The Hawthorne Effect suggests that subjects act differently merely because they have been given special attention, such as treatment.
4. Experimenter effects means that a treatment is more or less effective because of the personality of a particular experimenter.

In short, factors influencing the external validity of experiments are related to the interpret ability of the experimental results outside of the experimental setting. It should be noted, however, that use of a no-treatment control group (i.e., a group that is similar to the experimental group, but gets no special treatment at), compared to a control group that gets a placebo, does not generally result in a Hawthorne Effect (Adair, Sharpe, & Huynh, 1989).

Ideally, experiments should be designed that minimize threats to both external and internal validity. As previously noted, those advocating the use of the experimental approach often are more concerned with internal than with external validity. One experimental design that does minimize threats to internal and external validity is the posttest-only control group design (Campbell & Stanley, 1963):

R X O
R   O

Note that in this design both randomization and multiple groups are used, but pretests are not. All threats to internal validity are controlled and the testing threat to external validity is also controlled. Issues of ecological validity, however, still need to be addressed.

Ecological Validity

Ecologically valid experiments seem to take the best from the two worlds of experimental and naturalistic research. Following Bronfenbrenner's (1979) conception, ecologically valid experiments involve observing children in their natural habitat, such as a preschool classroom, and designing an analogue experimental situation. The designing of the experimental analogue should be such that children are in a similar environment as their classroom. Similarity involves similar physical props (e.g., toys), social configurations (e.g., number and gender of playmates), and mental-demand characteristics (e.g., children are assigned by teachers to play in certain areas at certain times). Comparisons should be made between the same or similar children in both the natural and experimental environments. Similarity of results documents ecological validity. An example of such a study was conducted by A. D. Pellegrini and Perlmutter (1989). The play behavior of preschool children was observed while they were in the classroom. Based on these observations, it was determined that children played in same-gender dyads, without adults. Further, the attractiveness of play props was determined for boys and girls. An experimental analogue to the classroom was designed whereby the children played in same-gender dyads with the same toys. Children were expected to play with both male and female preference toys. This regimen was not unlike that made by teachers in their requiring children to interact with a variety of play results in the classroom. The results were such that children's play was similar in both contexts. Consequently, the experiment was ecologically valid.

The value of such an approach is that we can make causal statements about the effects of toys (due to the experimental manipulations), while simultaneously knowing that children play in like ways in their natural environments. For educational researchers ecologically valid experiments are a necessity, not a luxury. We need to know that an experimental results effect children's real experiences and can be generalized to classrooms. It is of some interest knowing that children can behave in an experiment in a certain way. We need to know how they actually behave in their everyday context.

THE EXPERIMENTAL APPROACH EVALUATED: ADVANTAGES AND DISADVANTAGES

As we have discussed throughout this chapter the real advantage of the experimental approach is its controlled nature. This control of threats to internal validity allows the researcher to begin to make cause–effect statements about certain sets of variables. The awareness of causal relations among variables is necessary in order to understand the nature of the phenomena being examined. The objective nature of experiments, along with other empirical forms of inquiry, is also advantageous. The explicit description of experimental methods and results allows other researchers to attempt to replicate and interpret previous experiments. As noted earlier, objectivity is not the sole property of experiments; it characterizes all good scientific research.

There are also disadvantages to the experimental approach. The controlled nature of experiments is often inversely related to the experiment's external validity. That is, the more controlled an experiment is the less it approximates real-world conditions. The behaviors elicited in experimental situations may be characteristic only of those settings, not characteristic of behavior in analogous real-world situations. As Bronfenbrenner (1979) noted, the study of human development is becoming the study of children in strange situations for brief periods of times. Further, in most applied settings we often cannot meet the assumptions of laboratory experiments. For example, the director of children's programs in a local museum cannot assume that all children will react to a set of exhibits the way one or two groups have reacted. It may be that the children in the first two groups are very different than the groups to follow; thus, results from the first two groups is not generalizable to either groups. In this case, the educational coordinator will have to make connections between specific samples of children and the effects of certain exhibits.

Remediation of Weaknesses

How do we remediate the problems of the experimental approach? There are at least two possible answers. The first may be by the utilization of field experiments. This methodology is particularly important for the study of school children. The work of P. K. Smith and Connolly (1980) is particularly important here. These researchers used field experiments to systematically manipulate aspects of the school environment and the curriculum content.

A second possibility is in line with Bronfenbrenner's (1979) notion of ecological validity and recent approaches to cross-cultural psychology described earlier. In order to understand children, we should observe them in a number of different contexts, both natural and experimental. For example, in order to understand the way children play with toys we should observe them in school, in the laboratory, and at home. Our choice of laboratory analogues should be grounded in meaningful and familiar contexts.

CONCLUSIONS

In this chapter we have examined one way to study children. The use of the experimental method is questioned by a number of researchers who rightly noted that humans are different form chemical compounds. They recommended more naturalistic approaches to child study. Experimentalists, on the other hand, often point their fingers at naturalistic researchers and scorn their "unscientific" or "soft" approaches. Such dichotomous, often hostile, camps exist today in some aspects of child study. This my-paradigm-is-better-than-your-paradigm attitude in child study is counterproductive at best and vicious at worst. If we have learned anything in our discussion of different methodologies, it should be that, first, different methods are used to answer different questions. Second, we should view experimental and naturalistic contexts as different contexts in which we can study children. Indeed, children should be studied in both. If we find that children act in the same way in both contexts we can be sure of the reliability of that finding. The description of context specific behavior, however, is also important. Children are expected to behave very differently in different situations, so it is important to describe the behavior eliciting properties of different contexts. In short, we recommend a multimethodological approach to child study.

6

Observational Methods

In this chapter we outline general procedures that can be used to observe children's behavior and the behavior of those with whom they interact. These observational procedures are similar to the traditional procedures used in educational, psychological, ethological, and some anthropological research. With this methodology we gather information about children by systematically watching them. Here we discuss only a portion of the procedures needed to conduct observational research: category formation and measurement, sampling and recording rules, reliability and validity, entering the field, and recording media; these are the bare-bones skills necessary, we feel. The reader interested in more detail is referred to a more thorough treatment in A. D. Pellegrini (1996).

OUR ORIENTATION AND ASSUMPTIONS

We can watch children in either natural contexts (e.g., playgrounds) or in contrived contexts (e.g., experimental playrooms). In both cases, however, the observer minimally interferes with the behavior of the child being observed.

The notion of minimal interference should be stressed to the extent that observers typically have an effect on those that are being observed albeit an unintentional influence. It is crucial that observers recognize the effects they have on those being observed and try to minimize them. In the final analyses, observers must also account for these effects on the behavior of those being observed. These ideas will be expanded on later in the chapter.

A basic assumption guiding our orientation to observational methods, and indeed to child study, is what might be called a *quantitative* or *objective* perspective. This perspective is contrasted with a qualitative perspective. We only briefly discuss these distinctions, as they are more thoroughly differenti-ated in the next chapter when we discuss ethology and ethnography. Suffice it to say for now that we think that people can describe others' behavior with reasonable agreement (i.e., objectivity) and that these descriptions are reason-able approximations of the worlds of those being observed. The "reasonable-ness" of these descriptions, of course, relates directly to the theory guiding our selection of what is to be observed and the meaning we assign to those observations.

A second assumption guiding our orientation to studying and observing children is that children and their environments interact transactionally. That is, children influence their environments and their environments influence them. For example, specific groups of children will "furnish" a play area in a kindergarten class in very specific ways. One group may be comprised of a specific social "clique" who like to pile blocks in tall towers. This organization of the blocks influences the theme of the play. On the other hand, the blocks influence the play in that children will play with them in rather predicable ways, compared, for example, to play with replica figures (see A. D. Pellegrini & Perlmutter, 1989).

The implication for observational methods of assuming that children and environments influence each other is that we, as observers, should take care to describe both the behaviors and the contexts in which they occur. Of course, theory determines the relevance of specific aspects of behavior and context.

The Role of Theory in Conducting Observations

Theory is our guide to framing interesting questions, categorizing behaviors, and interpreting those behaviors. We simply cannot observe "everything" and have categories "emerge" as if by magic. A couple of examples should make this clear. First, let us consider what is to be observed. Contemplate the general and common problem of observing a mother and a child playing together. At one level, theory might suggest that we examine emotional components of the interaction, such as mother's use of emotional terms and comforting gestures. Continuing with consideration of the emotional dimensions of interaction, we could make observations of mother and child heart rate, galvanic skin response, or sample hormones from saliva or blood! What we choose to observe, in short, is guided by theory.

In terms of forming categories, different theories have us focus on different aspects of human behavior, but there are some rules that can be followed to systematize the ways in which we form categories. They too are guided by theory.

CHOOSING AND FORMING CATEGORIES

The system we use to categorize behavior can be either "borrowed" from a system already developed, or we can develop our own. Although borrowing is easier, there are risks associated with such a choice. Researchers usually develop category systems with a specific set of questions in mind for a specific group of children. As we see in the chapter on play, Rubin et al. (1983) developed a system to category the play of children in their preschool class-rooms. The systems remains an excellent choice for researchers or teachers interested in studying social cognitive dimensions of play for preschool-age children indoors.

The system does not work, however, if it is used with older children or with preschoolers interacting outdoors. When it is used in such an inappropriate way, we quickly find that most of the behaviors exhibited by children do not readily fit into the categories.

If you have a need to form your own category system, you can form them in one of three ways (Martin & Bateson, 1993), as displayed in Table 6.1.

First, categories can be formed using physical descriptions. Physical descriptions are descriptions of muscle contraction, and usually expressed in terms of strength, degree, and patterning. Physical descriptions that co-occur can be considered part of a category. Take the example of describing children's rough-and-tumble (R & T) play where the following physical descriptions could be considered constitutive: *run, pull/push, grapple, kick at, hit at,* and *smile.* When behaviors of this sort co-occur, they are considered R & T.

Descriptions by consequence, on the other hand, are much more subjective and based on the result of a behavior or set of behaviors, rather than the co-occurrence of a set of behaviors. For example, we might categorize all those behaviors which lead to children affiliating with another child. For example, *plays with same toys, cooperates,* and *talks* might be considered affiliative behaviors.

Finally, we consider relational descriptions. These descriptions category all those behaviors that occur in a specific place into one category. For example, all behavior that children exhibit on the playground would be categorized as play.

Once we have decided on the method by which we will form categories, we should take care that they have the following characteristics.

Characteristics of Categories

The characteristics of categories are summarized in Table 6.2.

Despite the type of category system used, the categories should be objec-

TABLE 6.1
Three Types of Categories

Category	Description	Example
Physical	Muscle contraction	Wide smile
Consequence	Stimulus orientation	Makes friends
Relational	Environmental relations	Play on playground

TABLE 6.2
Characteristics of Categories

Characteristic	Definition	Example
Objective	Observable terms	Wide grin
Mutually exclusive	Fits in one place	Wide grin/Slight grin
Homogeneous	Components have shared meaning	Hit, bite, cry
Exhaustive	Accounts for all behavior	

tively defined such that observers can clearly understand them and make behavior category discriminations. Most simply, this means that categories should be defined in terms of objective language, which can be directly observed, and which is minimally inferential. For example, use of the term "grin" is preferable to "happy." The former term is observable and makes no inferences about motivations. Happy, on the other hand, clearly has us moving from a behavior to inference about the meaning of a behavior.

Categories should also be mutually exclusive, or independent of each other; a behavior should fit into one and only one category. For example, in a system of molar categories of play including functional and dramatic play and games with rules, a behavior should fit into one and only one category.

Relatedly, *molar categories*, or categories with a variety of subcomponents, should be homogenous. That is, the subcomponents of a category, although independent of each other, should share at least one dimension. Another play-related example should make the point. McLoyd's (1980) system of children's verbalized fantasy has two molar categories, object transformations and ideational transformations. Within each molar category there are a number of molecular categories, or subcomponents. Within ideational transformations we have, for example, situation attributions and role attributions. Although these categories are independent to the extent that the former denotes a child's use of language to define a fantasy situation (e.g., "This is my office") and the latter has language used to define fantasy roles (e.g., "I'll be the doctor.") they each involve children using language to redefine a realistic situation into fantasy. Consequently, the categories are at once mutually exclusive and homogeneous.

A final aspect of behavioral category systems is that they, in the best possible world, should be exhaustive. That is, the categories should account for all of the behavior under consideration during an observational period. For example, in observing mother–child book reading episodes, an exhaustive category system would account for all behavior observed. Although an exhaustive system is desirable, it is neither necessary nor practical in most situations. More often than not we are interested in observing specific behavior, not describing the total event.

Exhaustive systems are, however, necessary if we are interested in examining sequences of behavior; for example, we could describe the behaviors that immediately follow a child entering a room for the first time. In order to examine the transitions from State 1 (that is, room entry) to State 2 (that is, a child's immediate next behavior) we must account for all possible behaviors. We might have categories like *smile, cry, run, walk*, and *other*. The other category can be a "waste basket" category to the extent that it includes all behavior not explicitly mentioned. It is a necessary category, however, so that we can have a behavior to put in the State 2 slot. We discuss sequences of behavior further later in the chapter.

Measuring Categories

Once we have our categories we must decide how we will measure them. Following A. D. Pellegrini (1996), we discuss four measures of behavior: latency, frequency, duration, and intensity. These measures are summarized in Table 6.3.

Latency is a measure of time, typically expressed in seconds, minutes, hours, days, and so forth. It is the time from a specific behavior or event (e.g. presentation of a flash card to a child with the word *heart* on it) to the beginning of the behavior of interest (e.g., reading the word *heart*). It may be that one child has a 2-second latency in reading the word, whereas another has a 5-second latency.

Frequency is the number of occurrences of the behavior(s) of interest *per* time unit. For example, a child leaves his mother's lap 10 times during 15 minutes in the waiting room of the pediatrician's office. The comparison of behavior against a time interval helps makes the behavior meaningful. For example, knowing that a behavior occurred a total of 10 times, or accounted for 20% of the total behavior, is very ambiguous. Was the period 10 minutes, 20 minutes, 1 hour, 2 hours, 4 hours? Consequently, a time-unit comparison must be included in frequency data.

Duration is the length of time for the single occurrence of a behavior; for example, the average duration of a preschooler's nap time is 45 minutes. Again, we need a base time against which to compare the duration measure. Is it 45:60, 45:90, 45:120? It should also be noted that frequency and duration measures often provide different and complementary information. For example, the frequency with which a child engages in social interaction (e.g., compared to

TABLE 6.3
Measures of Behaviors

Measure	Definition	Example
Latency	Time between response	Stimulus and reaction time
Frequency	Occurrence during a specified interval	Five cases of aggression a school day
Duration	Length of time for an occurrence	Naps the last 20 minutes of the school day
Intensity	Amplitude	Highly aggressive

solitary) tells us one thing and the duration of these interactions (e.g., they may be relatively long or short) tells us something very different.

Intensity is a more ambiguous measure. It generally refers to amplitude. For example, the intensity of children's R & T play can be rated from 1 (*not intense*) to 7 (*very intense*). In an effort to disambiguate the concept of intensity, it can be measured by the presence or absence of certain behaviors that are present during high-intensity and absent during low-intensity behaviors. For example, for very intense R & T the following behaviors must be present: *chase, hit-at,* and *pounce, wrestle,* and *play face.* To index intensity, we would then use a local rate measure (Martin & Bateson, 1993), or the occurrence of specific behavior(s), such as pounce per time unit. We might have an R & T bout with a local rate of 2 per minute and another with a local rate of 4 per minute, with the latter being more intense than the former.

RECORDING AND SAMPLING STRATEGIES

In observing behavior we should follow two types of rules: sampling and recording (Martin & Bateson, 1986). *Sampling rules* refer to who to watch and when to watch them. *Recording rules* refer to how the behaviors are recorded. The four sampling rules to be discussed include *ad libitum* sampling, focal sampling, scan sampling, and behavior sampling. The recording rules include continuous, 0/1, and instantaneous recording rules. A summary of the use of these rules is displayed in Table 6.4.

Before the specific rules of sampling are discussed the concept of sampling is addressed. Sampling is a concept used in many aspects of child study, as well as in most of the social sciences. In sampling, we gather aspects of behavior that represent children's total behavioral repertoires. That is, we recognize that children have large behavioral repertoires; these repertoires are the universe of their behaviors. Because observers typically do not have the time to observe the universe of behaviors, they sample representative slices of it.

Deciding on the representativeness of a sample, or the extent to which the sample approximates the population, is not a clear-cut issue. Although more specific recommendations are made in the following discussions of sampling and recording rules, some general comment is made here to foreground the

TABLE 6.4
Sampling and Recording Rules

Sampling Rules	Recording Rules		
	Continuous	0/1	Instantaneous
Ad libitum			
Focal	x	x	x
Scan	x		
Behavior	x	x	

importance of this issue. The most general and often-heard rule of thumb is: The more, the better. Numerous researchers have suggested that children and adults should be observed in more than one session, particularly if they are observed in a contrived situation. These numerous observations within similar contexts, such as mother reading to child, should be aggregated, or combined, and considered a single sample. Another rule of thumb: Aggregated data are more representative than single instances. Simply put, the larger the sample, the closer it approximates the universe about which you are hoping to make inference.

Within observation sessions we, too, must make sampling decisions; for example, do we use time or behavior sampling? Within time sampling, what is the time interval? Answers to these specific questions are addressed later. At this point it is sufficient to say that sampling involves examining portions of children's behavioral repertoires. We often make inferences about all of their behaviors, however, based on our analyses of samples of behavior. The important question that must be addressed in all sampling choices is the extent to which are samples results generalize to the population at large. A strong test of the generalizability of results involves the extent to which the results from one sample are replicated in another. The various samplings to be outlined in the following are differentially effective in meeting this criterion.

Ad libitum sampling is the least systematic type of sampling to the extent that there are no established rules for the observer to follow. He or she simply writes down what he or she wants, when he or she wants to. The obvious problem with such a procedure is that such observations are biased toward the most visible individuals and the most notable behavior. There are two saving graces of this method. First, it can be used to record rarely occurring events. For example, if physical aggression is very rare on school playgrounds, *ad libitum* sampling can be used to describe aggression when it occurs. Second, it can be used in very preliminary stages of observations. For example, when an observer enters an unfamiliar setting, such a strategy may be useful in providing initial but limited information.

Focal sampling, or focal child sampling, involves observing an individual (or group) for a specified period of time. For example, on Mondays we may have a list of children who are to be observed in a specified order for 15 minutes each. During these focal samples all of the focal child's behavior is recorded. In using focal sampling it is also helpful to describe the behaviors of those with whom the focal child interacts; for example, who initiates and responds to behaviors. A problem with focal sampling is that a child may "disappear" for a period during the observation period, for instance, if a child runs from the playscape into a playhouse. Rules such as "terminate observation when child is out of sight for 30 seconds" are necessary. Further, the observer should note the time that the child is out of sight. Focal children's behavior can be recorded according to any of the three recording rules: continuous recording, instantaneous sampling, and 0/1 sampling. These recording rules are discussed below. Finally, Martin and Bateson (1986) suggested that focal sampling is the most preferred sampling rule in studying groups.

Scan sampling involves the rapid scanning, or sampling, of behavior at specific intervals. The specific behavior of all individuals in a group is instantaneously sampled at predetermined time intervals. For example, we may choose to scan sample a classroom for on-task/off-task behavior every 15 minutes. In such a case the on-task/off-task behavior of each child in the class is sampled. In a class of 25 students this should take about 2 minutes; this procedure is then repeated every 15 minutes. Scan sampling is useful in gathering census data, such as the on-task behavior of a classroom.

The issue of the independence of scan sampling data is particularly relevant. For example, if Jack is scanned for four successive 15-minute intervals, the separate scans are not independent. Jack's behavior at Scan 1 may be coded as off-task because he is tired; consequently, he's likely to be off-task in subsequent scans because he continues to be tired. In cases where subjects are observed repeatedly in one session it would make sense to average the individual scans into one score. In the case of Jack, he would have one score, the mean of his four scans, rather than four separate scans.

An alternative would be to separate the scans by longer time intervals; for example, scans separated by one or two hours or one or more days are more likely to be independent of each other and, consequently, can be treated as separate scores. P. K. Smith (1985) has recommended using 4 minutes between scans to minimize interdependence of scans.

Behavior sampling involves the observing of a group and recording a particular behavior. This technique is useful in observing rare behavior such as physical aggression.

Specific recording rules should be applied to the sampling rules just described. It should be stressed that sampling rules and recording rules are different from each other (Martin & Bateson, 1986). There are two such recording rules: Continuous recording and time sampling.

Continuous recording involves recording all behaviors of interest. With such a recording strategy we can derive frequency, duration, and latency scores. Continuous recording can be used when we are interested in the structure of behavioral states; for example, what is the sequence leading from parallel to social play or from R & T to games with rules? In short, continuous recording should be used if we are interested in the details (e.g., duration and sequence) of particular behaviors. An example of continuous recording using focal child sampling is used here illustratively. Frank is the focal child being observed for a 5 minute period. The observer records all his behavior as it occurs by speaking into a tape recorder.

Time sampling involves sampling behavior as a function of time whereby the observation period is divided into sampling intervals. The interval will vary according to the number of categories to be observed. As noted earlier, the shorter the interval the more the sample will approximate the measure. For example, if the universe of recess time is 20 minutes we will more closely approximate the universe if we sample every 1 minute than if we sample every 5 minutes.

There are two types of time sampling: instantaneous and 0/1 sampling. Instantaneous sampling involves recording whether a behavior has occurred or not occurred at specific sample points; for example, behavior is coded when a beeper sounds every 30 seconds; behavior immediately preceding and succeeding the beep does not influence the coding. As noted earlier, the shorter the interval, the more the sample will approximate the universe. For example, we could use instantaneous sampling at 30-second intervals within a scan-sampling schedule by recording on-task behavior within a classroom. This interval will more closely approximate the universe of classroom behaviors than a 5-minute interval. The scores generated from instantaneous sampling are relative frequencies; that is, relative occurrence to total sample intervals.

With instantaneous sampling we do not get time frequencies (i.e., how often a behavior occurs within a period) or duration scores. If sampling intervals are short, for example, every 1 minute, instantaneous sampling data resembles continuously sampled data—we are sampling larger portions of the universe. Instantaneous sampling is useful for recording states that occur or do not occur at specific time intervals, such as on-task/off-task, sleeping/awake, running/not running. It is not useful with rare behavior; behavior sampling would be appropriate in that case.

0/1 sampling is similar to instantaneous sampling to the extent that observational periods are segmented into short sample intervals; behavior is recorded as occurring or not occurring during whole sampling intervals. That a behavior occurs once or more than once during an interval is not noted however. For example, we are observing students' looking at teacher in 30-second intervals; 0/1 sampling does not differentiate students who looked at teachers 10 times during that 30-second interval from those who looked once. The behavior is simply coded as having occurred or not occurred for the whole duration. The resultant scores from 0/1 sampling are relative frequencies (i.e., relative to total intervals) and neither true frequencies nor durations can be derived. Indeed, this technique tends to overestimate duration in that behavior is recorded per interval; thus, the same score is derived for short and long durations. Similarly, frequency is underestimated in that only one score per interval can be recorded. The shorter the sampling interval, the more closely 0/1 sampling approximates instantaneous sampling.

Sequences of behavior may be of interest. As noted earlier, behavioral sampling is necessary here to the extent that we are interested in maintaining the integrity of the behavioral state (Bakeman & Gottman, 1986); further an exhaustive category system is needed. We may be interested in the ways in which specific behaviors unfold, such as the sequence of children entering a strange group, or the ways in which one state changes into another, such as play fighting into real fighting. In such cases behavioral samples of a target behavior should be identified and recorded until they end; for example, one can record the play fighting bout from beginning until it changes into another state, such as aggression, games with rules, or children separating. We can then calculate the probability of our target behavior being followed by a specific behavior. For example, using a behavior sampling strategy, we are interested in specific behaviors, games with rules or aggression, which follow R & T play. As such we can note onset of R & T (Lag 0) with an A and use a B to note when R & T is followed immediately (at Lag 1) by games, and C to denote aggression. The frequencies can be arranged into a 3 x 3 matrix where A can be followed by A, B, or C and B followed by A, B, or C.

Based on this data set we can calculate conditional probabilities of R & T being followed by games and aggression. Simple probabilities are percents of the target behavior to total behavior observed for that row. For example, the simple probability of A being followed by B is .50 and for A being followed for C is .50.

Conditional probabilities provide interesting insight into possible functions of behaviors. In the aforementioned case, does R & T serve a function of leading into games or into aggression? The data in Table 6.5 suggest it may serve both functions.

RECORDING MEDIA

We have a number of options in the ways in which we can record observational data, but we discuss only a few here: video recorders, audio recorders, verbal descriptions, and check sheets. Although there are other recording media, such as computerized recording techniques, they are not discussed here, but the interested reader is referred to A. D. Pellegrini (1996).

TABLE 6.5
A Two-State Behavioral Model

Lag 0	Lag 1			
	A	B	C	
A	0	4	4	8
B	4	0	4	8
C	2	4	0	6
				22

A reasonable rule of thumb is that mechanical and computerized recording media should not be introduced into the observational field until the participants are used to the observer's presence. The observer's presence is obtrusive enough at first; to introduce devices which remind the participants that they are being observed is all the more obtrusive.

Video recorders provide excellent behavioral records to the extent that both visual and audio data can be preserved. In cases where both sources of information are necessary it should be the method of choice. For example, visual and audio information are important dimensions of mother–child book-reading styles. The pointing, page turning, and the language used provide important information. The added benefits of video recorders is that they can be used in a variety of ways. For example, we may have started off interested in book handling behaviors in mother–child dyads but later become interested in parental teaching, management techniques, or both. The audiovisual record preserves the event such that such data can be utilized in different ways. Another advantage of video cameras relates to reliability checks. The lasting record again enables us to code and recode behavior.

There are disadvantages, however, associated with video cameras. First, they are obtrusive. The behavior of participants is likely to be altered by the presence of one. This can be minimized by a hidden camera, such as one that films through a one-way mirror, and by repeated observations. In the latter case, participants will act more naturally with repeated observations.

A second disadvantage is related to the inability of video cameras to accurately record language from a distance. For example, we could visually record children's playground behavior from a great distance, but we would not be able to record corresponding language. One option here is to fit the children with radio microphones that are connected to the video camera. This, of course, entails more expense.

Audio recorders provide another way in which to record behavior. They have the benefit of providing verbatim records of language and of being less obtrusive than video cameras. Tape recorders, for example, can be unobtrusively hidden under a table on which children are doing puzzles. As noted earlier, wireless radio microphones, in conjunction with audio recorders, provide excellent language records for mobile subjects. For example, in a study of preschoolers' language we fitted children with wireless microphones in vests (Galda et al., 1989) After a few observations children seemed to hardly be aware of their vests and we had high-quality language samples.

Audio recorders can also be used by observers to describe behavior. For example, in a study of children's playground behavior observers described children's behavior into a microphone (A. D. Pellegrini, 1988). This technique is useful when the participants are very mobile and when there are many behaviors of interest. Speaking into a microphone allows us to continue to observe behavior while simultaneously recording behavior. Writing narrative descriptions or writing checklists do not allow such flexibility.

Interestingly, children get used to observer presence quickly, as long as the observers do not move too close to the subjects and they avoid eye and social contact. This technique is very useful for recording behavior and less useful for recording language because of maintaining physical distance from the participants.

Checklists, too, are a important recording device (Martin & Bateson, 1986). They are typically designed with columns for different behavioral categories and rows for successive sampling intervals. Behavior is recorded in the appropriate space at the appropriate interval. For example, in Fig. 6.1 we have a checklist for playground behavior. As Martin and Bateson (1986) noted focal, scan, and *ad libitum* sampling can be used with checklists.

Further, the three recording rules can also be used. Both frequency and sequence scores can also be derived from coding sheets.

RELIABILITY AND VALIDITY

As we all know, reliability and validity are hallmarks of objective data, and observational data are no exception. That reliability is necessary but not sufficient for validity is equally well known. Reliable measures are "good" measures to the extent that they meet four criteria (Martin & Bateson, 1993). First, is the measure precise? That is, to what extent is the measure free from random error? Precision, to use Martin and Bateson's example, may be a characteristic of a clock that tells time to the minute and second, but the time may be inaccurate. Accuracy is relevant to validity, not reliability.

The second criterion, sensitivity, tells us the extent to which small changes in values lead to changes in measured values. For example, are children's different levels of intensity in R & T play reflected in different observational ratings of those behaviors? Third and fourth are resolution, or identifying the smallest change in the behavior that can be detected, and consistency, or repeated observations of the same behavior producing similar results.

Reliability is typically determined by one or more than person repeatedly examining behaviors. The one person case is intrarater reliability and the multiple person care is interrater reliability. An example of the interrater reliability would involve the same person coding and then recoding infants' smiles from videotapes.

By interrater reliability we mean the extent to which observers in the same study agree that they see the same thing. Interrater and intrarater agreement statistics can be expressed in terms of percentages of agreement or correlation coefficients between different observations of the same behavior. The percentage of agreement, the simpler of the two, is calculated by comparing the occurrence of agreement to total occurrence of behavior. For example, two

```
Date ————————————

Time ————————————

Name ————————————

          R & T    Games    Aggression    Social Interact    Parallel    Solitary

 1 ———————————————————————————————————

 2 ———————————————————————————————————

 3 ———————————————————————————————————

 4 ———————————————————————————————————

 5 ———————————————————————————————————

 6 ———————————————————————————————————

 7 ———————————————————————————————————

 8 ———————————————————————————————————

 9 ———————————————————————————————————

10 ———————————————————————————————————

11 ———————————————————————————————————

12 ———————————————————————————————————

13 ———————————————————————————————————

14 ———————————————————————————————————

15 ———————————————————————————————————

TOTAL ——————————————————————————————
```

FIG. 6.1.   Behavioral checklist.

observers are noting the occurrence of egocentric behavior in preschoolers. They each make 100 observations of the same child; on 86 occasions they agreed that they saw the same behaviors and they disagreed on the other occasions. The interrater agreement would be calculated by dividing the number of agreements by the total number of observations: 86/100 = 86%.

Interrater agreement can be accomplished in a least two ways (Sackett, Gluck, & Ruppertral, 1978). First, observers can view samples of videotape of children's behaviors. For example, researchers may have 200 videotapes of children's social interaction. The researchers can randomly choose 20% of these tapes (40) and have more than one observer recode the desired behaviors. The scores of the observers would then be compared. Perfect reliability (i.e., 100%) can be achieved by filmed data using the consensus method. With this method two or more people observe the same behaviors until they can agree, or reach consensus, on the coding.

A second way of obtaining interrater agreement involves having more than one person observing the same child simultaneously. Again, interrater agreement is calculated by dividing agreements by total observations. Other more detailed methods for assessing reliability can be found in A. D. Pellegrini (1996).

Reliability is necessary, but not sufficient for validity, wherein validity refers to the true value of the data observed. That is, our observations can be perfectly reliable, but they may not be truthful. In determining the validity of a measure, its accuracy and specifically must be considered (Martin & Bateson, 1986). Accuracy refers to the presence or absence of systematic error in a measure and specifically involves the extent to which the measure describes what it purports to describe and nothing else. The specificity criterion is particularly important. Does our measure describe what it purports to measure? Consider the following. In my university-level child study class I give the students a test of single-digit addition. I assume that the measurement will be reliable. For example, they should get the same score from time 1 to time 2 and the scores should reach perfect agreement on what counts as right and wrong. But is this a valid test of child study? No is the obvious answer.

Validity, unlike reliability, cannot be measured directly. It is assessed by relating one aspect of measurement (e.g., a test score or an observation) to another theoretically relevant construct. For example, we could relate a behavioral measure of aggression to a teacher's rating of the child's aggression. As such, validity involves making a connection between theoretically relevant variables, some of which are directly observable, and others of which are not. In the remainder of this section, we present some ways of doing this. (For more detailed discussions of validity see A. D. Pellegrini, 1996.)

This is often done with observational data by using procedures to infer predictive and construct validity (Kerlinger, 1973). Predictive validity, as noted earlier, involves the observable behavior predicting other future behaviors. For example, if we are observing children's "egocentric" behavior we might be concerned with observing their solitary and parallel play. These play categories would have predictive validity if they predicted later aspects of children's egocentricism (e.g., low social-perspective-taking status).

Construct validity refers to the measurement of psychological constructs. In the aforementioned noted example, egocentricism is a psychological construct. The notion of solitary or parallel play being related to other contemporaneous measures of egocentricism reflects the important role of a theory in the establishing of construct validity. Theories suggest different measures that should be related to a common construct. Solitary and parallel play would have construct validity if they were positively related to other measures of children's egocentricism (e.g., absence of role playing).

Now that we have a set of reliable and valid measures, we are ready to enter the field.

ENTERING THE OBSERVATIONAL FIELD

The first step in conducting an observation should involve preliminary observation periods. These preliminary observations help observers refine the research questions and determine the appropriate measures and recording methods to be used (Martin & Bateson, 1993). First, regarding the research question formulation, some firsthand knowledge of the group that is to be observed is necessary if an intelligible research question is to be generated. For example, if one is interested in aggression on the elementary school playground, preliminary observations may indicate that behavior previously considered aggression, such as playful wrestling, are very different from actual physical aggression, like punching (see A. D. Pellegrini, 1995). Such insight might result in the following question reformulation: What are the different consequences of play fighting and real fighting? Second, regarding specific measures, if one is interested in children's aggression at school preliminary observations would be necessary to the extent that some contexts more readily elicit aggression than others. Although physical aggression is rare in elementary schools, verbal aggression is not. Further, aggression is more likely to occur in contexts that are unsupervised by adults; thus, the researcher interested in observing aggression would spend time observing children in contexts where they are usually unsupervised, such as at their lockers. Preliminary observations would thus sharpen the specific aspect of behavior to be observed.

Preliminary observations are also helpful in terms of helping the observer accurately, or reliably, record the behaviors of interest. Generally, categorizations of behaviors at the beginning of an observational study are less accurate than later in the study. Such observer drift is usually the result of observers becoming more accurate discriminators of the behaviors of interest. The preliminary observation period should thus be used as a time to develop and practice using the relevant observational categories. Additionally, this preliminary period should also be used as a time during which the participants are habituating, or getting used to, the presence of the observer. As children and adults get used to observer presence, their behavior will more closely approximate "normal" behavior. Consequently, preliminary data should not be used in the final data analysis to the extent that they are generally unreliable and not valid, as participants' behavior is maximally effected by observer presence at this stage.

OBSERVER EFFECTS

Although people's behavior is sensitive to the social contexts in which it is embedded, the behavior of children is yet more responsive to contextual effects. Indeed, chapter 3 explicates this point by showing the ways in which adult and child behavior can be very different depending on the specific activities in which they are engaged (e.g., playing with blocks vs. doing a puzzle), the social composition of the activity (e.g., the presence of an adult suppresses children's aggression), and specific materials in the environment (e.g., children will act differently in a crowded vs. a spacious room; number of toys present affects children's social interaction).

Observational research typically involves introducing a foreign participant, no matter how unobtrusive, into a natural environment (e.g., an observer in a classroom and a video camera) or taking children out of their natural environment and observing them in experimental environments (e.g., observing parents and children playing in an experimental playroom). Each of these scenarios involves children encountering a foreign (i.e., not typically present in the natural environment) participant or environment. These foreign participants and materials may have minimum or great effects of the behavior of those we are observing. Obviously minimal effects are the result of observational techniques that are minimally obtrusive; for example, observations being made by a regular participant in the behavior setting, such as a teacher, or teachers' aid, a nurse, or a parent. Other techniques that minimally effect participants' behavior involve the use of blinds or hiding from the participant. For example, children's playground aggression and play fighting can be viewed remotely, with binoculars from an adjacent building or with a telephoto lens on video camera. In such cases what is gained in unobtrusiveness is lost in the ability to record behavior that requires close proximity, such as hearing children's language and accurately recording facial expressions that demonstrate aggression from play.

The ethics of observing children, or anybody for that matter, with such remote recording devices may be of concern. It is imperative, as in all cases of research, that the participants in the research and their parents be informed of the techniques used.

It should be noted, however, that many human subjects boards permit researchers to observe subjects in the public arena, such as in parks or in supermarkets, without informed consent. The subjects' behavior in public places is public and consequently can be recorded.

Often minimally obtrusive techniques involve the use of remote recording devices, such as remote microphones or cameras. Again the obtrusiveness of these techniques depends on their being "remote." Many laboratory schools and clinics are equipped with such devices whereby behavior is recorded through a one-way mirror or from a blind. Where such facilities are not available, such as in home-based observations, participants typically "perform" for the camera or microphone. This is particularly evident with young children who make funny faces into cameras or speak loudly into microphones. In such cases, numerous observations should be conducted so that participants habituate to the devices. Although total habituation to devices as obtrusive as video cameras or tape recorders in one's living room is probably a myth there is less "performance for the camera" as time passes.

An example from our own work with preschool children might help here. In our study of preschool children's use of oral language during free play we had children wear wireless microphones during their free-play periods (see Galda, Pellegrini, & Cox, 1989). Children wore their microphones for 15-minute sessions for two school years. We found that (i.e., during the first two to three observations) children initially were very conscience of the microphones to the extent that they would talk loudly into their own microphones and those of their peers. For example, "Can you hear me?!" "I'm Jack." After this initial phase, however, children seemed to forget that they had them on as evidenced by their use of language that their teachers did not tolerate, such as calling other children nasty names and cursing.

In short, repeated observations minimize obtrusive but probably do not eliminate it. We should, consequently, "hedge" our conclusions with the strong possibility that observer presence has some effect. The results of such presence typically has participants behaving in ways they think observers want them to behave; this phenomenon is known as *reactivity*. For example, in observations of parent–child interaction we are unlikely to observe behaviors that parents think are contrary to those expected by the observer, such as spanking. Similarly, we are likely to observe behaviors that parents think the observer values, such as allowing their boys to play with female-preferred toys.

Another example relevant to observer effects is known as the Hawthorne Effect. This effect has participants behaving differently because they are being given special attention. For example, in a school-based literary project, children's reading-related behaviors will probably change. The change may be due to the project per se or to the special or different treatment children and teachers received due to the project. Consequently, comparison groups may be needed whereby teachers and children get special or different attention (e.g., weekly visits to the classroom by someone saying what good teachers and students they are as well as literacy-related attention). Where such comparisons are not desired or not possible, observers must recognize the possibility of a Hawthorne Effect.

7

Naturalistic Inquiry: Ethological and Interpretive Methods

This chapter outlines different methodologies for data collection that are relatively unobtrusive and occur in those situations children actually inhabit, such as schools, neighborhoods, and playgrounds. In contrast to more controlled and contrived approaches (see chapters on Tests and Experiments), the methods outlined in this chapter stress the importance of observing children in their natural conditions.

In this chapter we discuss two general groups of methods that could be characterized as more naturalistic. Both ethological and interpretive traditions are concerned with the ways in which children and their environments interact with each other, and both approaches assume that inferences about the meaning of behavior can be made most accurately when we consider the situations in which the behavior is embedded. Thus, in most cases these approaches assume that behavior and context influence, or are in a transactional relationship with, each other.

An example should help clarify this notion of transaction between context and behavior. Children choose to play in an environment, and in the course of their play, they change the environment, say by building a fort in the woods with sticks. Thus children have an impact on the environment by choosing it from among others and then changing, or "furnishing" it to suit their needs. The environment, in turn, affects children, by its limitations (e.g., rules of conduct) and its affordances (an availability of building materials and peers).

Naturalistic approaches are easily contrasted with the more contrived modes of inquiry, such as laboratory and testing approaches previously discussed.

Whereas the more controlled approaches to child study (which are rooted in the physical sciences) take children out of their natural environments and place them in situations that elicit and control behavior, naturalistic approaches (which are rooted in the natural sciences) are more often concerned with describing children's everyday functioning in their natural environments.

Generally, naturalistic researchers believe that in order to construct an accurate picture of children's behavioral repertoires, youngsters should be observed in contexts in which they are expected to exhibit those behaviors. For example, naturalistic researchers interested in children's reading achievement would observe reading behaviors in those situations where they are expected to read: school reading groups, library time, sustained silent reading time in school, and so on. Simply put, this approach suggests that children should be studied in those contexts in which we wish to understand them. We should not study them, so the argument goes, in analogue situations, and then make generalizations to the natural situation. Part of this bias is rooted in the notion the children's behavior is specific to certain contexts and that there are few generalizations that can be made from one situation to another.

Another reason that many researchers favor studying children in their natural habitats is the fact that children often suppress exhibiting the highest levels of competence in contrived situations. When children are put into a strange or anxiety-producing situations they do not exhibit high levels of competence because they are unsure of the consequences of these actions. This, as discussed in the chapters on testing and experimentation, is a prime reason for children's inconsistent performance in many testing and laboratory situations.

Following from this stress on the interdependence between behavior and context, most naturalistic researchers "induce" categories by which to study children that are unique to a particular study site. Consequently, categories used in studies of kindergarten children's playground behavior in rural Athens, Georgia, might be different from those developed in urban Minneapolis.

This inductive approach is in contrast to the cases where researchers generate categories based on a theory and then observe those categories, assuming little contextual variation. For example, Researcher 1 may, a priori, consider wrestling as a component of the category "aggression." In fact, this may be the case with certain groups of children but for other children wrestling may be a subset of playful, not aggressive behavior. Researcher 2 may have discovered this through category induction.

In this chapter we discuss two modes of naturalistic inquiry: Ethology and interpretive methods. Although ethology also can be experimental, the reliance of observational methods of children in their everyday environments contexts and the use of inductive procedures to define behavioral categories in the initial phases of child study deem it a form of naturalistic inquiry (Lancy, 1993).

ETHOLOGY

Ethology is biological study of behavior (Martin & Bateson, 1993) and is concerned with making sense of everyday behavior with minimal reliance on preexistent categories (Medawar, 1976). For example, a researcher may observe children on the playground and see what looks like wrestling. Further, wrestling seems to co-occur with other behaviors, such as laughing and turn taking. From these observations, a category of play fighting may be induced.

As noted earlier, ethology has a preference for the examination of children in their natural habitats, use of inductive strategies, and observational methods. In the ethological case the important of the interrelation between behavior and natural environment is a result of its Darwinian origins: Behavior of organisms is a result of the adaptation to natural environment. Further, ethologists do, in some cases, resort to experimental manipulation of environments to identify the causal mechanisms in behavior (see P. K. Smith & Connolly, 1980, for interesting examples). For example, the number of children in a preschool classroom can be experimentally manipulated to determine the effect of social density of children's social behavior (P. K. Smith & Connolly, 1980).

Although its biological orientation sets ethology apart from some of its naturalistic cousins (such as ethnography), its emphasis on "the objective" sets it apart from other branches of interpretive research. By stress on the objective, we mean that ethologists believe that observers can make consistent observations of children and behavior and that these behaviors at some level reflect a shared objectivity. This objectivity is often reflected in the fact that ethologies stress interobserver agreement between and among observers. With this agreement as a base, observers can then describe children's behavior in terms of those categories. The stress on replication of research results is another indicator of objectivity: If findings are objective, they should exist repeatedly.

An essential part of an ethological study is to describe, extensively, the behavior of the subjects in their natural habit. Such descriptions are known as *ethograms*. Ethograms typically include physical descriptions, or descriptions of motor patterns (e.g., *wide smile, run, hit at*) and descriptions of the participants (e.g, number and age of boys and girls) and descriptions of resources available (e.g., number and types of toys; Hinde, 1959, 1983; A. D. Pellegrini, 1996).

Obviously, it is very difficult to construct total ethograms for complex species such as human children. As a result, we must choose the types of behaviors and environments in which we wish to observe children. When this decision is made, the observer should record the behavior with a combination of media (i.e., written protocols, audio recordings, and audiovisual recording). The behaviors recorded are typically molecular descriptions (to use a term discussed in an earlier chapter) of physical movements. An example of such a behavioral repertoire can be found in Table 7.1. This is an ethogram of primary school children's playground behavior that we developed.

TABLE 7.1
Ethogram of Playground Behavior (Pellegrini, 1996)

1. Passive/noninteract
    sits
    stands
    lies
    eats
    watches
    waits turn
    reads/writes
2. Passive/interact
    talks to adult
    talked to by adult
    talks to peer
    talked to by peer
    gives comfort
    receives comfort
    grooms
    is groomed
    dresses
    is dressed
    offers object
    receives object
    refuses object
3. Aggression
    takes
    takes from
    kicks
    kicked
    swears
    sworn at
    hops
    dances
    balances
    climbs
    swings
    pushes on swing
    runs
    walks, following group or individuals
    jumps
    catches
    throws
4. Distress
    cries
	5. Football
	    runs with ball
	    runs without ball
	    stands with ball
	    watches in game
	    gets attention
	    catches
	    tackles
	    touches/tags
	    throws
	6. R & T
	    play face
	    plays/hits/kicks
	    hits/kicks at
	    play fights/wrestles (top)
	    play fights/wrestles (bottom)
	    carried
	    carries
	    pounces
	    pushes
	    is pushed
	7. Locomotion
	    chases
	    is chased
	    walks
	    skips
	8. Games
	    follow leader
	    jumps rope
	    plays ball
	    claps/sings
	9. Object
	    touches/explores
	    throws
	    holds
	10. Utterances
	    social rules/norm statements
	    aversive language
	    threats
	    contentions

Note. From *Observing Children in their Natural Worlds* (p. 18), by A. D. Pellegrini, 1996, Mahwah, NJ: Lawrence Erlbaum Associates. Copyright © 1996 by A. D. Pellegrini. Reprinted with permission.

In this table, we inventoried children's social behaviors while on the playground during school recess. Other ethologists who have examined and described children's social behaviors in school settings (mostly preschool settings) are Blurton Jones (1972b), McGrew (1972a, 1972b), A. D. Pellegrini (1992), and P. K. Smith and Connolly (1972, 1980). Connolly and Dalgleish (1989) have studied infants' tool use, and Ainsworth and Bell (1970) and J. Anderson (1972) have studied mother–child interaction.

Needless to say, the construction of ethogram is a tedious task. Hours of detailed observation are needed. Ethologists believe, however, that such descriptions are necessary in order to both understand behavior and to describe it such that results can be replicated by other research teams in similar settings. Once an ethogram has been constructed, the meaning, or functions, of these behaviors can be examined by subjecting them to Tinbergen's (1963) "Whys."

The four whys are, first, how does it work? Is the behavior due to proximate factors? Do factors internal and external to the organism cause the behavior? Second, how did the behavior develop during the lifetime of the individual? Specifically, how does a behavior assemble, or develop, within individuals across the life span. Third, what is the function of behavior? By function, biologists mean reproductive value; we, however, can consider the extent to which a behavior has beneficial consequences for an individual. Fourth, and finally, how did the behavior evolve across the history of the species?

An example of the application of these four questions may be helpful in understanding their importance. Take a hypothetical kindergarten child, Adam, as he is sitting listening to his teacher reading *The Tale of Peter Rabbit*. After finishing a page of reading the teacher looks at Adam, and without mentioning his name asks, "And what will Peter do now?" Adam says, "Run" and then smiles; the teacher nods, returns the smile, and says, "Very good, Adam." At the first level, we can explain Adam's behavior in terms of antecedents: Teacher asks him a question and he responds to that specific question. The second, developmental, question allows us to put Adam's verbalization into the context of his having learned the appropriate social rules of interacting with a teacher in a school literacy event: He has learned the rule of responding to teachers' questions, even when he knows that the teacher already knows the answer to the question. The third, functional, question points to an examination of the functional importance of Adam's response. He responded in such a way so as to gain the teacher's praise. The fourth, phylogenetic question, can be answered by looking at the similarities between affilative gestures and vocalizations across different primate species: Smiles can signal affiliation and acceptance.

These observations should also provide the bases of the theories that can later be tested experimentally. Unlike the experimental approach to child study, ethologists believe that extensive observation is needed before a theory can be advanced or behavioral categories formed. Theory without such an objective basis is, according to ethologists, often introspective and unscientific (Blurton Jones, 1972b). Furthermore, experimental analogues in ethology pay very close attention to constructing experimental situations that mirror the natural habitat as closely as possible.

One might ask the necessity of such thorough descriptions of children in their environments. In other words, what does the ethological approach have to offer those of us interested in studying children? First, ethologists help us generate objective measures of children's behaviors (Blurton Jones, 1972b). Because the molecular categories of behavior are so painstakingly described there seems to be little problem with the miscommunication of meaning. For example, when ethologists talk of play they define it explicitly in terms of a number of behaviors; for example, rough-and-tumble play is composed of the following behaviors: run, jump, laugh, play face, hit at, and wrestle (Blurton Jones, 1972a; A. D. Pellegrini, 1989a).

Such detailed description of labeled behaviors invites replication. Thus, the test of the objectivity of a category for an ethologist is the extent to which other research teams can replicate his or her category descriptions. This notion of replication seems particularly important in child study settings. Before making policy affecting children, families, and schools we should be sure that our observations and conclusions have been replicated across time and settings.

How to Conduct an Ethological Child Study

We have, in the preceding pages, outlined some of the theoretical constructs of the ethological method of child study. In this section of the chapter we outline the process by which such a study can be conducted. Fassnacht (1982) has outlined three phases of an ethological child study: exploratory observation, ethnogram, and systematic observation. These steps are outlined in Table 7.2.

Exploratory observations has the researcher observing the target children over an extended period of time.

The purpose of this stage is to establish behavioral categories. As previously noted, categories are usually molecular descriptions of movements and are the result of extensive observation. Categories of molecular behavior, such as twitching, often are combined into more molar categories, such as anxiety. These molar categories, however, are formed only after they have been scrutinized with the following series of questions: What do we mean by this? How do we know when we see it? Is it one thing or more than one thing, or nothing at all? (Blurton Jones, 1972b). The purpose of this scrutiny is to have objective and replicable molar categories. Such a technique has been applied to areas within child study, such as attachment (J. Anderson, 1972) and children's behavior in preschools (e.g., P. K. Smith & Connolly, 1972, 1980).

The second phase in the ethological process involves the construction of an ethogram (Fassnacht, 1982; A. D. Pellegrini, 1989b). Ethograms catalog the

TABLE 7.2
Steps in Conducting an Ethological Child Study

1. Exploratory observation
    a. Molar categories
    b. Molecular categories
2. Ethogram
    a. Physical descriptions
    b. Descriptions by consequence
3. Four questions
    a. Immediate cause
    b. Development
    c. Survival value
    d. Why done in this way

categories of behaviors established in the exploratory observations. These categories are further distinguished in terms of their being physical descriptions and description by consequence. For example, we have established an ethogram for elementary school children's playground behavior (A. D. Pellegrini, 1995, 1996).

The third phase of an ethological observation involves addressing each of Tinbergen's (1963) four questions: What was the immediate cause of the behavior? How did the behavior develop within this individual? What is the value of the behavior? Why does this individual solve this particular survival problem in this way?

To conclude this section, we have examined an exact method of observing children in natural environments. Ethologists view human beings in their evolutionary contexts and try to explain behavior in these terms. As such, children must be observed in their everyday environment. Further, antecedents and consequences of specific behavior help us understand the target behavior.

Ethology is very different in a number of important ways from other methods of studying children that we have described. First, behavioral categories are formed only after extensive observation. Second, behavior, if it is to be understood, must be examined in its natural environment. Third, hypotheses are tested only after objective observational categories have been formed. The values of the system are clear: It is objective and views behavior as being embedded within the natural environment. The disadvantage may lie in the molecular approach to human behavior: Human behavior may be something other than the sum of the discrete subcategories. Another disadvantage to some aspects of ethology, especially older forms, is the almost total lack of concern with cognition. Because ethology came out of studies with animals, examination of thought processes has, until recently, not been of concern. Now, however, many ethologists have begun to make inferences about animals' cognition based on their behavior (see Cheyne & Seyfarth, 1990). Indeed, some ethologists have gone so far as to suggest that we add a fifth question, to Tinbergen's (1963) four, concerning cognitive processes.

INTERPRETIVE METHODS

In this section we continue our examination of naturalistic methods by discussing two forms of interpretive research: ethnography and case study. The label *interpretive* has come to mean a collection of research methods, often labeled as qualitative methods, and ethnography. They most generally attempt to understand the meaning of the situation from the point of view of the participants (F. Erickson, 1986). A number of scholars have listed defining attributes of this form of research. For example, Walsh, Tobin, and Graue (1993) listed three defining attributes of interpretive research: conducting research in a natural setting, having questions and methods emerge during the process of field work, and stressing the participants' perspective. In listing the defining attributes of ethnography, K. Wilcox (1982) also stressed the importance of getting the participants' perspective on events, context–behavior relations, and emergent categories, but extended the defintion by stressing also the role of theory in guiding one's search. Interpretative researchers, as we discuss in the following, use a variety of methods, such as observations and interviews to gather information.

K. Wilcox (1982) accurately noted that a researcher cannot study or observe "everything," so a guiding theory is necessary. Theory guides us, generally, about where to look and what may count as relevant. Importantly, Wilcox also stressed the role of description and the meaning of these descriptive categories for the participants.

Focusing on the meaning of categories for participants is seen by some interpretive researchers as the most crucial task. Hymes (1972), one of the founding fathers of educational anthropology, suggested that the defining attribute of "qualitative" research is its search for the ways in which behaviors are meaningful to participants. Hymes noted that the meaning of identical behaviors may be different for different groups. In one group a specific behavior (such as a push) may be viewed as a hostile way to enter a group, whereas in another group it may be indicative of closeness and affiliation with that group. The job of interpretive researchers, according to Hymes, is to search for these differences in meaning. To merely count instances of pushing behavior would be missing the point of the underlying meaning of the behaviors. In short, we need to know what the behaviors mean before we can count them. To the extent that the "same" behaviors have different meaning across groups precludes their being counted together.

Because of its popularity in the fields of education and child study, we discuss ethnography first.

Ethnography

Ethnography originated in the field of anthropology, but has a considerable history in various aspects of child study as well. In regard to child study, it is most generally concerned with the interface between culture and childhood. For example, it has been used to study child-rearing practices in different cultures (e.g., Harkness & Super, 1993; M. Mead, 1954); children's language development and use (Blount, 1972, 1984; Hymes, 1972a); and children's experiences in schools (e.g., Harkness & Super, 1993; Heath, 1983; Mehan, 1978, 1979; Ogbu, 1974; Rist, 1970). The methods employed are useful for observing children in their natural environments.

Additionally, ethnographic methods can be extremely useful in the study of child development. For example, if we are interested in the development of particular habits, such as sleep patterns, ethnographic methods, as they are currently being applied in cross-cultural psychology, provide important information on the effects of specific cultural context (Rogoff & Morelli, 1989). Continuing with the example of sleep habits, we find that infants' habits are culturally determined to the extent that American infants' (4 to 5 months) sleeping uninterruptedly for 8 hours is determined by both neurological maturation and parents and children sleeping in separate rooms. In other cultures, where mothers and infants sleep together for continuous nursing, less stress is put on sleeping through the night and infants wake every 4 hours (Super, 1976).

In short, ethnographic approaches are important in the study of development in that they provide insight into the contexts in which specific phenomena develop. Much, but not all (see Lancy, 1996), of the current ethnographic work in the area of child study follows a context-specific approach to the study of development (e.g., Cole, 1988; Rogoff & Morelli, 1989; Wertsch, 1985). This approach, which is guided by Vygotsky's (1978; Wertsch, 1985) sociohistorical theory, posits that children learn and develop skills in specific contexts by interacting with a member of society who is facile with those skills. In this apprenticeship-like arrangement, children and their tutors define tasks according to cultural values. In this way culture is both constructed (between participants) and transmitted (to the child). More specific discussion of this Vygotskian approach can be found in chapter 8. In the remainder of this section we examine some processes used in conducting an ethnographic child study.

Ethnographers typically use observational methods in their work. Ethnographic field work regimens include, but are not limited to, participant observation. This practice involves the observer actually taking part in the communities which he or she studies. Cazden's (see Mehan, 1978) participant observation study of primary school teaching remains a classic example. Field notes are typically used to record behavior, events, and states; as well as analytic reflection on the recorded data (F. Erickson, 1986).

As noted in the beginning of this chapter, ethnography tends not to use preexistent data collection categories. They stress the use of emergent categories to the extent that the meaning of behaviors for participants probably varies from situation to situation and certainly from one study to the next. Part of the meaning-explication process in ethnography involves creating behavior categories that are meaningful to participants. The naive might say that ethnographers should enter child study with no preexistent ideas and induce categories based purely on experiences in the field. A more reasonable idea is for the ethnographers to recognize and be more explicit in their preconceptions and guard against their unwarranted intrusion into the data.

At the risk of possibly oversimplifying the point, ethnographers use theory to guide their observations. The theory is not used to generate observational categories a priori; it is used to inform the research as to where to look and what might count as relevant. Further, ethnographers attempt to go beyond behavioral observations in trying to understand a culture. To this end, they might actually take a participant role in the culture and interview participants. For example, theory would tell us that mother–child interaction might be important for peer relations. We would begin by looking at these cases but form relevant categories of interaction after extensive observation. We might also ask mother about the meaning of the behaviors we observe to help us assign meaning to them.

The data-collection process itself should start global and gradually become more focused. That is, ethnographers start off observing the general life of a community, such as all the events involving mother and child. Progressively, the observations may become more focused, concentrating on mother–child interaction when other children are present. The object of study thus also becomes more focused. This differentiation process, however, enables the ethnographer to place the specific phenomenon being examined in its larger context.

Throughout this process copious field notes, mechanical recordings, or both are often made. Simultaneously, the notes and recordings are rewritten or transcribed. This process is an important procedure in the interpretation and categorization of the recorded behaviors. That is, by reexamining notes and tapes we assign meaning to them. It should be noted that machine-recorded data, because they are retrievable, are less prone to the error of premature interpretation, inaccurate interpretation, or both (F. Erickson, 1986). This is not a trivial issue to the extent that inducing participants' meaning from observed behavior is the primary job of the ethnographer.

Ethnographic reports typically contain "thick descriptions" of the context being observed (e.g., Heath, 1983). That is, the researcher thoroughly describes the community and its members before describing the behavior under consideration. The reason for such description relates to a basic assumption of ethnography: Behavior occurs in response to contextual and cultural demands. Thus, in the quest to understand why particular behaviors occur, one must understand the culture of the participants generating the behaviors. For example, in describing the types of books parents read to their children, we must understand aspects of the parents' value system. Heath (1983) has shown that the low-SES white parents in her study put a high value on their religious commitment. Knowledge of this value is necessary in order to understand why these parents often read religious books to their children.

A way in which to check one's interpretation of events is through a collaborative relationship with a focal informant (F. Erickson, 1986). For example, we assume that boys' ability to greet each other with an elaborate handshake is necessary for membership in a particular clique; the validity of this claim can be tested by asking a member of the clique with whom we share mutual knowledge and trust.

Conducting an Ethnographic Child Study

In this section we briefly outline some basic procedures involved in conducting an ethnographic child study. In the next subsection we describe an example of a particular form of ethnography, *constitutive ethnography*.

Ethnographers generally attempt to construct detailed (i.e., molecular) descriptions of everyday behavioral patterns. A basic concern of ethnographers is to construct events from the points of view of the participants being observed. This "emic" (derived from phonemic) stance attempts to derive the participants meaning of events. In order to accomplish this goal, ethnographers utilize a participant-observer strategy. With this strategy, the observer tries to become a member of the group being observed and then tries to describe the behaviors involved in specific social events. Good examples of participant-observer researcher include Cazden's role as a teacher-researcher in a San Diego public school classroom (see Mehan, 1979, for a thorough description) and M. Mead's (1928, 1930) study of children's sexual development.

Although direct observations are important, ethnographers supplement their observations by interviewing different members of the group being observed. Such interview practices serve a number of functions. First, they may provide the observer with information from the point of view of a member for the target group. A problem with interviews, however, is that the interviewer may not get objective information. Those being interviewed may give information they think the interviewer wants to hear or otherwise intentionally mislead the interviewer.

A second function of interview data is that they allow researchers to check their interpretations of events. These interviews, however, such be informal, and not characterized by "leading" questions. For example, a participant-observer may have assumed mothers weaned their babies early so that the mothers could return to work; such an interpretation could be checked in interviews by asking mothers why they wean children at a particular age. This interview might be part of a larger discussion of childrearing practices

Ethnographers also examine artifacts produced by a group. For example, an ethnographer of schooling might examine children's homework or seatwork and teachers' lesson plans, whereas social ethnographers may collect Cub Scout projects.

The validity of an ethnographer's interpretation of events is determined by the triangulation, or convergence, of data sources. That is, different data sources, such as observations and interviews, provide different sources of information about the same events. Validity exists when multiple data sources give the same interpretation. For example, triangulation was provided when both interview and observation data suggested that mothers weaned their babies so that they could return to work.

CASE STUDY

Case study can be part of ethnography or a separate mode of inquiry and involves the examination of a single topic. Cases can be individual children, parents, a school, an event, or any other single entity. Most important, case studies should be used when we want to gain very specific information about a specific case. For example, physicians might construct a case study of a child's experience with a therapeutic regimen. Similarly, economists sometimes use case studies to examine successful corporations.

Case studies, therefore, offer information about the particular. To accentuate the particular, case studies often take the form of narratives, or stories. Good narratives, or narratives that grip the reader, typically provide detailed and varied information about the case and the general context in which it is embedded. Specifically, historical background, information on the physical setting, other relevant cases, and information about other informants add life to case studies.

There a three types of case studies. An intrinsic case study is undertaken because the researcher has intrinsic, or self-motivated, reasons for conducting the research. The particular case is not chosen for any specific reason; for example, it may not be representative or successful, but the researcher finds the case interesting. Family histories are often intrinsic case studies.

Instrumental case studies, on the other hand, are used to inform practice or theory. For example, my son's first-grade classroom and teachers were an interesting example of a cooperative social unit. It would be interesting to conduct case studies with those same teachers in subsequent years. Following up on family history, histories of families from specific groups might be used to gain information about the ways in which a certain group lived in history (L. Stone, 1976).

Collective cases involve the aggregation of numerous studies that shed light on a common problem. The result would be a more general picture than a single case could provide. For example, it would be interesting to examine, in separate case studies, the ways in which cooperation does and does not develop between those same teachers and different groups of children. Separate family histories from a specific county during a specific period would also provide a more general picture.

CONCLUSION

In this chapter we have examined two general approaches to child study. Of the different methodologies reviewed in this chapter, although they have different assumptions, two methods (ethology and ethnography) use observation as a primary mode of data collection. By observing children, they attempt to describe behaviors and attempt to make inferences about those behaviors. Unlike the more controlled methods discussed in previous chapters, naturalistic methods are typically unobtrusive. That is, they do not try to elicit information from children (by such procedures as tests); they observe and categorize behaviors elicited in a number of contexts.

The observational categories used in both ethological and ethnographic methods, however, try to minimize their reliance on preexistent observational categories. Instead, these researchers try to form categories only after they have extensively observed the topic of interest in natural settings; categories are typically induced (A. D. Pellegrini, 1996). The context of the behavior and the behaviors themselves are seen as interdependent. As such, both are extensively described.

The choice of a methodology depends on the question being asked by the researcher. Seldom is there a simple answer to the question "What's the best methodology?" For those of us interested in studying children in applied settings a combination of methodologies seems to be the best answer. In order to understand children we obviously should examine them in their natural environments: in schools, hospitals, playgrounds, and in the home. Experimental and psychometric approaches should be used as adjuncts to observations. Following the advice of the ethologists, it seems that we should understand behaviors in their context before we can generate interesting hypotheses to test in laboratories. Indeed, the observation of behavior often provides testable hypotheses.

No matter what methodology is used, those studying children need to keep in mind the notion that different situations elicit different behaviors which may be unique. For this reason we need to observe children in many different situations in order to begin to understand them.

Despite the often vitriolic debates between different schools of research, it seems to us that interpretive and ethological methods share much common ground: They both stress the role of studying children in their natural environments, often utilizing extensive behavioral observations to do so (A. D. Pellegrini, 1996; Wolcott, 1982). This reliance on understanding behavior in context has lead both groups to stress the role of inductive category formation in their studies. The stress on meaning is also a shared attribute. Whereas ethnographers might use "key informants" and other forms of interviews and questionnaires, ethologists infer meaning, or function by utilizing the 4 whys (Tinbergen, 1963).

ACKNOWLEDGMENT

We acknowledge David Lancy's comments on this chapter.

8

Children's Learning, Thinking, and Remembering

No one can remember what 4-year-old Jason did to get his father so upset, but whatever it was, his father wanted no more of it.

"Jason, I want you to go over to that corner and just *think* about all this for a while," his father yelled.

Instead of following his father's orders, Jason stood where he was, not defiantly, but with a confused look and quivering lips, as if he were trying to say something but was afraid to.

"What's the matter now?" his father asked, his irritation still showing.

"But, Daddy," Jason said, "I don't know *how* to think."

Obviously, 4-year-old Jason did know how to think; he just didn't know that he did. The term *thinking* has a fairly specific meaning for most people. People "think" when they need to solve a difficult problem; something that can be done easily and automatically is said to be done "without thinking." Perception and attention involve important cognitive abilities, but recognizing a face or attending to a stimulus is not what people generally mean by "thinking." In this chapter, we focus on those activities that come to mind for most people when they think about "thinking": learning, problem-solving strategies, memory, and metacognition (what children know about their own thinking).

We first examine traditional topics of learning: classical and operant conditioning, followed by a look at Bandura's influential social cognitive theory, the contemporary version of his earlier social learning theory. Piaget's account of cognitive development is then reviewed. We next look at information-processing perspectives of development, stressing the topics of strategies, memory, metacognition, and theory of mind. We conclude the chapter with a very different perspective on cognitive development, Vygotsky's sociocultural approach, which focuses not just on the child's intellectual development, but views the child *and* his or her social environment as the level of analysis for cognitive development.

LEARNING

Classical and Operant Conditioning

Thinking and remembering imply learning—the acquisition of new knowledge through experience. In the early part of this century, the primary theoretical approach to learning was *behaviorism,* which held that behavior and development are shaped by environmental influences. Two principal types of learning were described: classical conditioning and operant conditioning.

In *classical conditioning,* discovered experimentally by Russian scientist Ivan Pavlov, a previously neutral stimulus is paired with another stimulus that elicits some response. For example, a particular tone might be paired with a puff of air to the eye. The tone is initially neutral in that it elicits no response from a person. The puff of air to the eye, however, does elicit a response—an eye blink. After repeated pairings of the tone with the puff of air, eventually the tone will produce an eye blink even without the puff of air. In this example, the puff of air is referred to as the *unconditioned stimulus* and the tone as the *conditioned stimulus.* Emotional responses seem to be learned through classical conditioning. When a child associates a previously neutral stimulus with a stimulus that already elicits some response, eventually the new stimulus will elicit the emotion.

The most famous study of classical conditioning of emotion was performed nearly 80 years ago (Watson & Raynor, 1920). In that study, Watson and Raynor conditioned a young boy named Albert to be afraid of a white rat by sounding a loud gong each time the boy was shown the rat. Albert's innate fear of the loud sound quickly became associated with the rat. After the experimental trials, the child showed fear to the rat alone, a conditioned or learned response to a previously neutral stimulus.

The other basic form of learning is *operant conditioning,* or learning through reward and punishment. In operant conditioning, some behavior of the child is reinforced, or rewarded, causing a change in the probability of that behavior in the future. For example, children who receive a reward (candy, money, praise) for good behavior can be expected to continue to show good behavior in the future. Patterns of reinforcement—that is, the distribution or frequency of rewards received for particular behaviors—can greatly affect learning (Reynolds, 1968); aversive stimuli (mild shocks for rats, spankings or a reprimand for children) can also affect behavior.

Learning in Infancy

Although infants were once thought to be dumb, passive creatures, oblivious to the world around them, research over the last 40 years has clearly shown that babies are actively learning about their world from birth and before (see D. F. Bjorklund, 1995). Research has shown that infants less than a week old can learn to discriminate between the odor of their mothers and other women (Macfarlane, 1975) and that some learning of basic auditory patterns occurs prenatally (DeCasper & Spence, 1986).

Operant conditioning of newborns is relatively easy: They will modify their behavior in order to receive some type of reward. The trick is to find a behavior that infants can control themselves and something that they find rewarding. Behaviors that newborns can control include sucking, head turning, and kicking, all of which have been used in operant-conditioning experiments. Reinforcements have included milk, human voices, and music (Lipsitt, 1982). For example, in one experiment, newborns would suck on a pacifier in order to hear music as opposed to nonrhythmic noise (Butterfield & Siperstein, 1972), demonstrating both an ability to learn and an innate preference for patterned sound.

Classical conditioning also seems to be within the capability of newborns (Fitzgerald & Brackbill, 1976), although it is limited to a few biologically prepared reflexes, such as sucking and blinking. However, the length of time between the neutral stimulus and the unconditioned stimulus must be shorter in young infants than in older children for conditioning to occur (Lintz, Fitzgerald, & Brackbill,1967; Little, Lipsitt, & Rovee-Collier, 1984). Presumably, young infants cannot process information as efficiently and require more time to make the connection between the conditioned and unconditioned stimuli before learning takes place.

Behavior Modification

Principles of classical and (especially) operant conditioning are used frequently by parents and teachers to control children's behavior and establish discipline. In fact, *behavior modification*—the use of operant conditioning principles to change behavior—is the basis of many parenting programs and popular books aimed at instructing parents in how to manage their children. Yet although the principles of conditioning are as valid today as they were 50 years ago, contemporary researchers believe that operant and classical conditioning alone are not adequate to account for most of the learning that children do. One complaint about behavior-modification techniques is that children who are rewarded for desired behaviors often resort to earlier behaviors once the rewards are removed. That is, although behavior-modification techniques clearly work in controlling a child's current actions, they are less successful in shaping future behavior when rewards are no longer provided. In fact, children who are induced to comply by rewards (or punishments) may lose their intrinsic motivation for the behavior in question and be *less* likely to engage in it on their own (Fabes, Fultz, Eisenberg, May-Plumlee, & Christopher, 1989; Lepper, Greene, & Nisbett, 1973). For example, a study by Fabes and his colleagues (1989) investigated the relationship between experience with instrumental rewards (if you do X, you get Y) and prosocial motivation in elementary school children. To assess mothers' attitudes and practices regarding the use of tangible rewards for activities that children did not find attractive, the researchers asked mothers to respond to items on a 5-point scale, depending on how well it described their beliefs or behavior. Some examples of the items are:

The use of rewards to motivate children can be considered a type of bribery.

The use of rewards to motivate children can help produce desired behavior.

The use of rewards to motivate children makes them stop working when the rewards are no longer available.

To what extent do you provide your child with a reward for behaving properly?

To what extent do you give your child a reward for doing something he or she does not like to do?

The children of these mothers were seen separately and given the opportunity to help make a game for kids in the hospital by arranging pieces of paper according to color. Some of the children were offered a reward for helping (a small toy); other children were not. Later in the session, all children were given a second chance to "help the sick children," but rewards were not offered to anyone (free-choice period). Fabes and his colleagues reported that the offer of rewards increased helping behavior in the first situation. However, during the free-choice period, previously rewarded children were less likely to help, and this effect was greatest for those children whose mothers put a high value on instrumental rewards. Thus, although the use of rewards may enhance prosocial behavior immediately, "they may also undermine subsequent prosocial motivation in situations where rewards are no longer forthcoming" (Fabes et al., 1989, p. 514).

These results do not mean that children should never be offered a reward for good behavior. They mean that the desired behavior is more likely to occur if rewards for prosocial behavior are used with other techniques, such as modeling prosocial behavior (B. S. Moore & Eisenberg, 1984). In fact, modeling has been found to be a very effective technique for inducing prosocial behavior in children, especially when the model is perceived as warm, influential, and powerful (see Shaffer, 1993).

SOCIAL COGNITIVE THEORY

Learning by Observation

The primary limitation of operant and classical conditioning in explaining how children learn is that children (and adults) learn much about their world simply by watching. We do not need to be explicitly reinforced to learn something new. We can simply watch a model, retain the observed behavior, and be able to reproduce it at some later time. Not only can we learn overt behaviors from observing models, we can also learn attitudes and standards of judgment (Bandura, 1989b).

Recognizing the importance of learning by observation, a group of psychologists in the 1930s and 1940s developed a new theoretical approach known as "social learning theory" (Dollard, Doob, Miller, Mowrer, & Sears, 1939; N. E. Miller & Dollard, 1941). According to this theory, imitation is the primary learning mechanism for most social behaviors. Social learning theory was later championed by Bandura and his colleagues (Bandura & Walters, 1963), who initially proposed that children learn through observation by experiencing vicarious reinforcement; that is, they feel good (or bad) watching someone else get reinforced and modify their behavior accordingly. Over more than three decades, Bandura's theory has become less behavioral and more cognitive until, in its latest version, he has renamed it social cognitive theory (Bandura, 1986, 1989b). It is now the dominant approach to studying children's social development.

Unlike earlier social learning theory, social cognitive theory proposes that children play an active role in interacting with their environment. Bandura believes that children have as much effect on their environment as their environment has on them; he refers to this interaction as *reciprocal determinism*. Bandura (1989b) proposed that children's thoughts, feelings, and behaviors interact with the external environment. Children's emotions and thoughts will affect their actions (and vice versa), which, in turn, will affect how others perceive and act toward them. It is a human characteristic to make sense of our behavior (we rarely do anything for "no reason"), and we often modify our thinking and beliefs to make them consistent with our actions (Gazzaniga, 1985). Bandura's theory recognizes the complex web of factors that affect children's behaviors, from their own internal thoughts and feeling, their actions, and the thoughts, feelings, and actions of others in their environment.

Bandura proposed five abilities that influence children's learning about their social world, each of which develops: *symbolization, forethought, self-regulation, self-reflection*, and *vicarious learning*. Symbolization is the ability to think about our social behavior in words and images. Forethought is the ability to anticipate the consequences of our actions and the actions of others. Self-regulation involves adopting standards of appropriate behavior for ourselves—aspirations, or hoped-for levels of accomplishment, as well as social and moral standards. A capacity for self-reflection allows people to analyze their thoughts and actions. The fifth ability, vicarious learning, is the cornerstone of social cognitive theory. In contrast to earlier versions of social learning theory, children do not have to receive reinforcement for their modeling efforts nor even attempt to reproduce modeled behavior for learning to occur. They can watch a model and represent mentally what the model did; this mental symbol can then serve to guide their subsequent behavior, even if they never actually imitate what they observed. Bandura referred to this process as *observational learning*.

Bandura (1989b) proposed four subprocesses involved in observational learning: *attentional processes, retention processes, production processes*, and *motivational processes*. For observational learning to occur, to-be-learned behavior must first be attended to, then represented in memory for later retrieval, and finally the behavior must be performed at the appropriate time. Each of these factors develops, and problems in any one area (retention, for example) will impede successful observational learning.

Children can learn from observation without ever actually producing the behavior. For instance, although we "know" at some level what is appropriate male and female behavior in a range of contexts, most of us display only same-gender behavior. It is important for children to learn not only the behaviors and attitudes of same-gender adults in their society, but also the behaviors and attitudes of the opposite gender because it informs them what behaviors should complement their own. Yet despite "knowing" opposite-gender behavior, children tend to code it negatively and not imitate it, whereas they code same-gender behavior positively and incorporated into their behavior (Money & Ehrhardt, 1972).

Although imitation is not *necessary* for observational learning to occur, it is nonetheless an important component. Imitation is the clearest indication that children have learned through watching and the primary means by which children acquire new behaviors.

The Development of Imitation.   Imitation begins early in infancy and changes in character with the advent of language and other symbolic tools late in the second year of life. Bandura's account of observational learning begins with children's ability to symbolically code events and actions they have seen, store them in memory, and imitate them at some later time. This is what Piaget (1962) referred to as deferred imitation. Such imitative abilities, although apparently present to a limited extent early in the second year (Meltzoff, 1988), begin in earnest between 18 and 24 months of age (Piaget, 1962).

Following Bandura's model there are many components to observational learning. It is well known that young children have limited attention spans.

However, some things are more likely to be attended to than others. Events in which there is a lot of action, including aggression, are apt to catch children's attention, although keeping it is sometimes difficult. Educational television, such as Sesame Street, tries to keep young children's attention by limiting each segment to only a few minutes. Preschoolers may be able to attend to 2 minutes of "circles versus squares," but 4 and 5 minutes on such a topic would result in losing half, or more, of the audience. Young children's memory also shows substantial changes over early childhood, and how much and what children remember will influence greatly their ability to imitate. (Children's memory is discussed in greater detail later in this chapter.)

Even if children pay close attention to some modeled behavior, remember it accurately, and have the motivation to display it, it does not mean that they will be able to imitate it. A major limitation on children's imitation is their motor ability. Yet despite often obvious physical shortcomings, many preschool children believe they are more capable of imitating behavior than they actually are. Young children, in general, overestimate their physical and intellectual abilities (Plumert, 1995; Stipek, 1984), and thus often believe that they can imitate behaviors that are actually beyond their abilities.

Young children's knowledge of their imitative abilities was investigated in a study by D. F. Bjorklund, Gaultney, and Green (1993). In that study, mothers questioned their preschoolers about how well they thought they would be able to imitate certain behaviors, and then recorded their attempts. Children's underestimation was rare, occurring on only 4.7% of the observations. In fact, the most common response was overestimation, which occurred 55.5%, with children stating that they would be able to imitate some action, which they did not.

Young children have great confidence in their own abilities. For them to get better at observational learning, however, they must learn to monitor their behavior, compare their behavior to their memory of the modeled action, and correct mismatches. As children get better at these production processes, the discrepancy between what think they can do and what they actually can do declines (Bandura, 1989b).

Television as a Model for Learning

Children learn not only from watching other people, but also from watching film, videos, and television. There can be no question that television is an important socializing agent in today's society. American children between 3 and 14 years of age watch more than 3 hours of television per day, with the amount of TV viewing time decreasing some over adolescence into young adulthood (see Liebert & Sprafkin, 1988).

As a means of mass communication, television and its related technologies are the most important inventions of the 20th century. Television can serve as a great education tool, bringing knowledge in an easily understood visual form that doesn't require reading skills. But does it? What do children learn from watching TV?

TV and Education.   Many programs on public and commercial TV are aimed at educating children. Perhaps the best known and most successful of these is *Sesame Street*, which has the goal of fostering cognitive skills in preschool children.

Sesame Street has been a staple of children's television for nearly 30 years and is seen in more than 40 countries worldwide (Liebert & Sprafkin, 1988). Its intended audience was children from disadvantaged homes, with the goal of minimizing the gap in cognitive performance between advantaged and less advantaged preschool children. Its popularity has been enormous among children of all socioeconomic groups, and it is now viewed regularly by nearly 6 million American preschoolers.

Early studies that evaluated the effects of *Sesame Street* were impressive. During the first season of the show, Ball and Bogatz (1970) assessed preschool children's basic cognitive skills (including knowledge of letters, numbers, and geometric forms) prior to watching the program. Some children were then encouraged to watch *Sesame Street*, whereas others were not. Ball and Bogatz then divided children into four groups, based on the amount of time they had watched the program, and retested them. It was clear that watching the program had had the desired effect: The amount of cognitive gain children showed was directly related to how much they had watched the show.

More recent research has investigated the effect of watching *Sesame Street* on children's vocabulary development (Rice, Huston, Truglio, & Wright, 1990). Children ages 3 to 5 and 5 to 7 were observed for 2 years, and changes in their vocabulary were related to their TV viewing habits. It was found that *Sesame Street* had a positive effect on the vocabulary development of 3- to 5-year-old children, with lesser benefits for children older than 5. Other types of children's programs, such as cartoons, had no influence on the vocabulary of children of any age. These findings indicate that the program format of *Sesame Street* is well suited for preschool children's vocabulary development.

The* Sesame Street *Generation.   Television has been an everyday part of family life for the past 40 years. Many social critics blame television for the downslide in American children's school performance. Even *Sesame Street* has been criticized for shortening children's attention spans and making classroom learning seem boring by comparison to its rapid-fire visual format (Cook, Appelton, Conner, Shaffer, Tabkin, & Weber, 1975). It is widely believed that children's comprehension of television is fragmented and passive, promoting a passive attitude to thinking in general (Singer, 1980). A number of authors have suggested that the more television children watch, the poorer their school performance is. However, D. R. Anderson and Collins (1988), in reviewing the research evidence on the relationship between TV viewing and academic performance, found little evidence to support this assertion. They concluded that the impact of television is very small, particularly when children's IQs are considered, and that even for children most affected by television (those in low-ability groups), the effects are small and sometimes nonexistent. They conclude that "the most likely effects on schooling come directly from the central content of television programming most watched by children" (p. 70) and believe that television can have a major impact on what children know.

PIAGET'S THEORY

Five-year-old Heidi was watching her father prepare lunch. After spreading peanut butter and jam on one slice of bread and topping it with another, Dad cut the sandwich in two and then again into quarters. Seeing her sandwich cut into four pieces brought an immediate frown to Heidi's face. "Oh, Daddy," she sighed, "I only wanted you to cut it in *two* pieces. I'm not hungry enough to eat four!"

To us it may seem obvious that the amount of sandwich is the same regardless of whether it is cut into 2 pieces or 4 pieces or 40 pieces. But that's not the way it appears to young children, who sometimes draw erroneous (and humorous) conclusions about how the world works. Taking such pronouncements by young children seriously, Swiss psychologist Jean Piaget (1896–1980) formulated a grand theory to explain how thinking changes in quality over the course of development—a theory that has had unparalleled influence in child psychology.

ASSUMPTIONS AND PRINCIPLES OF PIAGET'S THEORY

Piaget's formal education was in biology, and he viewed intelligence as the way we as a species adapt to our environments. Basic assumptions of his theory (Piaget, 1967, 1983; Piaget & Inhelder, 1969) include the concepts of intrinsic activity, organization, and adaptation.

Intrinsic Activity

A fundamental assumption of Piaget's theory is that of *intrinsic activity*. Babies are not passive creatures waiting to be stimulated by external forces before they respond, but are themselves the prime movers and shakers of their world. They actively seek stimulation, initiating action on objects and people who come in contact with them. Thus, the motivation to learn and to develop is within the child. In short, Piaget believed that children play the central role in their own development—a view that minimizes the role of parents and teachers.

Children make sense of their surroundings by actively interpreting their experiences. Knowledge is not simply acquired; it is *constructed,* based on an interaction between the child and his or her environment. As a result, children of different ages hold very different beliefs about the world. A 3-month-old believes that a rattle that falls out of sight under the crib no longer exists; 4-year-olds believe that the sun follows them as they walk; 6-year-olds believe that in a group of seven dogs and four cats, there are more dogs than animals. To Piaget these examples demonstrated the constructive nature of cognition: Reality is not absolute, but a construction based on one's past experiences and current mental structures.

Functional Invariants

Piaget believed that there were two general processes, or functional invariants, that characterize intelligence and operate throughout the lifespan. He referred to these two processes as *organization* and *adaptation.*

Organization refers to the fact that every intellectual operation is related to all other acts of intelligence—that intellectual abilities are coordinated with one another. Organization thus implies a tendency to integrate mental abilities into higher order systems, or *structures.* A structure, or *scheme*, is some enduring knowledge base through which children interpret their world. It is these structures that are intrinsically active and that construct reality. For Piaget, cognitive development is the development of structures.

Piaget's second functional invariant, adaptation, refers to the fact that the child (or, more properly, the child's structures) must adjust to environmental demands. This simple concept has two complementary components: *assimilation* and *accommodation.*

Assimilation refers to the incorporation of new information into already-existing structures. This should not be viewed as the passive registration of new information, however. Assimilation is an active process, with the child sometimes distorting information to fit existing cognitive schemes. For example, after being read "Jack and the Beanstalk" the night before, 22-month-old Kristin greeted her parents in the morning with "Fee, Fi, Fo, Fum. I smell bacon and eggs." The line in the story "I smell the blood of an Englishman" made no sense to Kristin, so she distorted what she remembered in order to assimilate it into her current world knowledge.

The complement of assimilation is accommodation—changing a structure in order to incorporate new information. When children are confronted with something they cannot quite understand, they can modify their structures to make use of this new information. For example, a 2-year-old given a magnet for the first time would have difficulty understanding it if she treated it as she did any other small metal object; she would have to alter her underlying structures in order to take advantage of its special properties. In other words, she can incorporate the special properties of magnets into her behavioral repertoire only if she changes the way she thinks. This, according to Piaget, involves accommodation.

For another example of assimilation and accommodation, consider the 2-year-old who calls all men "Daddy." This child is using the verbal label she acquired for her father to refer to all adult males (assimilation). Now she must learn to restrict her use of the term "Daddy" to her father and find new terms for other men (accommodation), lest she cause embarrassment to her mother.

Piaget stated that all acts of cognition involve both assimilation and accommodation, although not always in equal portions. The purest form of assimilation is play. When playing, children assimilate whatever objects or people they are playing with into their own self-defined schemes. The chair is an engine, the table is the rest of the train, and the hassock is the caboose. At the other extreme is imitation, which Piaget believed was the purest form of accommodation. When successfully imitating another person, the child must modify his or her behavior to match that of the other person.

Piaget used the concepts of assimilation and accommodation to explain how thought develops. According to his theory, children strive to maintain a balance, or equilibrium, in their cognitive structures. When faced with information that does not fit their current thinking, they experience a state of disequilibrium, which is intrinsically unpleasant. To reestablish balance, they alter their cognitive structures, using accommodation to incorporate new information. Accommodation occurs, however, only when the discrepancy between new information and the child's present thinking is small; if it is too great, the child will either ignore the information or distort it. Piaget referred to this process of changing structures to maintain a cognitive balance as *equilibration*.

Piaget's view of development has important consequences for education. A teacher with a Piagetian perspective strives to present children with tasks that produce slight degrees of disequilibrium. Problems that are too easy can simply be assimilated, and thus no development has occurred. Problems or information too discrepant from what a child already knows cannot be accommodated, and thus they are either distorted or ignored. Learning and development are most apt to occur when problems are of some optimal level of discrepancy from what a child already knows.

Piaget also believed that the role of teachers should not be to *instruct* children (that is, to transmit knowledge), but rather to provide opportunities to *discover* knowledge. According to Piaget:

> Children should be able to do their own experimenting and their own research. Teachers, of course, can guide them by providing appropriate materials, but the essential thing is that in order for a child to understand something, he must construct it for himself; he must reinvent it. (Piaget, 1972, p.1).

Unlike conventional Western approaches to education, in which teachers are authority figures who transmit information to children, Piaget believed that the authority status of teachers actually hampered learning

> It is despite adult authority, and not because of it, that the child learns. And also it is to the extent that the intelligent teacher has known to efface him or herself, to become an equal and not a superior, to discuss and to examine, rather than to agree and constrain morally, that the traditional school has been able to render service. (Piaget, 1977, cited in Rogoff, 1997, p. 38)

As these quotes indicate, Piaget did not believe that children learn or develop much from interacting with adults. For Piaget, development is a process of discovery, and one cannot discover if one is instructed by an authority figure. However, Piaget proposed that children can learn and develop by interacting with *peers*. Peers are people of equal status, and it is through the inevitable conflict that comes with peer interaction that children's minds develop. The ideas of other children often conflict with a child's own. This results in disequlibration, which children seek to resolve. Because peers are equal in status, they must work together to resolve these conflicts and cognitive development is the consequence. (More is said about Piaget's perspective of peer interaction in play in chapters 10 and 11).

Stages of Development

The cornerstone of Piaget's theory is the idea of stages, with functioning at one stage being *qualitatively* different from functioning at other stages. Thus, children at any given stage have a unique way of viewing the world that is consistent with the rules they have derived so far and consistent with the reasoning of other children their age.

Piaget insisted that stages cannot be skipped. He believed that every structure in the psychology of intelligence is based on earlier structures, making it necessary for children to master the accomplishments of one stage before advancing to the next. Children may go through stages at different rates, and development may be arrested at a certain stage for some individuals, but the order in which children go through the stages is unalterable.

Piaget divided cognitive development into four major stages, or periods: *sensorimotor, preoperations, concrete* operations, and *formal operations* (see Table 8.1).

The Sensorimotor Period.   The first stage, which extends from birth to about 2 years, is known as the *sensorimotor period.* Mental functioning changes more drastically during these 2 years than during any other period in development. First, there is a change from an intelligence based on action to one based on symbols—that is, from cognition based on overt actions to one based on internal representations. Second, there is a related change in personal

perspective—from an undifferentiated world with no notion of a separate self to one in which self and other are clearly distinguished. Piaget (1952, 1954, 1962) described these monumental changes as occurring in six substages, which are described in Table 8.2.

At the earliest stage, that of *basic reflexes* (birth to 1 month), infants know the world only in terms of inherited reflexes. Piaget used the term *reflex* broadly to include not only behaviors such as sucking and grasping, but also behaviors such as eye movements, orientation to sound, and vocalizations. Basically, infants during this first stage apply their reflexes to objects. If an object, such as a nipple, fits a reflex, such as sucking, the infant applies the reflex to the object and assimilates the object to an existing scheme—in other words, the baby nurses.

In stage 2, *primary circular reactions* (1 to 4 months), infants extend their reflexes to acquire new patterns of behavior that were not part of the basic biological package they were born with. For example, there is no basic reflex for thumb sucking. However, there are inherited patterns for moving one's arms and hands and for sucking. When, as a result of chance, babies find their fists or thumbs in their mouths, sucking ensues. Because sucking is intrinsically pleasing, the infant attempts to re-create the pleasurable experience. Much trial and error follows, but the result is an infant who can suck its thumb at will. Although this may not seem an impressive act of intelligence, it is an example of infants' learning to control some aspect of their behavior.

Infants' control of their world expands during the third stage, *secondary circular reactions* (4 to 8 months), as they learn to control not only their own bodies, but events in the external world. For example, Bjorklund and Bjorklund (1992) described the behavior of their daughter during this stage of sensorimotor development:

> When our daughter Heidi was about 4 months old, she was lying in a playpen with a "crib gym" strung over it—a complex mobile with parts that spin when they are struck. While flailing her arms and legs, she hit the mobile, causing it to spin. She happened to be looking at the mobile, and its movement caught her attention. She immediately stopped moving and stared intently at the object over her head. When it ceased moving, she began to shake her arms and legs, to squirm, and finally, to cry. Again she hit the mobile, and again she froze and quieted, staring straight ahead at the wonderful event she had caused. (p 171)

This is an important step in intellectual development. In this stage, babies begin to realize that they have some control over their world. Although the initial event occurs accidentally, once under their control, the action is theirs to use whenever and wherever they please. Not only could Heidi spin the mobile in her playpen, she could apply this new behavior to other objects in other locations. She could switch hands or adjust the strength of her stroke to produce

TABLE 8.1

Piaget's Four Stages of Cognitive Development

Period	Approximate Age	Major Characteristics
Sensorimotor	Birth–2 years	Intelligence is limited to the infants' own actions on the environment. Cognition progresses from the exercise of reflexes to the beginning of symbolic representation.
Preoperations	2–7 years	Intelligence is symbolic; use of language and imagery enables children to represent and compare objects mentally. Thought is intuitive rather than logical.
Concrete operations	7–11 years	Intelligence is symbolic and logical, and less egocentric, but still limited to concrete phenomena and past experience.
Formal operations	11–16 years	Children are able to generate and test hypotheses, introspect about processes, and think abstractly.

Note. From *Children's Thinking: Developmental Function and Individual Differences,* p. 62, by D. F. Bjorklund, Copyright © 1995, 1989 Brooks/Cole Publishing Company, Pacific Grove, CA 93950, a division of International Thomson Publishing Inc. By permissions of the publisher.

TABLE 8.2

Substages of the Sensorimotor Period

Stage	Approximate Age	Major Characteristics
1. Basic reflexes	Birth–1 month	Cognition limited to inherited reflex patterns
2. Primary circular reactions	1–4 months	First acquired adaptations extension of basic reflexes
3. Secondary circular reactions	4–8 months	Beginning of control of objects and events external to infant
4. Coordination of secondary circular reactions	8–12 months	Coordination of two previously acquired schemes to achieve a goal (goal-directed behavior)
5. Tertiary circular reactions	12–18 months	Discovery of new means through active experimentation, trial and error
6. Mental combinations	18–24 months	First signs of symbolic functioning (language and imagery)

Note. From *Children's Thinking: Developmental Function and Individual Differences,* p. 64, by D. F. Bjorklund, Copyright © 1995, 1989 Brooks/Cole Publishing Company, Pacific Grove, CA 93950, a division of International Thomson Publishing Inc. By permissions of the publisher.

slightly different outcomes. She had begun to master her world by acting intentionally on objects around her.

Next in development infants learn to coordinate several of these accidental behavior patterns to achieve a goal. Piaget labeled this fourth stage *coordination of secondary circular reactions* (8 to 12 months). Suppose, for example, that a toy is set in front of a baby and an obstacle placed between the baby and the toy. At 6 or 7 months, babies are unable to get the desired toy, even though they are perfectly capable of moving the obstacle. Somewhere around 8 months, however, babies develop the ability to use one behavior (pushing an obstacle) in the service of another (retrieving a toy). This achievement of goal-directed behavior is a major advance in the development of intelligence.

Cognition takes a turn again beginning at about 12 months. Now, for the first time, infants invent slightly new behaviors to achieve their goals. They no longer have to wait until chance provides them with an interesting event; they can make interesting things happen themselves. Piaget called this fifth stage *tertiary circular reactions* (12 to 18 months). Sometimes these "interesting things" involve getting into things they should not, such as kitty litter, the bathroom cabinet, and the living room CD player. Children are discovering as much about their world as they can and are learning more about the control they have over their environment. They learn that their action is independent of their parents and that they do not have to comply if they don't want to. They also learn the consequences of this defiance, as they must, and they modify their behavior accordingly—most of the time.

Although children at this stage are wonderful problem solvers, their intelligence is still limited to actions on objects. Babies know things by acting on them; they cannot make mental comparisons or represent objects and events symbolically. It is not long, however, before infancy is left behind and a totally new way of understanding the world develops. Somewhere between the latter part of the second year and the beginning of the third, children become symbol users. They are able to make mental comparisons between objects, to retrieve memories from the past, and to anticipate the future. They no longer depend on their own direct actions to understand things; they can know the world through language and other symbols. This final stage of the sensorimotor period, *invention of new means through mental combinations* (18 to 24 months), is a transition between the action-oriented world of the infant and the symbol-oriented world of the child.

Perhaps the most studied aspect of Piaget's sensorimotor period is the concept of *object permanence*. According to Piaget, infants under 4 months have no concept of object permanence—no idea that objects have an existence in time and space independent of their own perceptions of or actions on those objects (Piaget, 1954). Thus, for example, 2- or 3-month-olds will follow their mother with their eyes, but when mother leaves their visual field, they will continue to gaze at the point where she disappeared and not anticipate her reappearance somewhere else.

The development of object permanence is gradual over infancy. For example, at around 4 months of age, infants will attempt to retrieve objects that disappear, but only if the object is still partially visible. Beginning at about 8 months, infants are able to retrieve a completely hidden object. To do this, infants must be able to use one behavior (removing an obstacle) in the service of another (retrieving a desired object). Object permanence is not yet complete, however, for if an object is hidden in one location and then moved to a second location, all while the child watches, the infant will search the first location and often act quite surprised not to find the object there.

At about 12 months, infants can solve the problem of consecutive hiding places. However, they still cannot solve what Piaget called "invisible displacements," in which an object is hidden in one container, then hidden under another container out of the child's direct vision. For example, Piaget (1954) related how his daughter Jacqueline at 18 months was perplexed when her father placed a potato in a box, put the box under a rug, and then brought out the empty box for her inspection, all while she watched. Jacqueline would look in the box and stare at the rug, but never search under it, despite having watched her father hide the potato and seeing a lump in the rug as evidence that something must be under there.

The sequence of object permanence described by Piaget has been replicated by other researchers (Kramer, Hill, & Cohen, 1975; Uzgiris & Hunt, 1975). More controversial, however, are the cognitive abilities that underlie object permanence. According to Piaget, failure to solve object-permanence tasks reflects an incomplete concept of objects: infants do not understand that objects are permanent in time and space. Other researchers have questioned this interpretation, providing evidence that infants have greater competence than Piaget proposed (see Baillargeon, 1987; Willatts, 1990). Some have suggested that a sense of object permanence is innate (Baillargeon, 1987; Spelke, 1991); others have suggested that failure to solve some object-permanence tasks is a function of other cognitive factors, including memory (Bower, 1982; Diamond, 1985) and the ability to inhibit a previously acquired response (Diamond, 1985).

We should note that it is not only the concept of object permanence that recent researchers have questioned. Although Piaget's observations of infants' development over the first 2 years of life have been repeatedly replicated (e.g., Kramer et al., 1975; McCall, Eichorn, & Hogarty, 1977; Uzgiris & Hunt, 1975), others have suggested that infants late in the first year of life have the rudiments of symbolic representation. For example, several researchers have demonstrated evidence of *deferred,* or *delayed imitation.* In these tasks, infants observe a model engage in some novel behavior (for example, playing with a new toy in an unfamiliar way), and some time later, ranging from minutes to months, are given the toy for the first time. Will they display the novel behavior that they had seen earlier? Compared to control children who did not witness the toy being played with earlier, evidence is that children as young as 9 months of age will imitate the novel behavior over delays ranging from 10 minutes to one year (Bauer, 1995). Evidence such as this has caused some scientists to question whether there ever is a period in life when children totally lack symbolic representation (Gelman & Williams, 1987; Mandler, 1997; Meltzoff, 1990).

Despite the evidence that infants have greater cognitive abilities than we once believed, Piaget's description of their thinking and behavior still provides an accurate description, we believe, of how most infants think and behave most of the time, although his account does greatly underestimate the actual cognitive abilities of infants and toddlers and may not focus on some important dimensions of cognitive development.

Preoperational Thought. The transition from the action-based cognition of the sensorimotor period to the symbol-based thinking of the *preoperational period* is seen most obviously in the child's use of language. Beginning around 18 months, children start stringing words together into sentences. Other examples of symbol use in young children are deferred imitation (discussed earlier), drawing, imagery, and symbolic play (for example, pretending a shoe is a telephone or feeding imaginary cereal to a doll). Each of these forms of cognition is available to most 2-year-olds, although how they use these symbols will improve dramatically over the next dozen years or so.

During the preoperational period, children's thinking, although symbolic, is not logical. For example, if a red stick is taller than a blue stick and a blue stick is taller than a green stick, then logically the red stick must be taller than the green one. This, however, is not an inescapable conclusion to 4- or 5-year-olds, who base their conclusions on what *seems* to be, regardless of what, by logic, must be. For example, if water is poured from a tall, skinny glass into a short, fat glass, the preoperational child is likely to say that the amount of water has changed. There seems to be less water in the short, fat glass because the height of the water is lower. For preoperational children, appearance is stronger than logic; they find no contradiction in stating that the amount of liquid changes when poured from one container to another. This is the intuitive nature of thought characteristic of the preoperational period.

Piaget described a number of characteristics of preoperatonal children's thought. For example, he stated that preoperational children's perception was centered on the most obvious dimension of a situation and that they attend to and make judgments based solely on that dimension. In the water-level problem, for example, their attention is centered only on the difference in height of the waterlines; according to Piaget, they are unable to consider the two dimensions of height and width simultaneously. Evidence of young children's perceptual *centration* can also be found in their everyday thinking. For example, Piaget (1969) noted that preoperational children often use people's height as a means to estimate their age. Tall people are older than shorter people. This developmental difference in how two children judge age is illustrated in the following transcript.

Nicholas, age 5½

Interviewer: "If a grown-up came into your classroom and asked you to guess how old he was, how do you think you would do it? What sort of things would you look at?"

Nicholas: "I don't know. I'd measure. I'd measure by how high he is."

Interviewer: "What if he was big?"

Nicholas: "He'd be old, like 15 or 100."

Interviewer: "OK. What if a new kid came to your school? How could you tell how old he was? What sort of things would you look at?"

Nicholas: "His fingers."

Interviewer: "His fingers? How could you tell by his fingers?"

Nicholas: "I'd see how many fingers he held up."

Interviewer: "Oh. What if he didn't hold up any fingers? How could you tell how old he was just by looking at him?"

Nicholas: "I don't know. How big he is. If he was big, he'd be old, like Russell. If he was like me, he'd be 5. If he was little, he'd be 4. Or maybe 3. If he was a baby, he'd be real tiny."

Kristina, age 8½

Interviewer: "If a grown-up came into your classroom and asked you to guess how old he was, how do you think you would do it? What sort of things would you look at?"

Kristina: "I would usually look at his hair. If he has a lot of hair or is bald. And if his legs are hairy, and whether he had hair coming out his nose. And his skin and stuff. If he would be old, his hair would be gray and his skin would be wrinkled."

Interviewer: "OK. What if a new kid came to your school? How could you tell how old he was? What sort of things would you look at?"

Kristina: "Usually, if they're tall like me or if they're like Marci's size, they'd be like 8. If they were smaller, they'd be like 7 or 6."

Interviewer: "So if they're taller they're older?"

Kristina: "Yes."

Interviewer: "Can you do the same thing with adults? Use how tall they are to tell how old they are?"

Kristina: "No. With the height you can't really tell with a grown-up. And also kids don't have gray hair and wrinkled skin."

This doesn't mean that children can't judge age on the basis of other features, such as faces. When the conditions are right they can (Montepare & McArthur, 1986). But when differences in height are present and substantial, young children have a difficult time ignoring the them.

Another characteristic of preoperational children's thought is their *egocentricity*. Piaget used this term to refer to the tendency to interpret objects and events only from one's own perspective—the inability to put oneself in someone else's shoes, as it were. Preoperational children are less egocentric than the sensorimotor child, but more self-centered in cognitive perspective than concrete operational children. According to Piaget, this egocentric perspective permeates the lives of young children, influencing their perceptions, language, and social interactions. For example, much research has examined young children's ability to take the visual perspective of another. In classic research by Piaget and Inhelder (1967), young children sat on one side of a display of three mountains and asked to tell what a doll placed at various positions around the mountains saw. Piaget and Inhelder reported that most children under 8 years of age gave an egocentric response and simply said that the doll saw what *they* saw. Other researchers have criticized Piaget and Inhelder's three-mountain task as overly difficult, and more recent research has shown that children will make nonegocentric responses when provided with less complicated visual displays (Borke, 1975; Gzesh & Surber, 1985). Some everyday examples of egocentricity in young children are given here:

> Egocentrism is easy to spot in young children. A kindergarten child will tell her parents a story about what happened to Billy at school and leave out much of the relevant information. *Everyone* knows about Billy. Surely that must include Mom and Dad.

> A telephone conversation with a 4-year-old can be interesting, but in the absence of face-to-face visual cues, much important information is often lost. For example, the voice on the other end of the phone asks, "What are you wearing today, Kelly?" and in response Kelly says "This," while looking down and pointing at her dress.

> Allen, the son of a high school math instructor, asks another 7-year-old, "What does your daddy teach?"—assuming that everyone's daddy must teach something. He knows there are other jobs in the world; in fact, *he's* going to be a fireman when he grows up. Nonetheless, daddies teach.

> Even young children are not consistently egocentric, however. At 5, my daughter Heidi still frequently demonstrated the classic egocentric attitude described by Piaget. For example, one evening in her bath she placed her head under the running water and excitedly called me in to hear the new sound. "Listen to this, Daddy," she said as she lowered her head under the faucet again while I watched. In a different context, however, this same child showed a keen ability to take the perspective of another. One evening, sometime before the bath episode, she and I were beginning a prebedtime card game and I was exhorting her to hurry because, I said, the game is more fun when you play it fast. Her response to that was quick. "No sir, Daddy," she said. "You only want to go fast so we can finish and you can put me to bed!" I had been caught. This child, who thought I could hear the rushing water when *her* head was under the faucet, in this instance, saw my perspective quite clearly.

> In general, each of us sees the world from a slightly different perspective, but with age and experience our perspectives expand, becoming less personal and more cultural. Our world and the world of the young child are not exactly the same, even though we may reside in the same house and live through the same events. We

should not be surprised that in telling the story of an afternoon together in the park, the child comes up with a different account of things than her father does. This is not necessarily due to the young child's poor memory; she may be remembering things very well. She just didn't see or experience the same things that her father did standing beside her. They saw and felt different things at the same place and time. This isn't a scene from *The Twilight Zone*, just the normal differences in thinking and perspective between children and adults. (Adapted from D. F. Bjorklund, 1986a, p. 8)

Concrete Operational Thought. By about the age of 7, children are no longer so easily taken in by appearances. They are able to *decenter* their perception—that is, they demonstrate *decentration*, the ability to separate themselves from the obvious aspects of a perceptual array and make decisions based on the entire perceptual field. They are also less egocentric than young children.

Perhaps the most critical difference between the preoperational and the concrete operational child is that the older child is able to think following rules of logic. The most important logical rule underlying mental operations is reversibility. In arithmetic, for example, subtraction is the inverse, or reverse, of addition. If 6 plus 3 equals 9, then 9 minus 3 must equal 6. Understanding this rule is critical for children to learn arithmetic, and children who do not appreciate the logical necessity of reversibility in arithmetic will be doing little more than rote memorization. Reversibility, more generally, is the logical idea that for any operation there exists another operation that compensates for the effects of the first. For example, if water is poured from a short, fat glass into a tall, thin one, the increased height of the water is compensated for by a decrease in the width of the column.

Piaget developed many tasks that differentiate the thinking of the preoperational from the concrete operational child, but perhaps the most studied, and for Piaget (1965a) the most important, were tasks that assessed conservation. Conservation refers to the understanding that an entity remains the same despite changes in its form. A classic example of a conservation task is the water-level problem discussed earlier. Do children realize that the amount of water remains the same after pouring it into a different container, even though there seems to be more (or less) than there was originally? The concept of conservation applies to any substance that can be measured and has been studied with respect to dimensions of length, number, mass, weight, area, and volume.

With respect to conservation, as with other aspects of his theory, Piaget believed that he was assessing children's competencies—their fundamental abilities. If this were the case, it should not be possible to train children to conserve unless they are in a transition stage, almost ready to learn to conserve on their own. However, a number of researchers, using a variety of techniques, have demonstrated that nonconservers as young as 4 can be trained to conserve (Brainerd & Allen, 1971; Gelman, 1969). Training effects are greater for older than for younger children (e.g., Brainerd, 1977), and few studies have successfully trained conservation in 3-year-old children (D. Field, 1987). However, about three quarters of all published studies in which preschool children were taught to conserve have been successful, with a smaller percentage showing generalization to other materials and over delays of a week or longer.

Formal Operations. Formal operations advance the logical rules acquired during the concrete operational period to the point that children can think about objects, ideas, events, and relations independent of their prior experience (Inhelder & Piaget, 1958). As one Piagetian scholar put it, "Concrete operations consist of thought thinking about the environment, but formal operations consist of thought thinking about itself" (Brainerd, 1978, p. 215). Formal operational thinkers are able to introspect about their own cognitions and produce new knowledge merely by reflecting on what they already know. They are also able to solve complex problems and to reason inductively, going from specific observations to broad generalizations, much as a scientist does when conducting experiments.

The hallmark of the formal operational period is the ability to think hypothetically—or, as Piaget put it, *hypothetico-deductive reasoning.* Possibilities are more important than what is real. Such thinking is critical for most forms of mathematics beyond arithmetic. If $3x + 3 = 15$, what does x equal? The problem does not deal with concrete entities such as marbles and pencils, only with numbers and letters.

Another characteristic of formal operational thought is *inductive reasoning*—going from specific observations to broad generalizations. This is the type of thinking that characterizes scientists, who generate hypotheses and then test them systematically in experiments. In other words, the ability to set up an experiment, test the effects that different variables have on an a dependent measure, and interpret the results properly (all of which were discussed in chapter 5), are abilities that children who have attained formal operational abilities posses, but children who are still in the concrete operational period have not yet mastered.

As with other aspects of Piaget's theory, there has been controversy concerning whether concrete operational children are capable of solving problems requiring scientific reasoning. In fact, researchers have been able to train young children to solve many formal operational problems (Siegler, Robinson, Liebert, & Liebert, 1973; C. A. Stone & Day, 1978), although they demonstrate these abilities only under limited conditions.

In other situations, however, research has shown that Piaget overestimated the tendency of adolescents and adults to use scientific-type reasoning. For example, Kuhn and her associates (D. Kuhn, Langer, Kohlberg, & Haan, 1977), using 265 adolescent and adult participants in a longitudinal study, administered a battery of formal operational tasks adapted from

Inhelder and Piaget, including tests of scientific reasoning. Based on these tests, only about 30% of the adults were classified as having completely achieved formal operations. Most adults were classified as transitional between concrete and formal operations, and 15% demonstrated no formal operational abilities at all.

Piaget and Individual Differences in Children's Thinking

Piaget was concerned with cognitive development—age-related changes in children's thinking that typify the species. He was less interested in individual differences, differences in thinking among children of the same age. This has not stopped other psychologists and educators, however, from applying Piaget's theory to the problem of assessing individual differences in children's thinking. For example, several researchers have reported that how well children perform on a battery of Piagetian tasks (for example, conservation) predicts their academic performance (e.g., Byrd & Gholson, 1985; Kaufman & Kaufman, 1972; Keating, 1975; Kingma, 1984; Lunzar, Dolan, & Wilkinson, 1976).

Perhaps the most impressive research relating children's performance on Piagetian tasks to academic performance and measures of IQ was performed by Humphreys and his colleagues (L. G. Humphreys, 1980; L. G. Humphreys & Parsons, 1979; L. G. Humphreys, Rich, & Davey, 1985). Humphreys and his associates administered IQ tests and batteries of Piagetian tasks to children of varying intellectual aptitudes (mentally retarded and normal children) and ages (6 to 18 years). The tasks included those that assessed early concrete operational abilities (e.g., conservation) to those evaluating formal operations (e.g., scientific reasoning).

Humphreys reported correlations between scores on the Piagetian tasks, IQ, and measures of academic performance in excess of .70. In fact, children's scores on the Piagetian tasks predicted academic performance nearly as well as IQ scores. Based on the pattern of correlations, Humphreys proposed that IQ tests and the Piagetian batteries are both valid measures of intelligence. Although there was overlap in the type of intelligence the two measures tapped, Humphreys noted that there were some differences between the tasks in terms of the intellectual skills they assessed. Humphreys was not able to specify the nature of these differences, but he stated that each measure is a valid index of intelligence (L. G. Humphreys et al., 1985).

INFORMATION-PROCESSING PERSPECTIVES OF CHILDREN'S COGNITION

Piaget's theory has been enormously influential, both in terms of providing scientists with a better understanding of child development and by helping educators to focus on ways in which children of different ages learn. But there is another approach to children's thinking that has also provided important insights into cognitive development, and that is the information-processing approach. Basically, this perspective views the human mind as being like a computer. We have certain hardware, such as limited-capacity memory stores, and are limited in how quickly we can process information. There are also aspects of our cognition that are analogous to software, for example, the strategies we use to solve problems. Both hardware (for example, how much information children can keep in mind at one time, speed of processing) and software (for example, knowledge that children possess and the strategies they have to act on that knowledge) change with age.

In this section, we examine several aspects of children's information processing. We will start by taking a look at the information-processing system, followed by an examination of strategies, focusing mainly on young children's early arithmetic strategies. We devote a bit more space to the important factor of memory, which influences all aspects of children's thinking. We conclude with a look at metacognition, and a particular type of metacognition termed theory of mind.

The Information-Processing System

Most contemporary theories of cognition assume that we have a limited capacity for thinking—a finite amount of mental resources. We can only think about one thing at a time, and many of our mental operations are effortful, in that they consume a portion of these resources, leaving less behind for other aspects of thinking (Atkinson & Shiffrin, 1971; Hasher & Zacks, 1979; Shiffrin & Schneider, 1977). Most theories also make a distinction between the short-term and long-term stores. The *long-term store* is our repository of permanent memories. Presumably, it can hold an infinite amount of information for an infinite amount of time, although forgetting does occur. The *short-term store*, on the other hand, can only hold a limited amount of information (in adults, 7 plus or minus 2 items) for a matter of seconds. The short-term store has also been referred to as primary memory, working memory, and the contents of consciousness. It is in the short-term store that information is consciously evaluated. The short-term store is where we live, cognitively speaking.

Memory Span.   One issue that has concerned developmental psychologists is age differences in the capacity of the short-term store. Can older children hold more information in consciousness at any one time than younger children? Early research found what appeared to be substantial and regular age differences, based on memory-span tasks. Memory span refers to the number of items one can recall perfectly after only a brief exposure (for example, hearing one item per second). Memory span for digits (digit span) is commonly used on tests of intelligence and shows very regular developmental changes (see Fig. 8.1).

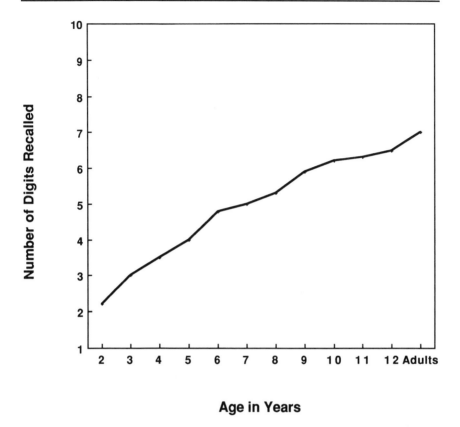

FIG. 8.1. Children's digit span shows regular increases with age. From "Memory Span: Sources of Individual and Development Differences," by F. N. Dempster, 1981, *Psychological Bulletin, 89*, p. 111. Copyright © 1981 by the American Psychological Association. Reprinted with permission.

Despite these impressive and robust findings, more recent research has seriously questioned the idea that the capacity of the short-term store increases substantially with age. For example, in one often-cited study, a group of graduate students at the University of Pittsburgh were given two simple memory tests. On one, they were read a series of numbers quickly (about one per second) and asked to recall them immediately in exact order. On a second test, they were shown briefly chess pieces on a chess board (again, about one chess piece per second), then given the pieces and asked to place them at their previous positions on the board. Their performance on these tasks was compared to that of a group of 10-year-olds. But, in all fairness, these were not typical 10-year-olds; they were all chess experts—winners of local tournaments or members of chess clubs. When memory for the chess positions was tested, the children outperformed the adults. This finding was probably not surprising, given the expert status of the children. But the critical question was, How would they do when remembering the numbers? Does being a chess expert cause one's memory capabilities to improve overall, or was the children's remarkable performance limited to what they knew best? The results support the latter interpretation. The adults, despite being outdone by the children when memory for chess positions was tested, were superior to the children when the test stimuli were numbers. The results of this experiment, conducted by Chi (1978), can be seen in Fig. 8.2.

What results such as these indicate is that children's short-term memory is not fixed but flexible. Under certain conditions, they can remember things as well as adults; in other situations, however, they act like kids. What this suggests is that the capacity of children's and adults' short-term stores is comparable; adults just make better use of it than do children (usually).

Efficiency of Processing.   This brings us to the idea of efficiency of processing. If that actual capacity of short-term memory is not much different between children and adults, what causes the substantial differences that are seen on most cognitive tasks? The simple answer is that older children and adults process information more efficiently than younger children (D. F. Bjorklund & Harnishfeger, 1990; Case, 1985; Dempster, 1985). With age, children process information faster (Kail, 1993; Kail & Salthouse, 1994), and faster processing translates directly into more efficient processing.

Why should having detailed knowledge about a subject result in improved memory performance? Bjorklund and his colleagues proposed that the better established information is in one's mind, the more easily it can be activated, bringing that information to consciousness (D. F. Bjorklund, 1987; D. F. Bjorklund, Muir-Broaddus, & Schneider, 1990; see also Kee & Davies, 1990). They are also able to integrate new information more easily the more they already know about a topic. In fact, when children are highly knowledgeable about a topic, they are able to learn and remember information about that topic very well. Because older children usually know more than younger children about things in general, they require less in the way of mental effort to activate common word meanings, leaving them with more mental space or mental energy to spend on the recall of additional words or on other cognitive operations.

We earlier gave an example of how chess-expert children have greater memory spans for chess position than chess-novice adults (e.g., Chi, 1978). Let us provide another example on a more complicated task of how children's knowledge for a topic can influence how much they remember and compensate for the effects of low academic ability. Schneider, Körkel, and Weinert (1989,

1990) compared the story comprehension of soccer expert and soccer novice third-, fifth-, and seventh-grade children on stories related to soccer. They also classified children as successful learners versus unsuccessful learners based on their classroom grades in German and mathematics and performance on IQ tests. This led to four groups of children at each grade: soccer experts/successful learners, soccer experts/unsuccessful learners, soccer novices/successful learners, and soccer novices/unsuccessful learners. Children were then read a story about soccer. Care was taken to ensure that most parts of the story would be easily understood even by the soccer novices. Children were then asked questions about the story or were asked to recall the story. The average number of idea units children remembered from the soccer story is presented in Fig. 8.3, collapsed across grades. First of all, expert children performed better than did novice children. What may be surprising, however, is that a child's learning ability did not influence performance; the soccer expert/unsuccessful learners remembered more than did the soccer novice/successful learners. In other words, what children knew about soccer determined how well they performed, independent of their general learning ability (see also Recht & Leslie, 1988; Schneider, D. F. Bjorklund, & Maier-Brückner, 1996; Walker, 1987).

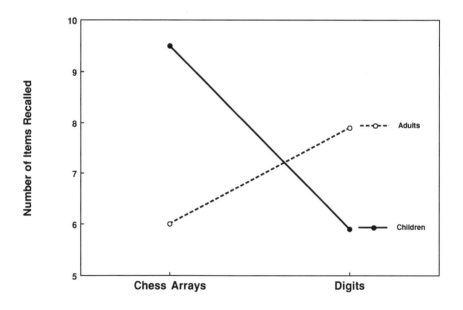

FIG 8.2.   Average memory span for digits and chess arrays by chess-expert children and college-educated adults. From "Knowledge Structure and Memory Development" (p. 74), by M. T. H. Chi in R. Siegler (Ed.), *Children's Thinking: What Develops?*, 1978, Hillsdale, NJ: Lawrence Erlbaum Associates. Copyright © 1978 by Lawrence Erlbaum Associates. Reprinted with permission.

We earlier gave an example of how chess-expert children have greater memory spans for chess position than chess-novice adults (e.g., Chi, 1978). Let us provide another example on a more complicated task of how children's knowledge for a topic can influence how much they remember and compensate for the effects of low academic ability. Schneider, Körkel, and Weinert (1989, 1990) compared the story comprehension of soccer expert and soccer novice third-, fifth-, and seventh-grade children on stories related to soccer. They also classified children as successful learners versus unsuccessful learners based on their classroom grades in German and mathematics and performance on IQ tests. This led to four groups of children at each grade: soccer experts/successful learners, soccer experts/unsuccessful learners, soccer novices/successful learners, and soccer novices/unsuccessful learners. Children were then read a story about soccer. Care was taken to ensure that most parts of the story would be easily understood even by the soccer novices. Children were then asked questions about the story or were asked to recall the story. The average number of idea units children remembered from the soccer story is presented in Fig. 8.3, collapsed across grades. First of all, expert children performed better than did novice children. What may be surprising, however, is that a child's learning ability did not influence performance; the soccer expert/unsuccessful learners remembered more than did the soccer novice/successful learners. In other words, what children knew about soccer determined how well they performed, independent of their general learning ability (see also Recht & Leslie, 1988; Schneider, D. F. Bjorklund, & Maier-Brückner, 1996; Walker, 1987).

Strategies

Much of cognition is automatic, in that it is done without a person's awareness. We are not conscious of the mental gymnastics that must be done to read the words on this page or identify the noise outside the window as the barking of our neighbor's St. Bernard. But much that we consider "thinking" does have a significant conscious and intentional component to it. We actively try to remember a phone number, figure out which can of deodorant is the best buy, or solve the problem of how to store our jumbled spices on the kitchen shelves.

Strategies are effortful processes, in that they consume a portion of one's limited mental resources. But the effort is usually well worth the mental cost because using a strategy typically results in better thinking. Strategies are generally defined as goal-directed mental operations used to facilitate task performance that are deliberately implemented and potentially available to consciousness (Harnishfeger & D. F. Bjorklund, 1990). According to some theorists, age differences in strategy use—more than any other single factor—are responsible for age differences in thinking (see D. F. Bjorklund & Miller, 1997).

Even infants seem to show some signs of strategic, goal-directed behavior as they search for missing toys or try to make their way around obstacles

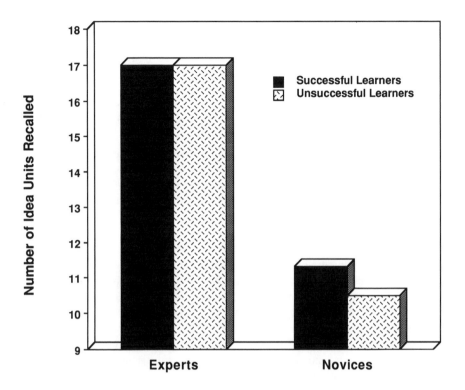

FIG. 8.3. Number of idea units remembered about a soccer story. From "Expert Knowledge, General Abilities, and Text Processing" (p. 112), by W. Schneider, J. Körkel, and F. E. Weinert, in W. Schneider and F. E. Weinert (Eds.), *Interactions Among Aptitude, Strategies, and Knowledge in Cognitive Performance*, 1990, New York:Springer-Verlag. Copyright © 1990 by Springer-Verlag. Reprinted with permission.

(Willatts, 1990). But the strategies of the infant and young child are ineffective compared to the strategies of older children and adults. In fact, a popular view in cognitive development during the 1960s and 1970s was that young children did not use strategies, at least not of their own accord. Most of these nonstrategic children could be easily trained to use simple strategies, and this resulted in improvements in their performance. This observation led Flavell (1970) to describe young children as having a *production deficiency*—they have ability to use a strategy but fail to produce one spontaneously. In contrast, children who showed a *mediation deficiency* (Reese, 1962) could not use a strategy even if it was demonstrated to them. (For a review of the history of research on strategy development, see Harnishfeger & D. F. Bjorklund, 1990.)

Today it is recognized that even young children use strategies, although the strategies of the preschool child may differ considerably from those used by older children (see D. F. Bjorklund, 1990; Wellman, 1988). P. H. Miller (1990, 1994) has identified a third "deficiency," which she called a *utilization deficiency,* meaning that children are able to use a strategy but the strategy doesn't help them much. For example, in a memory study by D. F. Bjorklund, Coyle, and Gaultney (1992), many third-grade children showed increases in a memory strategy over five trials, but no corresponding increases in how much they remembered. If the purpose of the strategy is to help children perform better, why do they use an effortful strategy when it doesn't help them? Utilization deficiencies are not rare, but have been found in most of the studies examined in which strategy use and performance can be evaluated independently (D. F. Bjorklund, Miller, Coyle, & Slawinski, 1997; P. H. Miller & Seier, 1994).

There have been several explanations utilization deficiencies (see D. F. Bjorklund & Coyle, 1995; P. H. Miller, 1994), the most common one being related to the effortful nature of strategies. Strategies use up a child's limited mental resources, and young children use their resources less efficiently than older children. That is, strategies have a cost in terms of mental effort, and young children exert so much mental effort carrying out the strategy that they do not have enough left to perform other aspects of the task effectively, such as remembering (D. F. Bjorklund & Harnishfeger, 1987; Case, Kurland, & Goldberg, 1982; Guttentag, 1984; Kee & Davies, 1988). However, children eventually show improvement in performance after repeated use of strategies. It has been proposed that many children are unaware that the strategy they are using is not doing them any good, and as a result don't get discouraged when their performance is actually not enhanced. One suggestion has been that children's lack of awareness of the relation between their strategy use and task performance is adaptive, and that a more cognitively aware child might stop using strategies that don't provide immediate benefits (D. F. Bjorklund, 1997).

How Do Strategies Develop?   One perspective that has gained much attention lately proposes that children have a variety of strategies available to them at any one time and use combinations of these strategies. That is, children do not simply develop from using a simple and ineffective strategy to using a more complicated and efficient one. Rather, both the simple and complicated strategies coexist with one another and compete for use. Such multiple- and variable-strategy use has been championed by Robert Siegler and his colleagues (e.g., Siegler, 1988, 1996; Siegler & Jenkins, 1989), and has been observed on a large variety of tasks including arithmetic (Siegler & Jenkins, 1989), spelling (Siegler, 1988), memory (Coyle & D. F. Bjorklund, 1997), and tic-tac-toe (Crowley & Siegler, 1993), among others.

Perhaps it is easiest to appreciate how children's multiple-strategy use by providing an example from children's early arithmetic. When children first learn to add, they often use a strategy that involves counting out loud both addends, starting from 1. So, for example, for the problem $4 + 2 = ?$, a child might say "1, 2, 3, 4 [pause], 6, 7." This is called the sum strategy. A more sophisticated counting strategy involves starting with the larger addend (in this case, 4), and counting up from there (for example, saying, "4 [pause], 6, 7"). The most sophisticated strategy for solving simple arithmetic problems is "just knowing" the answer, retrieving it directly and quickly from long-term memory. This strategy is called *fact retrieval*. A number of researchers have shown that as children get older they are more likely to use the more sophisticated strategy (e.g., Ashcraft, 1990; Groen & Parkman, 1972). However, these arithmetic strategies do not change like stages, with one replacing another. Rather, Siegler and his colleagues have shown that even after children are able to use fact retrieval for most problems, they still use some of the less sophisticated strategies more characteristics of younger children (Siegler, 1996). In fact, even college-educated adults will fall back on simpler counting strategies occasionally (Geary, 1994).

Memory

Memory plays a central role in thinking. We believe that it is safe to say that no complex cognitive task, and few simple ones, can be executed without involving memory. However, the act of remembering is also influenced by simpler cognitive operations, such as directing one's attention and storing information efficiently. Thus, memory represents a central stage around which both simple and complex processes revolve.

Recognition Versus Recall.   *Recognition* is the simplest form of re-membering. When we recognize something, we realize that what we are experiencing now is the same as something we have experienced before. Recognition requires relatively little mental effort. A stimulus, such as a song heard on the radio, either matches something one has heard before or it doesn't.

A more demanding form of remembering is *recall*. Unlike recognition, where a stimulus is presented and the person must simply state whether it has been experienced previously or not, recall involves the active retrieval of information. Who was the third president of the United States? How many chromosomes does a normal human have? Who are all the cousins on your father's side of the family? What are you supposed to buy at the grocery store for the big party this weekend? The retrieval question, or cue, can help a person focus on the right information. If you were cued, for example, by being reminded of the names of your father's brothers and sisters or that the big weekend party was to be a barbecue, you might have an easier time remembering the desired information.

Recognition memory is usually easier than recall memory, with *cued recall* falling somewhere between recognition and *free recall* (recall without specific prompts). A similar picture emerges when we look at development. Children's recognition memory is relatively good, and age differences are often quite small (A. L. Brown & Scott, 1971; Daehler & Bukatko, 1977). When recall is required, however, age differences are larger. In general, the ability to recall information increases with age, and as they get older children require fewer prompts to produce successful memory performance (D. F. Bjorklund & Muir, 1988). D. F. Bjorklund (1995) provided an example of the distinction between free and cued recall in a preschool child:

> A 5-year-old boy who had spent the afternoon with his grandparents seeing his first play, *The Little Shop of Horrors,* was asked by his mother, "Well, how was your afternoon?" The child replied "OK." The mother persisted, "Well, did you have a good time?" The child said "Yeah." However, when prompted by his grand-mother—"Tell your mother about Audrey II, the plant"—he provided copious details, telling how the plant ate some of the main characters, talked, sang, and how it took three people underneath it to make it move. The child had a wealth of information, but it could only be accessed when specific cues were provided. (p. 239).

The Development of Event Memory. There are many memory tasks that children are asked to perform on a regular basis. In schools, they may be asked to remember the names of al the U.S. presidents or the characteristics of the food pyramid. More commonly, however, children are asked to recall *events,* such as the 5-year-old in the example recalling the play he had seen. In most cases, children remember events from a personal perspective. That is, the events are something that happened to them, or that they witnessed. When we remember things that are related to the self is called *autobiographical memory.*

Research over the past 20 years has made it clear that children learn to remember events by incorporating new events in terms of what they already know. For example, children learn what happens when they go to a fast food restaurant. The develop a *script* for the event. A script is a form of representation that organizes real-world events in terms of their causal and temporal charac-teristics (K. Nelson, 1996). For example, a fast-food restaurant may include driving to the restaurant, going into the restaurant, standing in line, ordering, paying, taking your food on a tray to a table, sitting down, eating, and throwing away the trash when finished. Children learn what usually happens when, and use these scripts to interpret and then recall novel events (Farrar & Goodman, 1992; K. Nelson, 1996).

In recalling information about events, children need to learn to focus on the important parts of the event—to remember the who, what, where, and when of the event and the order in which things happened. How do they learn to do this? In large part, they seem to be guided by their parents. Several researchers have shown that American parents (especially mothers) provide their children with cues and ask the relevant questions to help their children recall events (e.g.,

Fivush & Hammond, 1990; Fivush & Reese, 1992; Hudson, 1990). Consistent with Vygotsky's position on cognitive development (to be discussed later in this chapter), Hudson (1990) has proposed that children learn how to remember by interacting with their parents, and that @147remembering can be viewed as an activity that is first jointly carried out by parent and child and then later performed by the child alone" (p. 172).

Let us provide an example of joint remembering between a young mother and her 19-month-old daughter, Brittany, after returning home after a trip to the zoo (from D. F. Bjorklund, 1995):

Mother:	Brittany, what did we see at the zoo?
Brittany:	Elphunts.
Mother:	That's right! We saw elephants. What else?
Brittany:	(shrugs and looks at her mother)
Mother:	Panda bear? Did we see a panda bear?
Brittany:	(smiles and nods her head)
Mother:	Can you say "panda bear?"
Brittany:	Panda bear.
Mother:	Good! Elephants and panda bears. What else?
Brittany:	Elphunts.
Mother:	That's right, elephants. And also a gorilla.
Brittany:	Go-rilla! (p. 259)

These observations make it clear that, in American culture anyway, parents play an important, and perhaps unconscious, role in helping children form narratives, or stories, in order to remember.

Children's Eyewitness Testimony.   Ever since the Salem Witch Trials of 1692, when children testified to seeing people transform themselves into animals or fly into the night, children have generally not been welcomed into the courtroom as witnesses. One major reason for this is the belief that children are highly suggestible and thus not reliable witnesses. Research over the past decade has shown that young children can often be reliable witnesses (see Ceci & Bruck, 1993, 1995). When asked free-recall questions for events they witnessed or experienced they rarely provide incorrect information (e.g., Cassel & D. F. Bjorklund, 1995; Poole & White, 1991). However, the absolute amount of information they do provide is low, making the use of leading questions necessary. When young children are asked more specific questions, such as "Tell me what the man looked like," they recall more correct information, but they also recall more incorrect information, reducing the overall accuracy to their recall (e.g., Cassel & D. F. Bjorklund, 1995).

Most research indicates that preschool children are indeed more suggestible than older children and adults (Ceci, Ross, & Toglia, 1987; Goodman & Reed, 1986; Ornstein, Gordon, & Larus, 1992). For example, in research by Ornstein and his colleagues (1992), 3- and 6-year-old children were asked misleading questions about a visit to a doctor's office 3 weeks earlier. Although both groups of children were generally correct, the 3-year-olds were less likely to reject the misleading suggestions of the interviewer than the 6-year-olds, suggesting somewhat greater suggestibility for the younger children. In other research, children watched a video of a theft and were asked sets of leading questions. If children did not agree with a question, they were immediately asked a more strongly worded follow-up question ("You do remember, don't you, that the girl said it was okay for the boy to take the bike?"). Five-year-olds were more likely to agree with the misleading questions than either 7- or 9-year-olds, with this difference being particularly large for the follow-up questions (Cassel, Roebers, & D. F. Bjorklund, 1996).

Although young children frequently comply with the misleading requests made by interviewers, this does not mean that they are actually "remembering" information incorrectly. At least a portion of young children's compliance with the misleading questions seems to be due to a desire to conform to the wishes of an adult (e.g., Cassel et al., 1996; Ceci et al., 1987). For example, after agreeing to the misleading questions of an interviewer, 5- and 7-year-old children later correctly identified the central factors in a bike theft, indicating that, although they changed their answers, they did not change their minds (Cassel et al., 1996).

Although much research indicates that children's long-term memories for events are only moderately influenced by misleading questions, another line of research shows that it can be relatively easy to get young children to create false memories. In research by Ceci, Loftus and their colleagues (Ceci, Crotteau-Huffman, Smith, & Loftus, 1994; Ceci, Loftus, Leictman, & Bruck, 1994), preschool children were asked to remember a series of events. Some of the events had actually happened to them, whereas others were invented by the interviewer (for example, "Got finger caught in a mousetrap and had to go to the hospital to get the trap off. Think real hard, and tell me if this ever happened to you. Do you remember going to the hospital with a mousetrap on your finger?"). Children were interviewed over a series of 10 or 11 weeks. In one study, 58% of the children produced at least one, often very detailed, false account, with one quarter of the children producing false stories to a majority of the false events. Moreover, many of the children in these studies refused to believe the interviewer and their parents when later debriefed and told that these events had not actually happened. In short, it was relatively easy, merely by repeatedly suggesting that an event had happened to them, to get preschool

children to generate false descriptions of these events, and many came to believe them to the extent that they
disbelieved their parents when told that the stories were made up.

Recall From Infancy and Early Childhood. The longer the delay between experiencing an event and recalling it, the less likely we are to remember it correctly, if at all; this is best illustrated by our general inability to remember events from infancy and early childhood (Cowan & Davidson, 1984; Sheingold & Tenney, 1982). In fact, when we do have memories of such long ago events, they are often not accurate:

> I have one vivid memory from my infancy. We were living at my grandparents' house, and I had the croup (I think it's called bronchitis today). My crib was covered by a sheet, but I remember looking past the bars into the living room. I can hear the whir of the vaporizer, feel the constriction in my chest, and smell the Vicks Vaporub. To this day the smell of Vicks makes my chest tighten. I can claim no other memories until close to my third birthday, and they are not as real for me as this memory is.

> Some years back, I related this memory to my mother. "David," she said, "you were such a healthy baby. You never had the croup. That was your brother, Dick. You were almost three years old then."

> The fact that my earliest memory is of an event that never happened doesn't make it any less real for me. The feelings it invokes are intense, and knowing that they didn't happen, at least not to me, does not lessen their impact. It's still *my* infant memory. It's just that the infant was my younger brother, and I was only an observer.

> Few of us have memories from our infancy, and for those of us who do, most can be explained as mine was. It's not a memory *of* infancy but a memory *about* infancy. In my case, it wasn't even a memory about my infancy, but rather about my brother's. (Adapted from D. F. Bjorklund, 1986b).

This inability to remember events from infancy and early childhood has been labeled *infantile amnesia*. There have been a number of hypotheses concerning why our recall of events from the early years of our life is so poor, including Freud's idea that the events of infancy are so painful that we actively repress them (see Spear, 1984; S. H. White & Pillemer, 1979). The most reasonable hypothesis, we believe, is that information is represented differently by very young children than it is by older children and adults. This perspective is consistent with the views of stage theorists such as Piaget, who contended that the nature of representation changes over childhood. The minds that reside in our heads now interpret information differently than did the minds that experienced the world when we were infants and toddlers. Other researchers have suggested similar explanations for infantile amnesia. For example, K. Nelson (1993, 1996) proposed that it is the ability to use language to form narratives that is responsible for autobiographical memory. Until we're good at forming and telling stories about our lives, something that happens at about 4 years of age, we won't be able to remember much of what we experience. In a similar vein, Howe and Courage (1993) proposed that autobiographical memory requires that children have a well-developed sense of self, and this, they propose, develops gradually over the preschool years.

Metacognition

Metacognition refers to a person's knowledge about his or her cognitive abilities. For every form of cognition, it is possible to think of a corresponding form of metacognition. Thus, for example, metamemory refers to one's knowledge about the working of one's memory, meta-attention refers to a knowledge of the factors that affect one's attention, and so on. Metacognition requires a conscious awareness. It is one thing to have complicated mental operations for solving problems, but it is another to know that you have these operations, to know when to use them, and to know how effective they are in arriving at answers.

Flavell and Wellman (1977) described three major classes of metacognitive knowledge variables: person, task, and strategy. Person variables include a person's knowledge of his or her own abilities and the abilities of other people with respect to thinking—for example, a knowledge that you can solve certain problems faster with visual than verbal information. Task variables involve knowledge of the requirements of tasks. Is there enough information provided to solve the task, or is more information needed? Strategy variables include a knowledge of what cognitive techniques one has available to solve a particular task and which strategies would be most appropriate for the task at hand. Does this task require my full concentration, or can it be accomplished with only a little study? What knowledge do I have that can be brought to bear on arriving at a solution?

One robust finding over the past 25 years has been age differences in children's metacognitive knowledge. Some research findings include: the ability to distinguish important from unimportant aspects of a written story improves with age (A. L. Brown & Smiley, 1978); an understanding of the factors that influence attention increases developmentally (Miller & Weiss, 1981); and young children do not effectively monitor information they have in memory, causing them to poorly predict their memory performance (Wellman, 1977). In general, age-related differences have been found on person, task, and strategy variables, with children becoming more aware with age of their own knowledge and how it can be applied.

Contemporary researchers stress the bidirectional relationship between cognitive and metacognition development (Flavell, 1978; Schneider, 1985). Metacognition is obviously an important component in children's cognitive development and certainly influences cognition; but the relationship also works in reverse, with competent cognition influencing metacognition. The two are intimately entwined, and the relationship varies depending on a child's age and the task involved.

One aspect of metacognition we have addressed earlier in this chapter concerns children's ability to predict how well they are able to perform certain tasks. Recall that preschool children greatly overestimated their imitative abilities, thinking they would be better able to imitate a model than they actually were (D. F. Bjorklund et al., 1993). Children's poor prediction skills have been found for a broad range of physical and cognitive tasks, from how accurately they can throw a ball or who are the smartest children in their class, to how many items they will remember on a memory task (e.g., Plumert, 1995; Schneider, 1991; Stipek, 1984; Yussen & Levy, 1975).

A good demonstration of developmental changes in metacognitive skills is seen in a study by Yussen and Levy (1975), in which children were asked to predict their own memory spans. Yussen and Levy presented children and college students with a set of 10 pictures and asked them to predict how many items they could recall in exact order; then they measured their actual recall. They found that 4-year-olds greatly overestimated their memory spans—estimating, on average, that they would recall slightly over 8 of the 10 items, whereas their actual recall was slightly greater than 3 of the 10 items (overestimation = 152%). Half the 4-year-olds predicted that they would recall all 10 items. Predictions were closer to reality for third-grade and college students (overestimation = 40% and 6%, respectively), and only 10% of third graders and 2% of college students predicted perfect recall. After the memory test, the preschoolers were aware of their failure to recall according to their predictions, but many were unperturbed, saying things such as, "If you gave me a different list like that, I could do it" (p. 507).

Young children's tendencies to overestimate their abilities is apparently not due entirely to a cognitive inability to make judgments of competency. For example, Stipek and her colleagues (Stipek, 1984; Stipek & Daniels, 1988) reported that young children can make relatively accurate assessments of other children's abilities and are overly optimistic only about their own performance. Stipek proposed that children's overly optimistic self-perception is due to *wishful thinking*, a concept originally introduced by Piaget (1930): children *wish* to hit a home run the next time at bat, and therefore they *expect* to hit a home run. By 8 or 9 years of age, children's evaluations of their own abilities are more in line with those of their teachers and other children.

Several people have proposed that young children's poor metacognition with respect to their abilities may actually be adaptive (e.g., D. F. Bjorklund & Green, 1992). Bandura (1989a) has stressed the importance of developing a positive sense of *self-efficacy* for success in life. Self-efficacy refers to the extent to which people view themselves as effective individuals, as having some control over their lives. Young children's overly optimistic (and unrealistic) opinions of their own abilities may foster their developing sense of self-efficacy. If they knew how poorly they did on most tasks, young children may get discouraged and quit. Being out of touch with their own abilities—believing that they know more than they actually do and can do more than they actually can—may provide them with positive perceptions of their own skills and encourage them to attempt things that they would not try if they had a more realistic idea of their abilities (D. F. Bjorklund & Green, 1992; Stipek, 1984). In fact, rather than seeing these poor metacognitive skills of young children as deficits to overcome, we should perhaps "try harder to design educational environments which maintain their optimism and eagerness" (Stipek, 1984, p. 53).

Although we believe that overestimating one's cognitive and physical abilities is generally adaptive for young children, there is a potential cost to such poor metacognition. For example, Plumert (1995) has shown that 6-year-olds who greatly overestimated their physical abilities in a laboratory task had a greater number of serious accidents than other children. Thus, young children's overly optimistic perspective of their abilities is a double-edged sword, and parents and teachers should be cautious neither to thwart young children's adventurous explorations nor to let them let them try anything they set their minds to.

Children's Theory of Mind

Over the past decade, perhaps the hottest research topic in the area of cognitive development has been children's *theory of mind*. In particular, researchers have been interested in when and how children appreciate that other peoples' behavior is motivated by their beliefs and desires, which are often quite different from their own (Flavell & Miller, 1997; Perner, 1991; Wellman, 1990). Most research has focused on children 4 years of age and younger.

A frequently used task in theory-of-mind research is the *false-belief task* (Wimmer & Perner, 1983). In this task, children watch as a toy or some other treat is hidden (in a box on a table, for instance). Another person, John, is there when the toy is hidden but leaves the room. Then, the toy is moved to another hidden location. When John returns, will he know where the toy is hidden? On this and similar tasks, most 4-year-olds are correct and state that John will look where the toy was originally hidden. In contrast, most 3-year-olds state quite confidently that John will look for the toy at the new hiding place, apparently not realizing that John had no way of knowing this (see, for example, Perner, 1991; Perner, Leekman, & Wimmer, 1987; Wimmer & Perner, 1983).

One reason why 3-year-olds fail the false-belief task may be due to a failure to remember what they had originally believed before any switch was made (Gopnik & Astington, 1988; Gopnik & Slaughter, 1991; Sullivan & Winner,

1993). For example, in a modification of the false-belief task, called the "Smarties" task, children are shown a box of Smarties (a type of candy in a distinctive box, with which British children are highly familiar) and asked what they think is in the box (Hogrefe, Wimmer, & Perner,1986). Children, of course, say "Smarties." But when the box is opened, the children see that it is filled with pencils. They are then asked what they believed was in the box before being shown the contents and to predict what another child (who doesn't know about the trick) will think is in the box. The correct answer to both of these questions, of course, is "Smarties," but most 3-year-olds say "pencils" to both questions. In other words, these young children seem to "forget" their earlier belief.

Interestingly, children 3 years of age and younger seem to be able to "read" another's mind when they are deliberately trying to deceive that person. For example, children played a game similar to the false-belief task but part of the game involved the intentional deception of another person (e.g., "Let's hide the treasure so that John won't know where it is when he gets back"; Chandler, Fritz, & Hala,1989; Hala, Chandler, & Fritz, 1991; see also Sullivan & Winner, 1993). Under these conditions, even 2 $\frac{1}{2}$-year-old children were able to use deception, implying that they had some idea of what the other person knew. Chandler et al. (1989) concluded that these findings "leave little room for doubt that even children as young as 2 $\frac{1}{2}$ are already capable of engaging in a variety of well-crafted deceptive practices, best interpreted as strategies aimed at instilling false beliefs in others" (p. 1274).

The picture is a complicated one, but it seems that 3-year-olds do have a limited "theory of mind"; however, one that is not nearly as sophisticated as it will be within a year.

VYGOTSKY'S SOCIOCULTURAL APPROACH

The theories and research we have examined to this point in the chapter have all focused squarely on the child as the unit of analysis. Information-processing approaches, Piaget's theory, and even Bandura's social-cognitive theory all view the child as processing or discovering information and changing mentally as a result. Each theory, of course, recognizes the environment as playing an important role in shaping development, but it is the child in active interaction with the environment that is responsible for development. A different perspective is represented by the sociocultural approach, emanating form the theory of the Soviet psychologist Lev Vygotsky (1962; 1978; and see Rogoff, 1990; Wertsch & Tulviste, 1992). Vygotsky (1896–1934), whose theories have come to light in the Western world only recently, proposed that cognition develops through the collaborations of members of one generation with another, and that one cannot examine the individual without also taking into consideration the community and activities that the individual is involved in. The child and his or her development are entwined with interactions with others in a culture, and development proceeds as children are guided through life in collaboration with others. Bandura's theory emphasized social learning, but his approach sees the child as internalizing social roles and behaviors from observation, and not as the result of active participation in social life. Piaget stressed that children develop through interactions with peers; but this was a minor part of his broader theory that emphasized the development of the child's individual structures and not the development of cultural understanding through participation of social life.

From a sociocultural perspective, it is children's participation in the social life of the community in which cognitive development occurs that must be considered. Vygotsky acknowledged maturationally paced differences in children's cognitive abilities, but proposed that children in different cultures have available to them different tools of intellectual adaptation, particularly suited for life in that culture. For example, it is common for children in Western cultures to be asked questions by a parent for which the parent already knows the answer (e.g., "What did we do at the park today?", "What's the name of Becky's new baby?"). This prepares children for life in school, where teachers ask children for information the teachers already know. Such a practice is not found in other parts of the world where formal education of the Western type is not practiced In fact, for the Wolof people, asking questions for which they already know the answer suggests a riddle or an aggressive challenge (Irvine, 1978). Another example of how middle-class American parents prepare their children for life in their culture was provided earlier in the section on memory development. Middle-class American mothers "teach" their children how to remember events by asking them questions, structured so that children learn the components that are important in constructing and remembering stories (e.g., Hudson, 1990).

Barbara Rogoff (1997), a leading sociocultural theorist, sees development as a process of *transformation of participation*. From this perspective:

> Evaluation of development focuses on how individuals participate in and contribute to ongoing activity rather than on "outcome" and individuals' possessions of concepts and skills. Evaluation of development examines the ways people transform their participation, analyzing how they coordinate with others in shared endeavors, with attention to the purposes and dynamic nature of the activity itself and its meaning in the community. The investigation of people's actual involvement and changing goals in activities becomes the basis of understanding development rather than simply the surface to try to get past. (p. 18)

Such a perspective makes clear the impossibility of separating the child's cognitive development from the greater social context.

The Zone of Proximal Development

Vygotsky proposed that cognitive development occurs in contexts in which a child's problem solving is guided by a more knowledgeable or skillful person, usually an adult or older child. Children are encouraged to participate in a sociocultural activity by someone with greater expertise, who assists them to perform an activity in a way they could not do on their own. Learning and development thus take place as the expert guides the novice in the execution of some task. Vygotsky referred to such a process as the *zone of proximal development*, defined by Vygotsky (1978) as the difference between a child's "actual developmental level as determined by independent problem solving" and his or her level of "potential development as determined through problem solving under adult guidance or in collaboration with more capable peers" (p. 86). Learning in the zone of proximal development is an active and dynamic process. Not only do children learn, and thus change, as a result of interactions with adults, but adults modify their behavior as children change.

Rogoff (1990) has described the transaction between children and adults as reflecting an "apprenticeship in thinking," with novice children improving their "skills and understanding through participation with more skilled partners in culturally organized activities" (1990, p. 39). This apprenticeship is not the sole responsibility of the adults, however. Vygotsky, like Piaget, saw children as playing an active role in their own development, and children frequently seek out adult attention in sociocultural contexts, increasing the level of engagement between themselves and adults, which in turn fosters development.

Scaffolding.   Related to the concept of the zone of proximal development is the concept of *scaffolding* (Wood, Bruner, & Ross, 1976). Scaffolding refers to a process in which experts respond contingently to novices' indications of understanding on a problem, gradually increasing the novices' grasp of the problem. Scaffolding is not just something that teachers do with students, but something that parents spontaneously do with their children. Scaffolding occurs when adults tailor their instructions to children, guide children to a level near the limits of their performance, and adjust instructions and feedback as a function of children's responses. For example, mothers of preschoolers gave their children more responsibility for solving a counting task as their children's performance improved, but provided more specific instructions following inaccurate trials (Saxe, Gearhart, & Gruberman, 1987).

An example should help clarify the concept of scaffolding. A mother and her 5-year-old daughter Emily are playing a game of Chutes and Ladders, but instead of a spinner to compute moves, players must determine their moves from a throw of two dice (D. F. Bjorklund & Reubens, 1997). After explaining the game to the child, Emily throws the dice. She just stares at the dice, saying nothing, and then looks at her mother. Her mother says, "How many is that?" Emily shrugs her shoulders. "Count them," her mother says. Emily shrugs again. Her mother then points to the dots on the first dice saying, "One, two, three," then to the dots on the second dice, saying "four, five. You have five. Now you count them." Emily does and moves her piece five spaces on the board. The mother then throws the dice and asks Emily, "How many do I have?" Emily shrugs, and her mother says, "Count them," which Emily does. The next five sets of moves continue this way. Then, on Emily's sixth move, she immediately counts the dice after her mother's question of "How many do you have?" She does the same on her mother's turn. Her mother then hesitates on the next several trials before asking Emily any questions. Eventually, Emily throws the dice and counts the dots herself, without her mother making any request, and this continues throughout most of the game. The mother corrected Emily when she counted wrong, but became less directive as Emily took more of the responsibility for the game herself.

Adults and children jointly determine the extent to which children are capable of functioning independently. More specifically, children who are less capable of independent problem solving will elicit more directive and less demanding strategies from parents. More competent children elicit less directive and less demanding strategies from parents. In short, with development, children assume more responsibility for the dyad's work. The more competent child is less in need of adult support, or scaffolding in order to solve a problem.

An important qualification here is that competence in this model is context-specific to the extent that learning and development occur by interacting around tasks that have very specific rules. Competence is not a psychological absolute in the Piagetian sense as a "central cognitive processor"; it is competence in specific tasks (Laboratory of Comparative Human Cognition, 1983).

Guided Participation. Rogoff (1990) developed the concept of *guided participation* to extend Vygotsky's concept of zone of proximal development. She defined guided participation as "the process and system of involvement of individuals with others, as they communicate and engage in shared activities" (Rogoff, 1990, p. 6). Although guided participation would include instances of scaffolding, where instruction is the explicit goal, it is not limited to such situations. Rather, it applies to all contexts in which "human learning occurs through people's diverse processes of participation in the activities of their varying communities" (Rogoff, 1997, p. 23). These would include the day-to-day activities in children's lives, such as helping to prepare meals, discussions around the dinner table, and eavesdropping on parents. It is during such mundane activities that children's cognition develops, as much or more so than in formal "educational" settings.

Peers as Collaborators

Vygotsky's primary focus was on children learning from adults. In recent years, the idea that cognitive development may occur as a result of collaboration among peers has caught the imagination of researchers and educators (e.g., Brandt, 1991; D. W. Johnson & Johnson, 1987, 1989; Rogoff, 1997; Slavin,

1990). Recall Piaget's proposal that cognitive development occurs only when peers interact, and not when children interact with adults. This perspective is not shared by the practitioners of sociocultural theory. In fact, when comparing the effectiveness of peers versus a parent in collaborative learning, parents usually provided better support, and thus better fostered learning, than slightly older children (e.g., Ellis & Rogoff, 1986).

However, in many situations, peers do learn to solve problems together in collaborative learning better than when trying to solve problems alone (e.g., Azmitia, 1992; Gauvain & Rogoff, 1989; D. W. Johnson & Johnson, 1987), and the children who gain the most are typically those who were initially less skilled than their partners (Azmitia, 1988; Tudge, 1992). In a meta-analysis of 378 studies that contrasted achievement of people working alone versus cooperatively, fewer than 10% of the studies produced better results when working individually, whereas working cooperatively yielded significantly better performance for greater than half of all studies (D. W. Johnson & Johnson, 1987).

Why does cooperative learning work? One reason seems to be motivation. Children working together on problems seem to be more motivated to work on the problems (D. W. Johnson & Johnson, 1989). The process of cooperative learning requires children to explain their ideas to one another, to attempt to persuade, and to resolve controversies. Each of these requires children to evaluate more closely what it is they actually believe and to convey that knowledge to someone else. The adage that one learns information best by teaching it is likely true in cooperative learning among peers. D. W. Johnson and Johnson also reported that cooperative learning promotes the use of high-quality cognitive strategies and metacognitive approaches. This results in children creating new ideas that none in the group could have created alone.

Peer collaborative learning is not a panacea for school systems, however. Fewer teachers cannot be hired based on the hope that they can be replaced by peer tutors. Collaborative learning does not always result in better performance, especially if the more competent peer lacks confidence in his or her knowledge or fails to modify instruction appropriately for the less skilled partner (Levin & Druyan, 1993; Tudge, 1992). In fact, research suggests that shared decision making is difficult for many American children (see Rogoff, 1997), although their abilities to make decisions cooperatively improves with practice (e.g., Socha & Socha, 1994). One reason for their difficulty is apparently related to the structure of American schools and the experience of teachers. Schools are not organized to promote cooperative learning, and children, accustomed to competitively structured individualistic classroom, have a difficult time knowing how to behave when cooperative techniques are use. When the structure of schools change to support peer collaboration, with teachers as participants in and not directors of the learning experience, cooperatively learning produces improved performance (see Rogoff, 1997).

9

Language Development

Language, more than any other single ability, is what distinguishes us from all other species. Children in all cultures acquire their mother tongue without the need of formal instruction. Language belongs to the class of innate abilities, such as sucking, grasping, and recognition of mother's odor, that are too important to be relegated to our conscious awareness and "free will" (Spelke & Newport, 1997). The reason for this, many people think, seems to be that the evolution of language made human thought possible (Bickerton, 1990; Donald, 1991; K. Nelson, 1996). The centrality of language to "humanness" requires that it be part of all groups of people and not subject to cultural peculiarities. Yet language is clearly influenced by environmental factors, as indicated by the fact that although all normal children acquire language over the preschool years in much the same way all over the world, the language they learn to speak is dependent on what is spoken around them. Language is thus a characteristic that is highly affected both by humans' general biological inheritance and by the uniqueness of the environments in which they grow up.

This chapter is about the development of language, the principal mode of human communication. Although a few nonhuman primates have shown simple language abilities (see Savage-Rumbaugh et al., 1993), none has approached the level found in all normal humans. Language enables individuals to communicate on a daily basis, but it also does much more. Language allows us to share the experience of others without having to be there ourselves. We listen to the firsthand reports of others and gain information about events happening in other parts of the world without traveling there. We read the conclusions others have reached after a lifetime of experience and absorb the knowledge without living that lifetime.

WHAT MAKES A COMMUNICATION SYSTEM A LANGUAGE?

Everyone knows what language is, yet differentiating language from other types of communication systems is something that linguists argue about. There are a number of features of language, however, that we think all, or most, linguistics and psycholinguists can agree on, and these include arbitrariness, productivity, semanticity, displacement, and duality (R. Brown, 1973). We define each of these briefly and then discuss different *aspects* of language, including phonology, morphology, syntax, semantics, and pragmatics.

Features of Language

1. *Arbitrariness* refers to the fact that a word is not inherently related to the concept it represents. For example, the fact that English refers to the orb in the nighttime sky as the *moon* and the brighter orb in the daytime sky as the *sun* is totally arbitrary. There is nothing about the features of these heavenly bodies that dictates their names. The exception to this, of course, are onomatopoeia words (for example, the *choo choo* sound resembles the sound a train makes and thus conveys the meaning of a train).

2. *Productivity* refers to the fact that speakers can combine a finite set of words to produce an infinite set of sentences. True language is *creative*, and speakers and listeners can produce and comprehend sentences that have never been uttered before. Language is not a limited set of utterances to be memorized. Rather, although the number of words of a language may be finite, these words can be put together via a system of rules (syntax, or grammar) to produce an infinite number of proper sentences.

3. *Semanticity* refers to the fact that language can represent events, ideas, actions, and objects symbolically.

4. *Displacement* refers the fact that what one speaks about need not be limited to the immediate context. Rather, one can talk about the past or the future, or events that are occurring a great distance from and out of the immediate perception of the speaker and listeners. All other animal communication systems deal with the here and now (with the possible exception of bees, whose dances seem to communicate the location of flowers some distance from the hive).

5. *Duality* refers to the fact that language is represented at two levels: *phonology*, the actual sound that a speaker produces, and the underlying abstract, meaning of language, reflected by the syntax (rules of putting words together) as well as semantics (meaning of those words and concepts).

The concept of duality implies that there are at least two different aspects of language, and in fact there are at least five different aspects: phonology, morphology, syntax, semantics, and pragmatics, and they all develop.

Aspects of Language

Phonology refers to the sounds of a language. The sounds infants and children make are limited by their physical structures (tongue, mouth, position of larynx in their throat), and, not surprisingly, the sounds that infants and children are able to produce change over time (Stoel-Gammon & Menn, 1997).

Related to the *production* of speech sounds is the *perception* of speech sounds. The basic units of speech are called to as *phonemes*. There is evidence that infants come into the word with the ability to perceive most, if not all, of the phonemes found in all human languages (see Aslin, Jusczyk, & Pisoni, 1997), suggesting substantial biological preparation for infants to learn language (but see Kuhl, 1987, for a counterinterpretation).

How can one tell if babies can perceive phonemes, or more importantly can discriminate one phoneme form another? One procedure relies on infants *habituating*, or decreasing responses to, a repeated stimulus. Phonemes such as "ba" and "pa" can be arranged along a continuum, so that the difference between hearing a "ba" sound and hearing a "pa" sound is gradual. Despite the lack of an absolute physical distinction between the "pa" and "ba" sounds, English-speaking adults "hear" the difference at a certain point on this continuum. Eimas and his colleagues (Eimas, Siqueland, Jusczyk, & Vigorito, 1971) presented infants with one "physical" example of the "ba/pa" continuum until they habituated to it, in this case by decreasing the rate at which they sucked on a pacifier. After habituating to this one example, infants were presented with other sounds at different points on the "ba/pa" continuum. If they perceived the new sound as being from the same phonemic category as the old one (for example, both "ba" sounds), they should continue to habituate to this new sound (that is, decrease their sucking). This is because even though the sound is physically different from the one they heard before, it is just another example of the sound they had just heard repeatedly (that is, just another "ba"). If, however, the new sound is perceived as a member of another phonemic category ("pa" instead of "ba," for example), they should increase their sucking rate (or *dishabituate*). One- and 4-month-old infants generally behaved on this task as if they classified the phonemes "ba" and "pa" the same way that older children and adults do. That is, young infants seem to categorize language sounds the same way as language-experienced speakers of a culture do, despite the fact that the physical distinction (that is, the acoustic signals) distinguishing these two sounds would seem to be arbitrary (see also Aslin et al., 1997; Grieser & Kuhl, 1989; Marean, Werner, & Kuhl, 1992).

Although infants can discriminate among the sounds of language at birth, or shortly thereafter, they eventually learn to distinguish the particular the sounds of their native tongue and have a difficult time telling the difference between many phonemes in other languages by as young as 6 months of age. For example, Japanese speakers have a difficult time distinguishing between the English "l" and "r" sounds, as adult English speakers have difficulty discriminating between phonemic contrasts that occur in Japanese or Czech but not in English. Yet research indicates that infants are able to discriminate foreign speech sounds that their parents cannot (Eilers, Gavin, & Wilson, 1979; Lasky, Syrdal-Lasky, & Klein, 1975; Werker, Gilbert, Humphrey, & Tees, 1981), whereas some sound discriminations are made only with experience. Such research findings suggest that infants can make some phonemic discriminations that adults speakers of their language cannot make, but with time lose the ability to discriminate sounds that are not heard in their mother tongue (see Colombo, 1986; Walley, Pisoni, & Aslin, 1981).

It is worth noting here that infants have some language experience before they are born. Sound gets through the abdominal wall, and fetuses are able to hear the voices of their mothers and other people months before birth. There is evidence, for example, that babies prefer their mothers' voices shortly after birth (and women's voices in general over men's; DeCasper & Fifer, 1980; Spence & Freeman, 1996), that they will prefer immediately after birth to listen to a story their mother had read out loud during the last weeks of pregnancy (DeCasper & Spence, 1986), and that newborns prefer to listen to the language their mother speaks rather than a foreign language, all suggesting that infants are learning something about the sound of language beginning before birth.

Morphology refers to the structure of something, and in the case of language morphology refers to the structure of words. Although we may think that the word is the smallest unit of meaning in spoken language, that isn't always so. In English, for example, we add sounds to words to make them plural (add an *s*) or past tense (add an *ed*), and these word endings are also units of meaning. The smallest unit of meaning in a language is called a *morpheme*, and they come in two types. *Free morphemes* can stand alone as a word, such as "dog," "chase," or "happy." *Bound morphemes* cannot stand alone but are attached to free morphemes. They convey meaning by changing the free morpheme they are attached to. These include the rules for making nouns plural (add an *s*), past tense (add an *ed*), forming the present progressive (add an *ing*), as well a prefixes (*un*happy) and suffixes (happi*ness*).

One clever way of assessing young children's knowledge of the rules of morphology is the "wug test" (Berko, 1958). Children are shown a picture of a novel object and told the name of this object (e.g., "This is a wug."). Children are then shown two of these creatures and told, "Now there are two of them. There are two ____." The correct response, of course, is "wugs." Using this and related techniques, children's knowledge of the regular rules of plurals, past tense (e.g., "This man knows how to rick. Yesterday he ____."), and the present progressive ("This man is _____.") can be evaluated (Marcus et al., 1992).

Syntax is the knowledge of sentence formation, or grammatical rules—rules for how words are combined into phrases and sentences and how sentences are transformed into other sentences. A competent speaker of a language can identify and create variations of a single sentence, each having different meanings. For example, the sentence, "The boy rode the horse," can be made negative ("The boy didn't ride the horse"), transformed to pose a question ("Did the boy ride the horse?"), or expressed in the passive voice ("The horse was ridden by the boy"). To do this requires a knowledge of the underlying structure, or syntax, of language. This knowledge need not be explicit, that is, available to conscious awareness. Few of us could state explicitly the rules by which we put words together to form sentences, but nonetheless, we are all linguistic experts when it comes to actual performance. Because we understand how English sentences are formed, we can recognize grammatical sentences (that is, sentences with proper syntax) even is they contain nonsense words. For example, the sentence "The grup was surfosed under his multex" is meaningless because "grup," "surfosed," and "multex" are all nonsense words. Yet, because you are an expert at English syntax, you know that "grup" is the subject of the sentence and some animate (and masculine) being, "surfosed" is a verb, specifically an action that was done to the "grup," and a "multex" is something (a noun) possessed by the "grup," possibly a body part. Not bad for nonsense.

Perhaps the primary focus of people who have studied language development has been the acquisition of syntax. How is it that children are able to make sense of the language they hear around them and come up with the rules for forming proper sentences in their mother tongue? Although there is a wide variety of syntactic rules in the over 4,000 languages that are currently spoken on Earth, there are some underlying similarities that psycholinguists have discovered (see Maratsos, 1997; Pinker, 1994). What has amazed most people who have studied language development is the complexity of language and the fact that children seem to master the basic syntax of their native tongue before they turn 5. They learn language easily despite the fact that the speech that surrounds them is full of errors. That is, the language that children hear is "degenerate," or imperfect. Somehow, children take the imperfect language that surrounds them and weave a theory of language (that is, syntax) that corresponds to that which their parents speaks. This, among other evidence, has caused many to propose that the learning of syntax has a strongly innate basis to it (see the later section on nativist theories). Anyone who has tried to learn the syntax of a foreign language as an adult has an appreciation of the difficulty of this task, yet in the span of several years children acquire language (that is, syntax), despite the fact that other aspects of their cognitive skills are seriously immature (see chapter 8 on thinking, learning, and remembering).

Semantics refers to meaning, specifically the meaning of language terms. "Meaning" here, however, refers to more than just a simple definition. Words refer to concepts or objects, but are also related to other concepts or objects. For example, children must learn not only that "dog" refers to a four-legged family pet called Spot, but to other perceptually similar creatures, who themselves are members of the larger group of "mammals" and "animals." They must also learn that the word "dog" does not refer to horses, goats, or pigs, and that it may be related to other objects such as cats and fire hydrants, although not in the same way it is related to animals.

Often times, the errors children make in using words provides us with a good indication of their level of semantic development. For example, children often make *overextensions*—using a word like "dog" to refer to objects that are not dogs, such as cats, horses, and cows. Overextensions indicate that children's boundary for what constitutes a semantic category is too large (in this case, all four-footed, hairy animals). At other times, children will make *underextensions*—for example, claiming that only their pet Spot is a "dog" and that other canines must go by another name. Underextensions indicate that children's boundary for a category is too narrow. Over the course of development, children learn to categorize words and concepts as adults in their culture do, although this process continues throughout life and it is likely that none of us has exactly the same meaning, or mental representation, for all common concepts used in our native language (K. Nelson, 1996).

Perhaps the most obvious indication of semantic development is a child's vocabulary. Children go from three or four words in their vocabularies at age 1 to about 10,000 words by age 6 (Carey, 1977; M. Smith, 1926). In fact, most changes in language development beyond the age of about 5 are not in syntax or phonology, but in semantics in the form of vocabulary growth.

Pragmatics relate to the use of language in social context, or the ability to use language to get things done in the world. It refers to knowledge about how language can be used and adjusted to fit different circumstances, such as using different tones when speaking to small children versus adults, and using more formal words when speaking to teachers and grandparents than to same-age friends (Rice, 1989). Knowing the phonology, morphology, syntax, and semantics of language does one little good in communicating unless one can use language appropriately in a social context.

Grice (1975) specified several conversational principles that children must learn. Messages should have the right *quantity* of information. For example, in administering an exam, an instructor might say to students, "Write your name at the top of the page." It would be inappropriate in this context to provide much more information, such as "Take a pencil, holding it so the graphite portion is pointed downward; pressing it against the top of the $8^{1}/_{2}$ x 11-inch paper, move the pencil so that the markings spell your name." Similarly, a message such as "Write name," would be a bit too ambiguous in this context. Children are more likely to provide too little as opposed to too much information in their attempts at communicating.

Messages must also have the proper *quality* of information, particularly that they be truthful. Exceptions are when one is joking or being sarcastic, and such situations are usually determined by the context or tone of voice.

Messages must be *relevant*, that is pertinent to the present context. If, in response to the request to "Write your name on the top of the page," a student were to ask, "Will it rain today in Chicago?", something is amiss. The question is irrelevant to the context.

Finally, there is a *manner* in which conversations occur. Speakers take turns and present their arguments in a coherent fashion.

None of us perfectly follows these conversational principles (our everyday language is filled with errors in syntax, semantics, and pragmatics), but children must learn the "how-tos" of conversation if they are to be taken seriously as conversation partners. All types of language knowledge (phonology, morphology, syntax, semantics, and pragmatics) are combined in a package called *communicative competence* (Hymes, 1972a). Generally, as children—or, indeed, adults—participate in varied context, they become communicatively more competent.

DIFFERENT THEORETICAL PERSPECTIVES
OF LANGUAGE DEVELOPMENT

Although philosophers have long been interested in questions of language development, in-depth scientific study did not begin until the 1950s. Since that time, however, children's language development has been one of the most popular research topics for developmental psychologists (Berko Gleason, 1997; L. Bloom, 1997; Maratsos, 1997; K. Nelson, 1996; Rice, 1989).

Behavioral Theories

The earliest historical mention of language learning was in the fourth century a.d., when the philosopher St. Augustine wrote in his autobiography that he remembered learning language as a very young child. Adults around him, he recalled, would point to objects and repeat the names for them, and after many repetitions he learned the language (Bruner, 1983).

St. Augustine's view of language acquisition essentially prevailed for 16 centuries, anticipating the behavioral theories of the early and mid-1900s (Skinner, 1957). Behaviorists held that language, like any other behavior, is learned by instruction, practice, imitation, conditioning, and reinforcement. According to this theory, children learn the meanings of words as St. Augustine described—by associating them with certain objects or events that are present when the words are used (Staat, 1971). Other learning occurs by operant conditioning, they theorized, when parents reward their children for saying words correctly and punish or ignore them when they say words incorrectly (Mowrer, 1960).

In most of their research, the early behaviorists focused on *words*, not communication or grammatical structure. Moreover, they emphasized the parents as models of and reinforcers for language. The behaviorists actually paid relatively little attention to children, who for generations had been producing perfectly understandable original sentences and phrases they could not have possibly learned through conditioning and imitation, such as "all-gone sticky" to announce that their hands have been washed.

Many claims of the behaviorists have not stood the test of time. For example, although words can be learned via conditioning principles in the laboratory, there is little evidence that such structured techniques are used by parents at home; yet almost all children are fluent in their native language before they reach school age (Berko Gleason, 1997; Hoff-Ginsberg, 1997). Other research has shown that parents seldom comment to children about the grammatical correctness of their spoken messages, only the meaningfulness of them (Hoff-Ginsberg, 1997); and although new words are obviously learned by imitation, new grammatical forms (such as plurals or the past tense) are typically not imitated until children are able to produce them spontaneously (Bloom, Hood, & Lightbown, 1974). All this makes it very unlikely that a behavioral theory of language development is adequate.

Nativist Theories

With the many shortcomings of the behavioral approach, the stage was set for a revolution. In the late 1950s, Chomsky (1957a) declared that for the study of language acquisition, learning theory was dead. In its place he offered a bold new theory. Children don't learn language the same way they learn to tie shoelaces; they learn language because it is a natural biological function of the human species. Language, he argued, was analogous to eating: we may exhibit different outward signs of these natural functions—eating rice and beans versus animal protein, or speaking English versus French—but the underlying structures of digestion and language are inborn.

Chomsky proposed that we acquire our native language via a language acquisition device (LAD) that is presumably located in the brain and programmed to recognize the deep structure—the underlying universal grammar—of any language. Once the child is exposed to a sample of his or her native tongue, the LAD sorts out the rules of grammar and proper usage automatically and the child is able to produce well-formed sentences regardless of his or her knowledge of the world or communication experience. What people actually speak—the outward manifestation of language—Chomsky referred to as surface structure.

With Chomsky's revolution came an increased interest in language development and new ways of looking at old problems. In the late 1960s and early 1970s, the focus turned from the *structure* of language to the *function* of language. Developmental psychologists discovered the riches that the study of language development had to offer and became some of the first practitioners of the new discipline of *developmental psycholinguistics*. For example, R. Brown (1973) and his colleagues did extensive work charting in detail the development of three children (Adam, Eve, and Sarah) from their first words through the early preschool years.

Chomsky's theory provided the major theoretical impetus for much of the research during this time. The linguistic approach, as practiced both today and in the decades immediately following the publication of Chomsky's theory, is focused on the *language* children learn to speak, not on the children themselves. Adherents of the linguistic approach believe that every language has a structure—a set of rules that all who speak that language understand, whether or not they are able to express them formally. As children gain experience with the language being spoken around them, they discover those rules for themselves. And once those basic rules are mastered, children can substitute words and create an endless number of sentences.

Most developmental psycholinguists following the Chomsky line believe that humans are biologically destined to use language. They offer as evidence the fact that all humans use language and that it develops similarly in all cultures and with very little or no formal training (Locke, 1993; Pinker, 1994).

Our understanding of language development was greatly enriched by Chomsky's theory. Liberated from the stranglehold of behaviorism, researchers were free to study language development in terms other than learning curves and acquisition rates. They could look at what the child was intending to express and why one word was learned more easily than another. The focus shifted to what the child was learning and why, not how quickly it was being learned.

But Chomsky's view was indeed a radical one, as extreme in one direction as learning theory had been in another. And although researchers had become dissatisfied with the behavioral approach, they had questions about the new biological approach as well. One researcher, George Miller, summed up the situation nicely: "Now we have *two* theories of language acquisition, one *impossible* and one *miraculous*" (cited in Bruner, 1983). As research on language acquisition progressed through the 1970s and 1980s, so did disagreement concerning how best to approach the topic. In fact, one researcher stated that by the end of the 1980s, language development was considered by some to be "the most contentious topic in developmental literature" (Rice, 1989, p. 149).

Research following the Chomsky tradition is thriving today (see Pinker, 1994), but so is research from many different perspectives. Many developmental psychologists now take an *interactivist approach,* looking not just at the structure of a child's developing language, but also at the cognitive and social factors that influence language development and, conversely, at the role that language plays in cognitive and social development.

Social Interactive Theories

Few theorists take either of the extreme positions exemplified by the behaviorist and nativist perspectives of language development. Most recognize that language development can best be understood as an interaction between a biologically prepared child and the language environment in which he or she grows up. It would be a misrepresentation to state that there is only one interactive perspective, but the one we feel is most relevant to our concerns is one that proposes that a child's social environment plays a significant in his or her acquisition of language.

Social Interactive approaches view the child's cognitive structures and social needs as interacting with the objects, people, and events in the environment to develop language. New language abilities, in turn, help develop new social and cognitive skills. This interactive perspective is well illustrated in the theorizing of Bruner (1983), who set out to fill the gap between "the miraculous and the impossible." He rejected the idea that language is encountered willy-nilly by the child and that the innate language acquisition device abstracts rules from this shower of spoken language. Instead, Bruner believes that language is carefully presented to children by the people around them. Not only is the content selected for the child's current abilities, but the presentation is executed to provide the best possible chance of learning. We illustrate how we believe this interactive process of language acquisition takes place by describing in the sections below how infants and children, in interaction with others, acquire their first language.

HOW CHILDREN ACQUIRE LANGUAGE

Children gradually acquire their native language over the course of the preschool years. It would be a mistake, however, to think that language development begins only with a child's first words. As we saw earlier, infants can perceive and tell the difference between phonemes shortly after birth or before. They also communicate effectively with their parents months before they speak their first words, and how parents respond and talk to their preverbal infants also have some consequences on children's developing communicative competence.

Early Nonlanguage Communication

Babies come into the world with a variety of abilities such as sucking, grasping, and turning their heads toward a nipple and away from a blanket covering their faces. They are also born with the ability to communicate with others to make their needs known and to establish the foundation of lifelong attachment bonds.

These and other early, well-formed abilities are not selected by chance; they are so vital to our survival that they must be present at birth. In some cases, such as sucking and head turning, the survival value is obvious. But early communication ability is also of crucial importance to human survival and development.

Adults' Speech to Infants.   Communication implies an interaction between individuals, and researchers have investigated the role that adults, especially mothers, play in early nonlanguage communication. Anyone who observes adults interacting with a baby will quickly realize that the adult end of the interaction involves a peculiar form of speech commonly known as "baby talk." ("Hello, Ben! How is the big boy today? Huh? How is Mama's big boy today? Did you go for a walk? Did you? Did you go for a walk with Daddy? Did you see the ducks? Did you? Did you see the ducks?").

Gelman and Shatz (1977) studied the way mothers talked to their infants and found certain commonalities: high-pitched voices, short phrases, lots of questions, many repetitions, and exaggerated emphasis. This style has been termed *infant-directed* (or *child-directed*) *speech,* and is found in many cultures, in both men and women, and in children as young as 4 years. (Infant-directed speech has also been referred to as "motherese," although research has shown that it is also practiced by fathers, babysitters, older siblings, and elderly gentlemen in supermarkets.)

Although not all cultures talk to babies in the same exaggerated way as American mothers frequently do, some aspects of infant-directed speech may be universal (Fernald, 1992; Kuhl et al., 1997). Several researchers have suggested that the special intonation patterns that mothers use with infants may have initially evolved as a means for the mother to control her infant's emotional state and to communicate her emotions to the infant (Fernald, 1992; Locke, 1993). Such nonverbal communication plays an important role in developing a secure attachment between mother and infant, and, according to Locke (1994), "Spoken language piggybacks on this open channel, taking advantage of mother–infant attachment by embedding new information in the same stream of cues" (p. 441). Although a secure attachment is not necessary for children to develop language, there is evidence that maltreated toddlers have significant delays in language acquisition (Cicchetti, 1989).

How do adults and older children know infant-directed speech? How have they learned what words to present to this particular infant and how to present them? Bruner (1983) suggested that people have a learning device in their brains that takes cues from a young child and interacts with the child's language acquisition device. Bruner suggests calling this the *language acquisition support system* (LASS).

One reason why people may use infant-directed speech with infants and young children is because that is the way babies expect and "want" to be spoken to. Infants show a preference for infant-directed speech. Four-month-old babies who have been taught to turn their heads to one side or the other to select which of two tapes they will listen to prefer tapes of infant-directed speech over conventional speech (see Fernald, 1992). Using other techniques, Cooper and Aslin (1990, 1994) reported a preference for infant-directed speech by 1-month-old infants. The results of these and other studies suggest that the auditory system of newborns is prepared to process certain types of language, and that the singsong speech adults often direct to babies is no accident, but reflects the type of language infants most readily discriminate and attend to.

Infants not only seem to prefer to listen to infant-directed speech, can but apparently discriminate between language sounds better when they are spoken in infant-directed as opposed to adult-directed speech. For example, 1- to 4-month-old infants were able to tell the difference between similar three-syllable sounds (such as "marana" vs. "malana") if they were spoken in an exaggerated style so that the middle syllable was accepted (ma-*ra*-na and ma-*la*-na) as in infant-directed speech. They could not tell the difference between such syllables when they were spoken in normal adult speech (Karzon, 1985; see Trehub, Trainor, & Unyk, 1993).

Infants' Social Vocalization.   If a mother talks to her 3-month-old baby, the behavior most likely to occur in the next 10 seconds is baby's vocalization. The second most likely behavior is baby's smile (Lewis & Freedle, 1973). During the first 6 months, infants vocalize along with speaking adults (Freedle & Lewis, 1977). By 7 or 8 months, babies will take turns vocalizing with an adult (Snow & Ferguson, 1977).

Language sounds in the form of cooing and laughter begin at 2 to 4 months and increase to 9 to 12 months, when they decline and one-word utterances begin. Sounds made during babbling vary widely, including sounds heard in the baby's native language and sounds that are not. Babbling sounds change with age. All of this caused some early theorists to conclude from diary studies that babbling served as an exotic smorgasbord of universal language sounds from which infants selected those they heard in the language being spoken around them, while gradually eliminating those they didn't hear (Jakobson, 1968). This popular theory is still cited today by some, but more recent research findings have not supported the early diary studies' data. Babbling does not contain all the sounds found in human language, only a small subset (Locke, 1983; Oller, 1980). The developmental changes in infants' language sounds over the first 6 months reflect anatomic changes in the vocal apparatus more than approximations toward the sounds of one's native language (Ingram, 1989).

Stark (1979) and Stoel-Gammon and Menn (1977) described the developmental stages of infants' babbling as follows:

Stage 1: *Reflexive vocalizations (birth to 2 months).* These include cries, coughs, and the sounds associated with feeding and breathing, such as burps. They may make a few vowel sounds, but the vocal tract of these young infants closely resembles that of nonhuman primates; their tongue fills their oral cavity and their larynx is high in their neck (which permits them to breath and swallow simultaneously). This arrangement limits greatly the range of sounds an infant can produce.

Stage 2: *Cooing and laughter (2 to 4 months).* Infants now begin to make pleasant noises, especially during social interaction. These are mostly vowel sounds such as "oooh" and are termed cooing because they resemble the sounds made by pigeons. A few of the sounds will also contain some consonants such as *g* and *k*. Crying decreases and takes distinct forms that convey meaning to caregivers—discomfort, call, and request. Sustained laughter appears.

Stage 3: *Vocal play (4 to 6 months).* This ia a transition between cooing and true babbling. Infants begin to utter single syllables with prolonged vowel or consonant sounds, including both very loud and very soft sounds.

Stage 4: *True babbling (6 months and older).* True babbling sounds appear, such as "bababa" and "nanana." Consonant–vowel patterns are repeated, and playful variations of pitch disappear. This type of vocalization is not just a response to caregiver's social interaction, but often occurs when no one is present. The feedback infants get from hearing their own babbling is important. This is demonstrated by the fact that deaf babies, although going through the first three stages, do not engage in true babbling at this time (Oller, 1980).

Stage 5: *Jargon (10 months and older).* Babbling consists of many nonrepeated consonant–vowel patterns. Jargon babbling is strings of sound filled with a variety of intonations and rhythms to sound like meaningful speech. Babies now often sound as if they are carrying on their end of a conversation, with the intonations sometimes reflecting questions or explanations, but their "words" are only babble sounds.

It has been suggested, however, that babbling plays a more important role in language development than just a poor attempt at spoken words (Sachs, 1977). Babbling may serve as a way to relate socially with family members long before the cognitive system is able to appreciate the intricacies of language—that certain sounds made in certain orders symbolize certain specific ideas.

Evidence for this is that although *sounds* of babbling don't gradually come to approximate speech, the *intonation* of babbling does. Infants begin to "converse" in many ways that do not involve words, but rather the conventions of speech. They develop the ability to take turns (Snow & Ferguson, 1977), match the speaker's tone of voice, pause between strings of syllables, end phrases with upward or downward inflections (Tonkova-Yompol'skaya, 1969), and match the pitch of adults speaking to them—higher for mother, lower for father (Lieberman, 1967).

The Second Year (12 to 24 Months)

Children show the beginnings of true language ability around the age of 10 to 13 months. It is at this time that they speak their first words that can be understood by family members and that consistently have the same meaning—for example, saying "dada" frequently to refer to the male parent and not to request a cookie or address the family cat.

Over the next 6 months or so, children increase their vocabularies a few words at a time, but their speech consists of one-word expressions. Nouns account for the single largest category of children's early words, many referring to familiar people, toys, and food (Bates et al., 1994; K. Nelson, 1974), although their pronunciation of these words is often dissimilar to those of adults.

Not only are young children's initial pronunciations of words often at odds from those of adults, but so also is their meaning. As we mentioned earlier, young children often *overextend* the meaning of words, using a word to denote things it should not (for example, using "doggie" to describe any furry mammal, including cats and horses). Overextensions often produce corrections from adults and thus can be viewed as a method for acquiring new information. In the example of a child overextending "doggie," the parent might respond, "That's not a *doggie*, it's a *kitty*" (J. R. Thompson & Chapman, 1977). The adult might also add other information, such as "We have a doggie at home, don't we? But this one is a kitty." Or "Doggies say 'woof-woof,' don't they? Kitties say 'meow.' Can you say that?" Thus, children's lack of knowledge and immature response can be adaptive here, leading to getting more information from their parents (D. F. Bjorklund & Green, 1992).

Although toddlers are greatly limited in their ability to express themselves through language *(productive language)*, they can understand substantially more *(receptive language)*. This includes not only words, but also some rather complex sentences. For example, Hirsh-Pasek and Golinkoff (1991) found that 16- to 18-month-old infants, most of whom could produce "sentences" no longer than one word, were able to tell the difference between sentences such as "Where is Big Bird washing Cookie Monster?" and "Where is Cookie Monster washing Big Bird?" This trend toward receptive language being more advanced than productive language is true not only for children in the one-word stage of language development, but also for older children (Hirsh-Pasek, Golinkoff, & Naigles, 1996) and adults.

Around 18 to 24 months, toddlers begin putting the few dozen words they know into short, usually two-word sentences or phrases. Children obviously talk about things that are familiar to them, including actions ("Timmy hit!"), possessions ("my ball"), location ("mommy kitchen"), recurrence ("more cookie"; "daddy again"), and nonexistence ("all gone"; de Villiers & de Villiers, 1979).

If toddlers' communication were restricted to these two-word utterences, they may have a difficult time getting understood. However, these beginning language users supplement their simple sentences and single words with gestures and intonations. For example, "MOMMY!" can be a clear cry of distress, whereas "Mommy?" can be ther initiation of a light conversation. Add a little hand waving and an empty cup and "Mommy" becomes a request for a drink refill. And coming from behind a chairback, "Mommy" can be the beginning of a round of peek-a-boo. Sometimes toddlers are even more obvious. For instance, one 18-month-old would get his mother's attention by climbing up next to her on the sofa, putting one hand on each of her cheeks, and turning her face toward his as he finally said "Cookie?" Another 2-year-old communicated to her mother that she did *not* want any more milk by giving a negative head shake as she was saying "More milk."

In their short tenure as language users, 2-year-olds have also learned pragmatics—adjusting language to circumstances. They watch their listener for signs that they are being understood (J. Wilcox & Webster, 1980). They know they must beclose to their listener in order to be heard and that if they are not close, they must speak louder (Wellman & Lempers, 1977).

The Preschool Years (2 to 5)

Sometimes usually between their second and third birthdays and by the time they're ready for kindergarten, children's productive language leaps from two-word phrases to adult-level proficiency. We can think of no other cognitive accomplishment that is so complicated and yet acquired so well in such a short period of time. And perhaps especially impressive is the fact that children master the syntax of their mother tongue with little if any formal instruction but normal social interaction with adults and older children.

Children increase the number of words they know and use and the length of the sentences they speak. Children's vocabulary increases drastically over the preschool years. It has been estimated that children learn an average of a dozen new words a day between 2 and 5 years of age, and that they know between 8,000 and 10,000 words by the time they start school (Anglin, 1993).

As children start to lenthen their sentences, they do so by using words that convey the most meaning and omitting the "little" words that make language easy to understand but that are not absolutely necessary for comprehension. For example, a child may say "I jump pool" or "Al me go store?" rather than "I'm going to jump into the pool" or "May Al and I go to the store?" When heard in context, the meaning of these truncated sentences are relatively straightforward. Children are economical in their word choice, using only the concrete and high-information words that are most important in conveying meaning. Such speech has been described as *telegraphic*, in that it is accomplished much as telegrams were written, including only the high-content words and leaving out all the ifs, ands, and buts (Brown & Fraser, 1963).

Researchers have found that the reliable increases with age in the length of their utterances shown by preschool age children is a good indication of early linguistic development, and this is measured by a child's *mean length of utterances* (MLU). MLU is measured by counting the number of *morphemes*, or meaningful language units, in children's speech. These include both the *free morphemes* that can stand by themselves (such as "hat," "walk," and "pretty"), and *bound morphemes* that are attached to a word's beginning or ending (such as un-,-s, -ing, and -ed). The relation between a child's linguistic sophistication and MLU is quite high, at least for MLUs up to 3.0 (that is, three morphemes per speech act; Rondal, Ghiotto, Bredart, & Bachelet, 1987).

Overregularization. Many of the morphemes children learn are word endings. For example, 2- and 3-year-old children learn that adding an -s to the end of a word makes it plural and adding an -ed makes a verb past tense. Once children learn these rules, they tend to apply them even when it is not correct to do so. This is referred to as *overregularization.* For example, once children learn the -ed rule, they often apply it incorrectly to words they previously used properly, such as *teached, goed* (or *wented*), and *comed* (or *camed*). Children who have been saying *teeth, mice,* and *cups of sugar* may suddenly and consistently switch to *tooths* or *teeths, mouses* or *mices,* and *cup of sugars.* They have learned a rule for regular words and generalize it to irregular words.

This can be assessed by using the "wug" test developed by Berko (1958) described earlier (see Fig. 9.1). Research has found that children begin to overregularize words typically around 20 months and continue to do so until about their third birthday, when they are more likely to use the irregular forms of verbs and nouns properly (Marcus, 1995; Marcus et al., 1992). This phenomenon is not limited to children learning English, but has been found in a wide variety of language, suggesting that children around the world approach the problem of language acquisition in a similar way (Slobin, 1970).

Negatives. Children do not need language to express a negative. An emphatic shaking of the head is often enough to express the concept "no" or "no way." When children start to express negative ideas linguistically, they do so by negating an entire phrase by putting a negative word such as "no" or "not" at the beginning. For instance, children may say, "No go store," or "Not Daddy do it." They may sometimes add the negative to the end of a sentence, as in "Wear sweater no" (Bellugi, 1967). Note that children who negate sentences in this way are also speaking telegraphically and have relatively short MLUs.

Following this stage, the negative term is moved inside the sentence and put next to the main verb, for example, "I no do it" or "We no run." In the final period, children learn to use auxiliaries much as adults do and as reflected in sentences such as, "I don't want to go," and "You can't have this." Obviously, these later forms are associated with longer sentences.

Questions. Questions also show a regular pattern of development in most children. Children's earliest questions are posed by adding a raised intonation at the end of declarative sentences, such as "Heidi go outside, Daddy?" or "Go soon?" This is a legitimate form of a *yes/no question* that adults often use.

More sophisticated questions involve use of "wh" words, such as *where, what, which, when, who, why,* and *how.* Proper use of "wh" questions involves inverting the order of the subject and auxiliary, so that the declarative sentence, "You are going to town" becomes "Why are you going to town." Children's earliest "wh" questions are asked by putting a "wh" word in front of a declarative sentence, as in "What dat?" or "Why Mommy go?" They later include the auxiliary, but fail to invert the subject and the verb as in, "Why you are going to town?" or "What you are doing?" In the final stage, usually achieved by the time children start kindergarten, children are forming their questions much as adults do.

Something that all parents of toddlers and preschool teachers know is that children will sometimes ask questions, particularly "Why" questions, for which there is often no good or simple answer. Some children we know, around the age of 2, began to use "why?" and "what?" in response to many things adults said to them. One child, after being told by her father that she couldn't go outside, asked "Why?" again, and he told her about the dark clouds gathering to the west. Her third "Why?" brought an explanation of the evaporation–precipitation cycle, and by her fourth "Why?" he was sure he had a scientific genius for a daughter. His wife burst his bubble by suggesting that perhaps their daughter was just interested in listening to Daddy talk. She had learned that "why?" was a magic word that caused adults to take a deep breath and explain *something* at great length.

Another child of 2 had her mother consulting the pediatrician about possible hearing impairment because she responded "What?" after everything her parents said to her. Again, it seems this child was using a "wh" word to extend conversations. When a parent said "Where is your bunny?" she would respond with "What?" This caused the adult to elaborate: "Your bunny, you know, the pink bunny that Grandma gave you? Where is it?" A second "What?" would bring another round of adult conversation: "Did you leave your bunny in the car when we went to the store? I hope you didn't leave it in the store."

The usage of "wh" words at an early age does not indicate acquisition of the concept of questions and answers. What it does illustrate is how social needs can advance ahead of true language abilities. Preschoolers like to converse with others and seldom let minor details, suhc as lack of language ability, get in their way.

Language development continues beyond age 5, of course, but the basic syntax of early schoolage children is remarkably similar to that used by adults. Children become more proficient at using infrequent grammatical structures, such as passive sentences, and they make fewer subject/verb agreement errors (for example, saying "They were going" instead of "They was going") and errors associated with use of the proper form of pronouns (for example, "He and she went" instead of "Him and her went"). But these are subtle changes and the "poor grammar" of the school-age child rarely interferes with communication. Vocabulary increases markedly over the school years, especially vocabulary that is encountered more in print than in speech (Schwanenflugel, 1991), and children's understanding of the pragmatics of communication still continues to develop.

One aspect of children's developing pragmatic abilities can be seen in their ability to monitor their own speech and evaluate whether they are being understood or not (Warren & McCloskey, 1997; Whitehurst & Sonnenschein, 1985). One way of assessing children's ability to monitor the effectiveness of their own speech is to look at the frequency with which they make *verbal repairs,* or correct themselves when talking to a listener. M. A. Evans (1985) looked at the verbal repairs of kindergarten and second-grade children during "show and tell" time at their schools. She found that second graders made significantly more verbal repairs than the kindergarten children. Following is an example of a story told by a second-grade girl that includes several verbal repairs:

> We went to—uh me and Don went to Aunt Judy's. And ... and uh my brother came down on Fri—Friday night, Uh there was a acc—came on the train, And there was an accident. And they thought uh ... that uh ... the—there was an accident with a—a van, And they thought—there was pig's blood in it, And they thought there was somebody hurt. But it was the pig.

Why should the older children make more repairs, indicative of errors, than younger children? Evans believed that it was not because the kindergarten children were the more effective communicators. Just the opposite. The second-grade children were more aware of their speech and the need to communicate effectively. This resulted in more self-monitoring of their speech and correcting themselves, or providing additional information, when necessary to improve communication. As children get older and are able to plan their speech more carefully, the frequency of verbal repairs declines (Sabin, Clemmer, O'Connell, & Kowal, 1979).

LANGUAGE IN CONTEXT

Although language seems to play an important role in how we represent the world and as a tool for thought (see the later section on language and thought), the explicit purpose of language is to communicate. Communication is a social phenomenon, and the fact that humans are social animals likely played a significant role in the evolution of language. Social factors are thus likely involved in how we use language. We have already discussed social-interactive ideas about how infants and young children acquire language, but social factors influence more than the initial acquisition of language, but also the type of language one speaks in any particular situation. Language occurs in social contexts. Social contexts are characterized as including different people, often of different social status and familiarity. Once a child learns the basic rules of a language, she must learn how to modify her speech as a function of the social situation. This can be seen as a form of pragmatics and includes children learning to be polite (saying "please" and "thank you"), as well as learning to use different language *codes*, or *registers*, in different social situations (Warren & McCloskey, 1997).

Speech Registers

We have already seen how children as young as 4 years of age modify their speech when talking to infants and young children. They simplify their language and use a tone or modulation of voice that serves to attract and maintain the attention of the younger child (infant-, or child-directed speech). This is a form of *speech register*. It is a distinct style of speaking that differs from the way children (and adults) talk to one another. It is used only is specific contexts (speaking to young children) and would be considered inappropriate if it were used in other contexts.

Perhaps more significant are speech registers that children learn to use in formal situations, with unfamiliar people, or both versus the speech registers that they used in informal situations with family and friends. The most obvious distinction for most children is between speech used in school with teachers (a school register) and speech used in informal social settings (a social register). Children, particularly those whose home language represents a nonstandard version of the majority language, need to differentiate these two types of speech registers and use the more formal one where appropriate if they are to get the most out of their schooling.

When the type of language children use at home differs noticeably from the language used at school, there is the potential for educational difficulties. In most cultures, families from middle-class backgrounds often speak a "standard" version of the language, one that is used in school, whereas families from lower socioeconomic backgrounds often speak a nonstandard version of the language, one that is different from that used in schools and one that is often regarded as "inferior" (e.g., Baugh, 1983; Bernstein, 1971). In the United States, the most prevalent language distinction between social and school registers for native speakers is often children whose home language is described as *Black English* (or more recently as *Ebonics*).

Black English

Most of us are familiar with Black English. Although used mostly by members of the African American community, not all African Americans speak it, and many non-African Americans do, so the term can be somewhat misleading. Black English is characterized by some special rules of pronunciation and syntax. Perhaps most obvious to speakers of standard English is Black English's use of the verb "to be." It is often not conjugated as in standard English (for example, "I be" or "They be," as opposed to "I am" or "They are"), and it is sometimes not used at all in a sentence, depending on the precise meaning that is trying to be conveyed. For example, the verb "to be" may be omitted if the sentence refers to a one-time or unusual occurrence of an event, for example, "He playing ball" for a person who doesn't usually play ball. But if the sentence refers to a recurrent event, the verb "to be" is inserted in the sentences, for example, "He be playing ball," to describe a person who regularly plays ball and is playing ball right now (Warren & McCloskey, 1997). Black English is not an inferior linguistic form of standard English. For the most part, the two share common syntax and vocabulary, but where they differ, one is not simply a degraded form of the other. Black English is a syntactically complex form of English capable of expressing complex ideas and emotions (Heath, 1989).

However, Black English is not the language of the schools, nor of the mainstream American marketplace. This means that children speaking Black English will often be misunderstood by their teachers (who have a difficult time understanding Black English), have a difficult time reading text or understanding directions expressed in standard English, and may be unjustly judged as intellectually inferior based on they language style they use to express themselves. Research has shown that the actual language abilities of young speakers of Black English may be underestimated when tests are administered only in standard English.

Although there has been some substantial debate over the years on the costs and benefits of providing children instruction in Black English, most young speakers of Black English seem to acquire some aspects of standard English and use it in school (DeStefano, 1972; Melmed, 1971). For example, DeStefano (1972) reported that the classroom speech of 8- to 11-year-old African American children contained more components of standard English than their speech out of school. Thus, even young elementary school children are able to switch dialects and registers, from social registers (Black English) to school registers (standard English). However, there is some evidence that many African American adolescents tend to *increase* their use of Black, compared to standard, English, over adolescence, as use of Black English becomes an important part of their social identity (Delpit, 1990).

The debate on how to educate children whose home dialect is substantially different from the dialect used by teachers and others in the school is a lively one, and we do not pretend to have an answer. It should be recognized, however, that Black English, or other regional dialects, are not inferior languages and that the language itself does not impede thought. It may impede educability, however, and the opportunity to partake fully in the American economy. Children of all social classes learn to use different registers. It may be more difficult for speakers of Black English, because the different registers are actually different dialects of the same language with some different syntactic and phonological rules. Moreover, language serves as a form of social identity, and children and adolescents may be reluctant to give up their language style merely for the sake of doing well in school. The ideal, seemingly, would be for children to master both dialects and have the flexibility to switch between them as the situation demands. These different dialects then truly become different registers, to be used when and where appropriate.

SECOND-LANGUAGE LEARNING

Learning to use different registers is something that most children readily learn to do, although this may be a bit more difficult then the social register is substantially different from the school register, as is the case for speakers of Black English. However, fewer children (in the United States, anyway) learn to speak different languages, but when they do they show sensitivity to social context, just as they do when using different registers. For example, young children who speak two languages usually use each language in specific contexts—one language for use at home and church and another for use at school. Second and third languages are a fact of life for children in some parts of the world, such as areas of Europe, for instance, where there may be several "official" languages in a single country. There is only one dominant language in the United States, but the influx of immigrants over the past decade has increased the number of children in schools who do not speak English as a first language. By understanding the way in which successful learners of English have mastered the language, we should be able to design educational environments to optimize instruction for children who are learning English as a second language.

Acculturation and Second-Language Learning

Several theorists have proposed that second-language learning is associated with the extent to which children are, or wish to become, integrated within the new culture (R. C. Gardner & Lambert, 1972; Schumann, 1993). This *acculturation hypothesis* holds "that learners will acquire the target language only to the degree to which they acculturate" (Hoff-Ginsburg, 1997, p. 364). For example, R. C. Gardner and Lambert (1972) proposed that there are two types of motivation for learning a second language: integrative and instrumental. *Integrative motivation* refers to a person's desire to learn the second language so that he or she can more easily associate with members of the majority culture. *Instrumental motivation* refers to a person's desire to learn the second language for more utilitarian purposes, such as getting a job. Gardner and Lambert found that people expressing integrative motivation were more successful at mastering a second language. In more recent research, J. S. Johnson and Newport (1989) reported that the only factors other than age of arrival to the United States that predicted Korean and Chinese immigrants' eventual language proficiency in English were self-consciousness and degree of American identification, both factors that would seem to be related to degree of acculturation.

But how do children who speak one language go about the process of learning a second language? The work of Fillmore (1979) is particularly relevant here. Generally, she has suggested that children develop a second language by putting themselves in social contexts that will facilitate the process of learning that language. She observed five children (5 to 7 years old) in school settings of second-language users and outlined the cognitive and social strategies that nonnative speakers of English used to learn English. These strategies are listed in the order in which they were used:

1. First, successful learners attempted to establish *social relations with native speakers*. In essence, the children were using the native speakers to provide them with the "input" to learn the language.

2. The first *cognitive* strategy used by the children was to *assume that what was being talked about in a specific situation was relevant to the situation at hand*. Children used the linguistic routines that were specific to these contexts in similar situations; for example, when recess ends, children may say, "Let's line up." Being exposed to this utterance and the context of recess ending and lining up should result in comprehension and production of the appropriate utterance in the appropriate context.

3. & 4. The second social strategy children used to learn the language was to *give the impression that they could speak the language.* In attempting to do so, the nonnative speaker had to use the second cognitive strategy: *use some expressions that you understand*. Children often began by using *routines* and formulaic expressions like "Yah," "What's happening!" and "Gimme" to participate in groups. The use of this type of strategy allows children to continue to participate in groups so that they may continue to learn the language. Such formulaic expressions allow children to use aspects of the second language long before they have mastered them.

5. The third cognitive strategy was for nonnative speakers to look for and *use recurring parts in the formulaic expressions they knew*. To do this, nonnative speakers must first notice how parts of the expression vary with the changes in situations, and then notice which parts of the expression resemble the parts of the meaning of the utterances known by them. By doing so, nonnative speakers can determine the meaning of the constituents of expression. For example, if the word *hungry* appears in a number of different phrases that are used in the presence of food, the nonnative speaker could deduce that *hungry* is related to eating.

6. The fourth cognitive strategy is to *make the most of what you've got*. Children use most frequently those strategies that they have mastered. This strategy may involve the overgeneralized use of a term, such as *sangwish* (sic) to refer to all food.

7. The fifth cognitive strategy is: *Work on the big things and save the details for later.* Successful learners of a second language used major constituents first and only later tried to sort out the grammatical details of the expression; they used phrases that they had already mastered to help them construct novel utterances.

8. The third social strategy used was to *count on friends*. Second-language users needed the help of someone else if they were to learn the new language

effectively. Friends had the belief that the nonnative speaking children could learn the new language. By doing so, they continued to interact with the language learner, often simplifying their speech in the process.

We have seen that children learn a new language most effectively when they have the desire to communicate with others and become part of the culture represented by the new language. Children are viewed as active learners who are motivated to learn new language forms by a desire to communicate ideas that they cannot express to others with their current linguistic repertoire. Fillmore's (1979) work also shows that learning a second language is not just a "linguistic" problem, but is affected by a child's cognitive and social skills and the presence of a supportive social environment of peers. Although the effect of the interaction of social, motivational, and linguistic factors is most obvious in the learning of a second language, it is also true for the acquisition of a child's first language (L. Bloom, 1997). Language is acquired in a social context, be it home or school, or with parents or with peers, and we must be mindful of these social and emotional factors when trying to explain language development.

The Role of Age in Learning a Second Language

Our earlier discussion concerned young children learning a second language. Would learning be easier if children were older or younger than the 5- to 7-year olds studied by Fillmore (1979)? The answer is obvious here: Younger is better when it comes to learning a second language. People who learn a second language only as adults rarely become proficient in that language. This is seen both in phonology ("foreign" accents) and syntax.

It is easy to spot almost anyone who learned a second language as an adult. Even if they are articulate, well-educated, and have an impressive vocabulary, they almost always have a noticeable accent. Research has confirmed this. Oyama (1976) studied Italian immigrants in the United States and assessed their accents as a function of (a) their age of arrival to the United States, and (b) how long they had resided in the United States. Only the first factor, age of arrival, and thus age at which they were first exposed to English, predicted the degree of their accents.

Perhaps more subtle is syntax. Presumably, people who live in a country for many years will eventually master "like a native" the syntax of a language, even if they retain an accent. This was tested in research by J. S. Johnson and Newport (1989), who examined second-language learning as a function of age. They tested 46 native Chinese or Korean speakers who had emigrated to the United States and learned English as a second language. The age of people at time of arrival in the United States ranged from 3 to 39 years, and they had lived in the United States between 3 and 26 years when they were tested.

J. S. Johnson and Newport (1989) reported that their subjects' grammatical proficiency in English was related to the age when language training began:

People who learned their second language early in childhood showed greater proficiency as adults than people who learned later in childhood. Such a result might not be so surprising if it concerned only people's pronunciation of words (phonology), but these data are for *syntax*, and indicate that it is the age at which one starts the second language, and not necessarily how long one has been speaking it, that determines eventual proficiency in a second language.

The Benefits of Bilingualism

Second-language learning is obviously necessary for children immigrating to a new country, but is it advisable for children from the majority culture to learn a second language? For better or worse, Americans have been able to function well in the modern world learning only English. The rest of the educated world learns English in order to speak to us. But with mass communications and an economy that is truly worldwide, learning a second language may make some sense. Is there any evidence of cognitive benefits or detriments of learning a second language, beyond the ability to converse in two tongues?

Researchers in the early part of this century noted that bilingual immigrants to the United States fared less well on a host of intellectual tasks than monolingual natives. They interpreted these results as indicating that it was the two languages of the new immigrants and not their lower socioeconomic status that was responsible for their intellectual deficits and argued strongly against teaching children a second language (see Hoff-Ginsburg, 1997). Later research turned this interpretation on its head, however. Peal and Lambert (1962) assessed Canadian children who were fluent in both French and English and found that bilinguals performed better on a series of cognitive tests than monolinguals from the same social class. Other research has confirmed these early findings (e.g., Ben-Zeev, 1977). Ben-Zeev proposed that bilingual children develop an ability to seek out the language rules and evaluate which are required for the circumstances. In general, these children may develop a keener sense of *metalinguistic awareness*, or a knowledge of how languages work (Diaz, 1983).

On the downside, children who acquire two languages at once may show some slowed development in each language (Ben-Zeev, 1977; Umbel, Pearson, Fernández, & Oller, 1992). Thus, although speaking two languages proficiently may be better than speaking one, it is likely not true that it is as easy to learn two languages as it is to learn one. However, it is true that if two languages are going to be learned, the earlier the better. The obvious pedagogical implications for this is that we should introduce children to a second language (whether it be English of Japanese) early and not wait for formal instruction to begin after the language-learning process becomes laborious.

IS THERE A CRITICAL PERIOD
FOR LEARNING LANGUAGE?

We would not be thought to be making a profound statement if we were to say that adults learn most things more easily than children. Children's cognitive limitations make it impossible for them to learn some things and others are learned only after much repetition. Yet, as we've just seen in our description of second-language learning, language seems to be an exception. Children are better at acquiring both first and second languages than are adults, and this has caused some people to propose that children are especially prepared by biology to learn language and that there is a critical period beyond which language acquisition becomes difficult (Lenneberg, 1966).

Locke (1993) stated that there are four types of evidence for a critical period for language acquisition. First, there is the evidence we cited earlier concerning the relation between age and second-language learning. Eventual proficiency of both phonology and syntax is greater the younger children begin learning the second language.

Second, there are cases of people who were socially deprived or isolated early in life and who, as a result, are able to develop only a tenuous mastery of syntax (Curtiss, 1977).

A third source of evidence comes from differences in proficiency in sign language in the deaf as a function when children were first exposed to sign language. The logic here is much the same as that in the J. S. Johnson and Newport (1989) study, except that now sign language is the first, not the second language, for these people. Newport (1990) reported findings very similar to those of J. S. Johnson and Newport (1989): the earlier children were exposed to American Sign Language, the greater their eventual proficiency.

A final source of evidence comes from recovery of language function as a result of brain damage. There are specific areas of the brain that are devoted to processing language (further evidence of the special biological basis for language). When these areas are damaged early in life, other areas of the brain can take over their function and eventual language proficiency can be nearly normal. Recovery of language function after brain damage is reduced with age, and there is little recovery when damage occurs in adolescence or later.

It is clear that the cognitive system of the young child is especially suited for language learning, of both a first and second language. This ability is gradually lost over childhood, and although adults are able to acquire a second language, they rarely attain the same proficiency that is achieved when language is acquired in childhood. This is evidence for the presence of a critical, or more appropriately, a sensitive, period for the acquisition of language. The window of opportunity seems to be relatively wide, however. But if children have not acquired a first language by adolescence, they may never fully acquire one; and if language instruction in a second language is delayed much past childhood, it is unlikely that phonological or syntactic proficiency will ever be attained.

LANGUAGE AND THOUGHT

When people think about thinking, they usually do so in terms of language. For most people, thought without language is unthinkable. Although language is not our only means of thought, it is certainly the basis for much of our cognitive processing.

The connection between language and thought is not a constant one but develops over childhood. Bruner (1980) argued that preschool children, although possessing language, represent their world primarily in terms of images. Not until the early school years do children begin to use language as a tool for thought. K. Nelson (1996) has similarly proposed that the children's acquisition of language over the preschool years transforms their thought, permitting them to classify objects into culturally defined categories, represent events in terms of narratives that can be remembered and communicated to others, and develop a sense of self and knowledge of other's minds that is so critical in human social and intellectual life. In the section that follows, we focus on the role of private speech in young children's thinking, a phenomenon that characterizes the preschool child. Although entire books have been written on the role of language on children's developing thought (e.g., K. Nelson, 1996), we believe that this brief section will introduce readers to some of the key issues and behaviors surrounding this important area.

The developmental relationship between language and thought was investigated earlier in this century by Vygotsky (1934/1962). He believed that thought and speech have different roots in development and that the two are initially independent. However, with development, thought and speech merge: thought becomes verbal, and speech becomes rational.

Vygotsky was particularly interested in the role of *egocentric,* or *private speech,* on children's thought. Private speech is overt language that is carried out with apparent satisfaction, even though it does not communicate. It can be observed when children are alone or in social settings.

Examples of private speech are the collective monologues described by Piaget (1955). In collective monologues, two (or more) children will be talking about some common activity, but not necessarily talking to one another. Take, for example, the "conversation" of two 5-year-old boys overheard not long ago. Michael described how his ghostcatcher was going to drive his ATV over to

Jimmy and catch some ghosts. Jimmy commented that his ghostcatcher had been slimed and he had to hurry back to the fire station (ghostcatcher headquarters). The conversation continued for some time, with both boys moving their toys and describing their actions; but what one boy said appeared to have little to do with what the other said or did.

Vygotsky believed language serves to guide children's behavior (and thus their thought), but young children cannot yet use language covertly, "in their heads." In order to guide their own behavior through language, they must talk out loud to themselves. With development, children become able to use inner speech. In other words, private speech serves as a cognitive self-guidance system and then goes "underground" as covert verbal thought.

In contrast to Vygotsky's view of the role of private speech in cognitive development is that of Piaget (1955), who believed that the egocentric speech of preschoolers reflects their general egocentric perspective of the world. As children become increasingly able to decenter their cognition and perception and see the point of view of another, private speech decreases. For Piaget, private speech plays no functional role in cognitive development but is merely symptomatic of ongoing mental activity.

Most research that has been done to examine the relationship between private speech and thought support Vygotsky's position (see Berk, 1992). For example, children's performance on school-type tasks often improves when accompanied by private speech (Behrend, Rosengren & Perlmutter, 1989; Berk & Spuhl, 1995), and children are more apt to talk to themselves on difficult as opposed to easy problems or after making errors (Berk, 1992). Also, brighter preschool children use more private speech to guide their problem solving than less bright preschoolers, although this pattern is reversed for older children (Berk, 1992; Kohlberg, Yaeger, & Hjertholm, 1968). This suggests that private speech peaks early in brighter children and persists in older children after it has gone "underground" as covert verbal thought for the brighter older students. And private speech does indeed "go underground," progressing from words and phrases, to whispers and mutterings, to inner speech (Bivens & Berk, 1990; Kohlberg et al., 1968). There is also evidence that preschool children are generally unaware that inner speech is even possible. Rather, they tend to believe that when a person is "thinking" he is *cannot* be simultaneously talking to himself. Moreover, when prompted to use inner speech (for example, "Silently think about how your name sounds"), preschool children are just as likely to say that they had a picture of their name in their head while thinking than to say that they said their name in their head (Flavell, Green, Flavell, & Grossman, 1997).

Vygotsky was apparently right about the role that private speech plays in young children's cognitive development. Preschool children who talk to themselves are most likely using their overt language to guide their problem solving.

Older children resort to overt, private speech when the faced with difficult problems, such as a thorny math assignment. And adults, including the authors of this book, sometime read out loud when trying to make sense of a particularly difficult passage. These findings also indicate that language, either spoken out loud or quietly "in one's head," is a powerful tool, not just for communicating with others, but for thought.

10

Children's Social Competence

In order to understand children fully we must study the interrelations among the social, cognitive, and affective aspects of their behavior and development. For example, if we were interested in studying what is typically considered a dimension of cognition—reading—we should be concerned with psycholinguistic processes, such as knowledge of letter–sound correspondence; social processes, such as the ways in which children's knowledge of the social conventions governs classroom discourse; and affect, such as achievement motivation. Similarly, in studying children's social behavior, such as cooperation with peers, we must consider cognitive processes, such as the ability to take another person's perspective. The reason for the examination of social, affective, and cognitive processes is simple: They affect each other.

In this chapter we examine children's social competence and the ways in which it develops. Social competence is a measure of children's adaptive or functional behaviors in their environments (Waters & Sroufe, 1983). Extending this to a developmental framework, there are different social competencies, or hallmarks of competence, at different ages. By implication, the hallmarks for toddlers should not be considered as unfinished or incomplete versions of adult behavior; they represent adaptations to that specific developmental niche.

In this chapter we also examine children's social competence in the context of different family, school, and peer contexts. We examine the ways in which children interact with parents, teachers, and peers and show how these processes affect children's subsequent social competence. The effects of toys and other people on children's social competence is also explored as well as children's popularity and friendship, both as important aspects of their peer relations.

We conclude with a discussion of various ways of assessing these different aspects of children's social competence.

WHAT IS SOCIAL COMPETENCE?

The term social competence has been used extensively in the fields of education and psychology. Social competence has been defined differently by a number of scholars (e.g., Anderson & Messick, 1974; Dodge, Petit, McClaskey, & Brown, 1986; Zigler & Tricket, 1978). As noted earlier, social competence involves cognitive, affective, and social processes. A socially competent child is functional in a specific environments. For example, competence in a kindergarten classroom would involve effective communication with peers and teachers, attending to class work, cooperating with peers, washing hands after going to the toilet, and attending school with regularity, to name but a few examples.A general definition of competence refers to "an ability to generate and coordinate flexible adaptive responses to demands and to generate and capitalize on opportunities in the environment" (Waters & Sroufe, 1983, p. 80). This definition is neither age- nor situation- nor skill-specific. Earlier however, we stressed a developmental approach to social competence such that there are hallmarks of social competence for different periods. This approach is consistent with the view of development, which stressed the integrity of individual developmental periods. For example, crying may be effective for an infant to secure food. It should not be considered an inferior variant of more mature behavior.

Scholars have attempted to measure social competence for a number of years, using tests for children (e.g., *Circus*, 1975), questionnaires completed by teachers or children (Pellegrini, Masten, Garmezy, & Ferrarese, 1987), and by direct observations of children in natural situations (B. White & Watts, 1973). Despite the data source, it is important to define the construct of social competence such that it reflects the integrity of children in different developmental periods.

Waters and Sroufe (1983) have provided such a model. Generally, they consider competence as "an integrated concept which refers broadly to an ability to generate and coordinate flexible, adaptive responses to demands and to generate and capitalize on opportunities in the environment" (p. 80). Waters and Sroufe further specified their definition of social competence by listing some of its subcomponents. First, individuals must contribute to situations. Responding to others (e.g., answering questions) or making one's own contributions (e.g., asking questions) to conversations are ways of contributing.

Second, children must recognize the opportunity or demand to respond. For example, in conversation children are obligated by the rules of social discourse to respond to questions. Third, children should possess a repertoire of response alternatives. For example, children should have an array of responses to others' discourse; they can ask for questions to be clarified, change the topic, or answer the question. Fourth, they should be able to choose alternatives that are appropriate to specific situations. For example, if a child does not understand another's questions, he or she should either repeat the question or ask for clarification of the question. Fifth, children should be motivated to respond. That is, children should want to engage in social discourse or interact with materials. As such, children should want to interact with different stimuli; they should be active, not passive. Sixth, children should persist at their interactions and change their responses to meet situational demands. For example, children's play with their peers should be sustained. Individual children may have to alter their social responses (e.g., sharing toys) in order for the interaction to be sustained. Last, children's responses should be fine tuned. That is, children should be able to decide quickly when to use certain types of behavior. In addition, they should be facile in using them in different areas.

This approach to social competence suggests that children should, initially, seek out different physical and social stimuli. Further, they should develop repertoires of behaviors within each context that are adaptive. That is, in each context they should act in such a way that their interaction is sustained.

How do these individual processes relate to specific developmental hallmarks? Waters and Sroufe (1983) have listed hallmarks through the preschool period. The issues presented in this table are meant to highlight those specific competencies that are appropriate for each age level. After mastery of one set of competencies, the child moves on to the next set of skills, each solving the problems germane to that specific period.

At the preschool period and into later childhood children's functioning in school becomes part of their social competence. Social competence in school has been effectively captured by the early work of Zigler and Trickett (1978) and S. Anderson and Messick (1974).

First, Zigler and Trickett (1978) suggested three general dimensions of social competence in school: children's physical health; formal cognitive ability, such as IQ, a Piagetian measure of cognition, or both; and measures of motivation and emotion. Social competence thus seems to be a global measure of the ways in which children can effectively take from and contribute to their environments. It is not living in a rich environment, it is the ability to coordinate social, emotional, and cognitive resources such that one functions optimally in one's environment.

The specific skills that might comprise young school age children's social competence have been outlined by Anderson and Messick (1974) and displayed in Table 10.1.

TABLE 10.1
Twenty-Nine Dimensions of Young Children's Social Competence

Competence	Example
1. Differentiated self-concept and identity consolidation	Child recognizes has different skills and a single identity
2. Self as initiating and controlling agent	Child feels responsible for own learning
3. Personal maintenance and care	Cleanliness
4. Realistic self-appraisal and feelings of self-worth	Recognizes how level of math competence fit with individual self-worth
5. Differentiation of feelings	Recognizes positive and negative feelings
6. Social relationship sensitivity and understanding	Understands different perspectives
7. Positive and affectionate relations	Stable friendships
8. Role perception and appreciation	Acts differently in different situations
9. Regulates antisocial behaviors	Isn't a bully
10. Morality and prosocial tendencies	Helps peers
11. Curiosity and exploratory behaviors	Examines new environments
12. Controls attention	Attends to a task
13. Perceptual skills	Discriminates units
14. Fine motor dexterity	Buttons shirt
15. Gross motor skills	Runs
16. Perceptual–motor skills	Handwriting
17. Language skills	Communicates ideas
18. Categorization skills	Recognizes similarities and differences
19. Memory skills	Remembers telephone
20. Critical thinking skills	Identifies and solves problems
21. Creative thinking	Novel responses
22. Problem solving	Solves similar problems
23. Flexible information-processing	Using color and shape to sort
24. Quantitative skills	Recognizes magnitude
25. General knowledge	Name of books
26. Competence motivation	Enjoys problem solving
27. Uses resources	Ask adults for help
28. Positive attitude to school	Low absentee rate
29. Enjoys play	Engages in make-believe

The Role Of Context

Different contexts elicit different sorts and levels of social competence. If we conceptualize competence as one's ability to take from one's environment, then those environments that differentiate between those who are capable or incapable of doing so are important. Generally, environments that are highly structured by adults elicit lower levels of competence from children than do less structured environments. Simply, when children and adults are together, adults often do most of the work that initiating and maintains social interaction. It may be for this reason that children with low levels of social competence choose to spend time with a teacher on the playground during recess than with peers: Teachers probably initiate and conversation and keep it going, whereas peers are probably less likely to do so.

This has been confirmed in a number of studies. For example, in an observational study of preschool children, M. Wright (1980) attempted to identify positive indicators of children's social competence. Her general definition of social competence, like others, was children's socially adaptive behavior. She identified a number of naturally occurring behaviors that were related to various measures of social adaptability. She did this by examining child–child and child–adult interactions and then relating these behaviors to children's test scores of adaptability in preschool. She found, first, that the child–adult behaviors tend *not* to be related to measures of adaptability. Three types of peer interactions were, however, related to social adaptability: the successful and positive seeking of peers' attention; successfully using peers as instrumental resources; and successfully leading peers. Children must exhibit higher levels of competence to secure resources around peers than around adults. Adults, it seems, do much of children's work for them.

These results seem to support Waters and Sroufe's (1983) notion that social competence involves children seeking out social stimuli and having an effect on those stimuli. Dodge and his colleagues (Dodge et al., 1986) have determined more exactly those processes involved in successful social interaction with peers. The process begins with children's accurate processing of social information. For example, do children accurately encode and interpret social information? Do they search for an appropriate social response? Do they then evaluate the effectiveness of their response? These actions, in turn, relate to peers' judgements of each other and their subsequent behaviors in peer groups.

SOCIAL COMPETENCE IN THE FAMILY
AND IN SCHOOLS

In this section we examine children's development and learning of social competence in family and school contexts. In order to understand children's behavior in school, and other public settings, we must understand the ways in which they were socialized and the effects of these socialization practices on them. Many would argue that the family context provides an important basis for children's social competence. For example, many argue that the quality of children's attachment to their mothers has implications for children's later social development (Bowlby, 1969; Bretherton & Waters, 1985; Mahler, Pine, & Bergman, 1975; Sroufe, 1979). Insecurely attached children may be less successful at establishing social relationships in later childhood. Further, the values and behaviors modeled by parents are thought to affect children's later behavior and aspirations.

Additionally, socialization theory predicts that the socialization models in the community impact children's social competence in school (Baumrind, 1980). In short, the family context has an important affect on children's social competence. In this section of the chapter we examine, first, two dominant theories of socialization in the family. Second, we briefly examine four different child-rearing schemes. We suggest that the processes described in the family socialization models can also be used to describe processes in the classroom. Parents and teachers alike use different socialization strategies in teaching children.

Theories

Social Cognitive Theory. Two dominant theories in the child socialization literature are social cognitive theory and interaction theory (Maccoby & Martin, 1983). Social cognitive theory is most closely identified with Bandura (1986, 1989a), and states that children learn specific behaviors for specific social contexts by observation and by imitation. Social cognitive theory does not stress the role of reinforcement in learning. Instead of reinforcement, social cognitive theorists stress the importance of contingent response and recognize cognitive contributions to learning. Contingent responses are responses to specific behaviors. An adult responding to a child's gaze would be a contingent response. If children are responded to by adults, children are more likely to exhibit those behaviors again. Reinforcement comes into play in order for a behavior to be maintained. Children generate behaviors learned by imitation or observation. Behaviors will be maintained if they are responded to contingently.

In this model children learn primarily by observing others' behaviors. Children, it seems, observe behaviors that are salient in specific contexts and subsequently imitate those behaviors in similar context. Children's behavior in a specific context may be a result of observing many different models. Children's subsequent behavior may be a model *configuration* of their recombining different models' behaviors. For example, a young girl's gender identity, an important component of the self-system, may be the result of her observing female teachers and bright female students. Gender identity is thus established by children applying social and cognitive processes to social phenomena. Children's imitations are creative to the extent that they seem to combine the behaviors of many different models. Children tend to imitate, however, people who are powerful, skillful, and nurturant.

In terms of parents as models, children's behaviors do not seem to result from their imitation of their same-sex parent. Maccoby and Martin (1983) and Maccoby (1988) suggested that children's behaviors seem to be a result of their observing and interacting with *a number* of same-sex models. It is suggested that children may build a *prototypic* behavior, based on a number of models, before using the behavior. As such this theory has children constructing behavioral repertoires, which are often novel, based on their viewing a number of different models.

Interaction/Escalation Theory.   Interaction theory is the second theory used to explain child socialization within the family (Maccoby & Martin, 1983). Where social cognitive theory stresses parental effects on children's behavior, interaction theory stresses the reciprocal effects of both children and parents. That is, parents influence children's behaviors but children also influence parents' behaviors. These reciprocal interactions have a ripple effect to the extent that earlier interactions influence later interactions. As such, children's and parents' social identities are products of these reciprocal interactions. The work of Patterson and colleagues is exemplary in this regard (Patterson, 1986; Patterson, DeBarsyshe, & Ramsey, 1989). For example, in discussing antisocial children, it is noted that children's antisocial behavior toward a parent may elicit a harsh response. This acts as a reinforcer for the children's antisocial behavior and, consequently, children exhibit more antisocial behavior; this in turn escalates into harsher parental response. This theory seems to be a more realistic account of how parents and children and peers actually affect each other. In short, social actions are interdependent to the extent that they are embedded in sequences of behavior.

Social Processes in the Family and School: Parenting and Teaching Patterns

As noted earlier, knowledge of parenting patterns are useful in child study in that they have predictable affects on children's behavior. Knowledge of these patterns may help us understand their behavior. Based on their extensive review of parent–child interactions, Maccoby and Martin (1983) have suggested a fourfold scheme of parental characteristics. As we suggested earlier, these processes can also be applied to socialization in the classroom.

Although this model did not initially address culturally diverse families, subsequent research by Steinberg and colleagues has shown that the model works the same in diverse ethnic and socioeconomic niches (Steinberg, Dornbusch, & Brown, 1992; Steinberg, Mounts, Lamborn, & Dornbusch, 1991).

The first category, the rejecting–demanding parent, is characterized by parents and teachers making demands on their children but not accepting their children's demands. This type of parent restricts children's expression of needs. This is the classical case of "Children should be seen but not heard." Adults' demands are neither questioned by children nor subject to discussion; children must obey the demands. Children are typically punished, often severely, when they do not comply with adult demands.

Children from such authoritarian families tend not to interact frequently with peers but when they do they are dominated by their peers. These children, thought obedient, lack spontaneity and affection. Additionally, they tend to perform poorly in school. In short, they do not seem to be socially competent. Preschool children from authoritarian families are dependent, socially withdrawn, and unhappy (Baumrind, 1967, 1971, cited in Maccoby & Martin 1983). When this type of child was examined in elementary school the girls did not show signs of social responsibility (e.g., altruism, cooperative interaction, and social imitation) and cognitive competence. In high school, these children achieve at low levels (Steinberg et al, 1992).

Indulgent–undemanding parents and teachers, are contrasted with the rejecting–demanding parents and teachers. They are characterized as being permissive with their children. They take a tolerant and accepting attitude toward children's impulses. They make few demands and do not impose restrictions on children. Children are allowed to regulate their own lives. These parents can be either a warm, caring group, or cool and uninvolved. Baumrind (1967, 1971, cited in Maccoby & Martin, 1983) found that children of permissive parents tended to lack impulse control, self-reliance, independence, and social responsibility.

The demanding child-centered orientation, is characterized by parents and teachers having clear expectations of mature child behavior, firmly enforcing rules, encouraging child independence, and recognizing rights of both children and adults. Based on Baumrind's research (1967, 1971, cited in Maccoby & Martin, 1983), children experiencing this form of parenting tend to be the most competent. Generally, children tend to be socially responsible and independent. Steinberg and colleagues suggested, specifically, that parental warmth and acceptance when paired with democracy (or considering children's points of view), and supervision of children are responsible for the positive outcomes.

Unresponsive–undemanding, is the last socialization style to be discussed. Generally, these adults minimize the time and effort spent with their children (Maccoby & Martin, 1983) and parents in this groups want to keep their children at a distance. As such, the behaviors related to children's long-range developmental status (e.g., establishing rules for doing homework) are not attended to by these parents. Parents attend only to those behaviors necessary for children's immediate survival (e.g., feeding). However, these parents sometimes even neglect these basic survival responsibilities. It has been reported that unresponsive–undemanding parents often abuse and neglect their children (Egeland & Sroufe, 1981, cited in Maccoby & Martin, 1983). In short, these parents are not interested in their children. What are the consequences of this type of parent for children? For preschoolers, parent noninvolvement was a good predictor of children's aggression and disobedience.

SOCIAL PROCESSES AND PEERS

The term *peer* refers to individuals of equal status. In child study we typically use the term to refer to same-age children. Children of the same age are often equal in status in a number of ways. Peers, as well as adults, influence children's socialization.

The study of peer interaction in the field of child study has recently experienced a rebirth. Until recently psychologists, educators, and others interested in children have been more concerned with the cognitive aspects of children's behavior than with the social aspects. Piaget, as noted earlier in this book, was concerned with peer interaction. Indeed, he stated that peer interactions was the best context for spurring children's cognitive and social development. In peer contexts children experience views discrepant from their own and often compromise their views. This accommodation of one's own point of view to another's is said to result in conceptual growth. As a result, different peer configurations have potent effects on children's behavior. To understand children's social competence we must understand their peer configurations because of this potent effect.

Children's ability to interact with peers, however, undergoes significant developmental change across the early childhood period. Piaget's (1970) popular notion of the egocentric preschooler was a dominant concept until recently. He noted that sensorimotor and preoperational children were socially egocentric to the extent that they were neither willing nor able to consider the point of view of others.

More recent psychological research has challenged Piaget's concept of egocentricism in young children (e.g., Garvey, 1977; Mueller, 1972; Mueller & Brenner, 1977; Mueller & Rich, 1976). Generally, this more recent body of research suggests that very young children (e.g., 6 months old) are very willing to interact with others, but their ability to coordinate social interaction continues to improve through the early and middle childhood period. Mueller (Mueller & Lucas, 1977) and Parten (1932) have documented the social interactive behaviors of infants and preschool-age children, respectively.

Infants' Social Interaction

Mueller's sequence of infant's social interaction begins in the object-centered stage. Here two infants spend more of their time together interacting with objects rather than with each other. The second stage, simple interaction, has infants responding to each other and attempting to regulate each other's behaviors. For example, children may imitate each other or laugh at each other. The complementary interactive stage is the third and final stage for infants' social interaction. Children engage in reciprocal role relationships such as chaser and chased, giver and taker, and hider and seeker. This trend continues throughout the early preschool period.

Social Participation in Preschoolers

Preschoolers' social interaction with peers has been described by Parten (1932). She generally, suggested that children's social participation with their peers progressed in a three-stage sequence, from solitary interaction to parallel interaction to cooperative interaction. Briefly, solitary interaction has a solitary child involved with a prop, not a social partner. Parallel interaction has two children next to each interacting with similar props, but not with each other. Cooperative interaction is sustained reciprocal interaction. More current research suggests that these patterns of social participation were not stages per se, but strategies used by children in different situations. For example, parallel interaction is often used by young children to enter a group. Once they have gained access, they engage in cooperative interaction. If they were unsuccessful in gaining access, they may use parallel interaction again. For this reason, children who spend a significant portion of the time in parallel interaction may lack social skills necessary to sustain peer interaction.

THE EFFECTS OF TOYS

As peer configurations affect social competence, so too does the variety, type, and number of toys available to children. From infancy, as we saw with Mueller's work, toys affect children's interactions with their peers. Generally, infants and toddlers are more socially interactive with peers when toys are not present (Hartup, 1983), as toys may divert children's attention from peers. Similarly, behavior is seen in preschoolers. An early study by M. Johnson (1935, cited in Hartup, 1983) found that when the availability of toys was decreased children experienced *both* more positive and more negative interactions. The specific types of toys with which children interact also affect their social behavior. A number of naturalistic and experimental studies have shown that when children interact with art materials they engage in nonsocial play (i.e., parallel and solitary; Pellegrini, 1984; Pellegrini & Perlmutter, 1989). When these same children interacted with dramatic props (e.g., dress-up clothes) or blocks they more frequently exhibited social, or cooperative, interaction.

The effect of toys on children's behavior is not a direct one, however. The ways in which children play with toys depends in part on their age, gender, gender of their playmates, and the level of sex-role stereotype of the toys. For example, when 3-year-old girls play together with a male-preferred toy, such as large wooden blocks, their play behavior is *more* sophisticated than the play of 5-year-old girls with the same toys (Pellegrini & Perlmutter, 1989). Girls seem to learn at a young age that they should not exhibit competence with

male-preferred toys. The lesson here is that toys do not have an effect, independent of personal variables, on children's behavior.

Research on the effects of toys on older children's behavior is, generally, not
available (Hartup, 1983). By the time children enter elementary school they are
not expected to interact with toys during class time.

THE EFFECTS OF OTHERS

Peers and Adults

The number and type of people, both adults and children, in an area also affects
children's behavior. As noted in the chapter on school context, social and spatial
densities have potent affects on children's behavior. Research suggests that
parents often *inhibit* children's social interaction with peers (T. Field, 1979;
Pellegrini, 1984). Hartup (1983) suggested that adults inhibit children's peer
interaction when both peers and adults are present because children interact
with them, not with peers. Pellegrini (1984) found that as the number of adults
increased within preschool activity centers, children's social interaction generally decreased. In classroom settings adult presence may facilitate children's
attention to physical activities and tasks, not social interaction.

Peer presence, on the other hand, is facilitative of children's social interaction. In the same study (Pellegrini, 1984) it was found that as numbers of
children in activity centers increased, so too did children's social interaction.
The comparisons of adult presence and child presence on children's social
interaction seems to support the Piagetian hypothesis that peer presence may
facilitate development (i.e., eliciting more advanced forms of behavior),
whereas adult presence may inhibit development (i.e., inhibiting advanced
forms of behavior). Further, playmates' gender, as noted earlier, also affects
behavior.

The influence of peers on children's social behavior can be interpreted from
a social cognitive theory as well as a Piagetian perspective. Peers serve as
models and reinforcers for each other by giving positive attention, approval,
affection, and personal acceptance, and by submitting to each other's wishes.
Peers also serve as models for each other. However, both positive and negative
behaviors are modeled and subsequently learned from peers. Children tend to
imitate those peers most similar to themselves (Hartup & Coates, 1967, cited
in Hetherington & Parke, 1979). Further, children are more likely to imitate
those peers who are warm, rewarding, and powerful (Hetherington & Parke,
1979). The notion of peer similarity and mutual reinforcement seems to be a
powerful determinant of children's behavior. In the following section on
friendship we see how these dimensions also influence children's friendship
choices and the stability of those friendships.

Friends. If we look at the nature of the relationships between peers, we find that children act differently with friends than they do with nonfriends. We defined *friendships* as dyadic and reciprocal relationships where two children both agree that they are friends with each other. If only one child considers him- or herself to be friends with another child and that nomination is not reciprocated, they would not be considered friends (Hartup, 1983, 1989).

The bases for friendship change from the preschool period through adolescence. During the early childhood period, friendships are based on children's common activities and similar expectations (Bigelow, 1977). Thus children of this age will be friends if they enjoy playing with the same toys. Next, in about fourth and fifth grade, friendships are based on sharing similar values toward rules. Finally, in about fifth through seventh grade friendships are based on mutual understandings, self-disclosure, and continued shared interests.

Friends also tend to be physically similar to each other, especially for preadolescent children (Hartup, 1983). As a result, age, race, and gender have pervasive effects on friendship choices and maintenance. Children's friends are typically same-age, same-race, and same-gender. These patterns persist even in situations where heterogeneous groups exist (Hartup, 1983). Behavioral and attitudinal similarities and shared interests do not predict children's friendships as well as ages, race, and gender. Of course, these findings are embedded in dominant societal values that reward such affiliations.

On the global level, preschool-age children spend more of their free time with friends (Lewis, Young, Brooks, & Michalson, 1975). The quality of these interactions is also different to the extent that more positive exchanges and mutuality is found among friends. Additionally, their social pretend play is more complex, compared to the play between nonfriends (Howes, 1992). Friends give and receive more positive reinforcement than do other acquainted children. Further, when friends are observed in unfamiliar, anxiety-producing situations they tend to generate more verbalizations and are more socially involved (Schwartz, 1972, cited in Hartup, 1983). Groups of nonfriends observed in similar anxious situations seem more anxious to the extent that they produce less behavior. Among school-age children, friends, compared to nonfriends, are more interactive, affective, and mutually directive in a group task situation (Newcomb, Brady, & Hartup, 1979).

Interestingly, however, friends, compared to nonfriends, also disagree with each other more frequently (Hartup, 1996). This probably reflects their friends' confidence and trust in each other. Correspondingly, friends, compared to nonfriends, also resolve their disagreements. All this is to say that friends' interactions resemble Piaget's conflict—resolution cycles, which result in conceptual growth. Indeed, the scarce literature that does compare friends and nonfriends in learning contexts suggests that when friends are in learning groups, such as story writing, their products are more sophisticated than nonfriends (I. Jones & A. D. Pellegrini, 1996).

Children without a least one friend seem to have difficulty adjusting to school (Hartup, 1996). A friend probably provides a buffer against some of the difficulties that youngsters experience in school.

Popularity

Whereas friendship is a dyadic and reciprocal relationship, popularity is a group and unilateral measure (Bukowski & Hoza, 1989). Popularity, as we see later, is typically defined in terms of children nominating or rating their peers in terms to "liking" and "disliking" them. Children who are liked more than they are disliked are popular whereas children who are disliked more than liked are rejected. Children who are not nominated as being liked or disliked are considered neglected. So, hypothetically, children can be rejected but still have a friend and popular and not have any friends.

Generally, children who are rejected by their peers often are at risk for a number of subsequent problems, such as delinquency and dropping out of school (Parker & Asher, 1987). Oftentimes, although not always rejection, especially for boys, is due to aggression.

To conclude this section, friendship and popularity are two important indicators of social competence. They are sensitive indicators of what children's peers think of them. Difficulty in either area should be treated seriously, with follow-up examinations in other areas.

METHODS OF MEASURING SOCIAL COMPETENCE

In this section we examine different methods by which to examine and assess children's social competence. As noted at the beginning of the chapter we recommended using different methods of measurement to achieve the most accurate picture of children's competence. With specific reference to social competence, we suggested that children's ability to function adaptably in a social world involves both cognitive and affective–social processes. As such, both psychometric and observational assessment methods were recommended. Here we review both psychometric and observational approaches to measuring specific aspects of children's social competence: social problem solving, friendship, and popularity.

Social Problem Solving

An important aspect of social competence is children's ability to manage interpersonal problems. The social-problem-solving paradigm is useful in determining the extent to which children can use different strategies in different situations. The work of Spivack and Shure (1974) represents one psychometrically oriented approach to social problem solving. With this procedure children are presented with a *hypothetical* problem situation, such as acquiring a toy from another child without angering the present adult. Testers elicit children's varied strategies in such hypothetical situations. Children's responses to these situations are judged along five dimensions: the general alternate solutions; consideration of consequences of their actions and the articulation of consequences; step-by-step outline of goal reaching plan; sensitivity to interpersonal problems; and understanding other's motives. Although Spivack and Shure do not recommend differentiating between prosocial (e.g., "I'd ask him to play with the kite and offer my ball as a trade") and antisocial (e.g., "I'd hit him and take the kite") problem solutions, research suggests that such responses differentiate prosocial from antisocial children (e.g., D. S. Pellegrini, Masten, Garmezy, & Ferrarese, 1987).

Further, Krasnor and Rubin (1981) suggested that such hypothetical measures of social problem solving may not be related to children's ability to solve problems in their everyday world. They suggested observing children interacting with others in goal-directed situations. Children's social-problem-solving strategies in naturalistic settings can be evaluated on these criteria: object transfer, action, attention and acknowledgment, instruction and information, and defense.

Object transfer has children soliciting desired goods from others. Children can achieve this goal assertively (e.g., grabbing, demands, questions) or prosocially (e.g., giving other objects to others). Success involves possession of the desired goods.Actions have goals involving the solicitation of behaviors from others (e.g., asking someone to tie a shoe or to play with them). Success or failure is determined by others' compliance with the action verbalization. The action is prosocial if it is directed toward another person.

Attention and acknowledgment goals require a response from the target. For example, a child can say "Look at this" and elicit a response from another. Prosocial aspects of this category have children commenting on each another's work without solicitation.

Instructional and informational goals involve the seeking of information (e.g., What's the answer?) or direction (e.g., Where's the juice?). When this information is offered it is considered prosocial. Defensive goals involve the maintenance of possessions. Prosocial defensive goals exist when children want to help another person maintain his or her possessions.

A CASE STUDY OF SOCIAL PROBLEM SOLVING

Anna is a four-year-old in a weekly play group. Anna and her friend Bridget are enacting a dramatic play theme wherein they are both cooking dinner. Anna solicits Bridget by saying, "Please can I have that pan." Bridget responds by saying, "Sure, Anna," and handing Anna the pan. The social problem criteria for this event would be:

Objects transfer: Goods were solicited.

Outcome: Successful.

Measuring Popularity and Friendship

Although friendship (i.e., a close dyadic relationship) and popularity (i.e., liked by members of a group) are quite distinct, we will not dwell on the conceptual differences (See Bukowski & Hoza, 1989, for a thorough discussion). *Sociometry* refers to the process of describing the interpersonal attraction among members of a group (Renshaw, 1981). The "classical" sociometric procedure developed by Moreno (1951) is known as the nominating of partial-rank-order procedure. This method involves asking children a number of questions relevant to a group's activities. An example of a question might be: With whom would you like to do homework? This type of question might be used to determine children's status in school-related activities, or popularity, as well as the specific children who choose to affiliate with each other, or friendship. For out-of-school activities, one might ask: With whom would you like to spend your next weekend? In short, questions asked should be relevant to specific contexts.

Popularity.   Popularity is a general measure of how well-liked a child is and can be measured using peer rating or nomination procedures. Peer-rating scales, like that displayed in Table 10.2, typically list all of the children in a group, such as a classroom, and have each student rate all of his or her peers on a scale of 1 to 5. This technique can be used like the traditional sociometric technique to measure different types of group structure; for example, homework groups, sports groups, or general popularity within the classroom.

Nomination procedures involve asking children to name those children they like and those they dislike. To promote an accurate inventory of all children in the class, this procedures typically begins with children being shown pictures of all of the members of their class (e.g., class roster or Polaroids are used), and asked to name each. Children are then asked to nominate three children they "Like the Most" and three children they "Don't Like." As noted earlier popular children are those who have more Likes than Dislikes nominations. Rejected children have more Disliked than Liked, and controversial children have equivalent numbers of both Likes and Dislikes. Neglected children are not nominated.

There may be some concern with asking children to identify those they don't like. Do children, after these procedures, treat those nominated as being disliked differently than before? Do they talk about those children nominated as dis-

TABLE 10.2
Peer Rating Scale

	Like Lots	Like	Not Sure	Don't Like	Really Don't Like
Child	5	4	3	2	1
John					
Harry					
Susan					
Quinn					
Nigel					
Dave					
Sarah					
Anna					
Jenifer					
Michael					

liked? Although very little research has been conducted in this sensitive area, the procedure does not seem to affect children's subsequent treatment. Children know very well who it is they like and dislike and given one opportunity to restate that does not seem to change things much.

Friendship.   Friendship should be assessed at three levels, according to Bukowski and Hoza (1989). First, the extent to which specific children have dyadic friendships should be determined. Second, the number of such dyadic relationships should be determined. Third, the quality of the relationships should be determined. In measuring the first dimension of friendship, either rating scales or nominations could be used to determine the extent to which children have dyadic friendships; children must rate each other similarly (i.e., 4 or above on a 5-point scale), nominate each other as friends, or both.

Second, the number of dyadic relationships that meet the aforementioned criteria can be used to document the extent of children's friendships. Third, quality of friendship can be assessed by asking children open-ended questions about friends such as, What makes him or her fun to be with?, close-ended questions such as, How often does he or she help you when you have too much to do?, or both (Berndt, Hawkins, & Hoyle, 1986).

CONCLUSION

In this chapter we have examined children's social competence because the construct represents the processes children must use in order to be a functioning member of society. Further, the notion of social competence includes both social and cognitive behavioral measures. As we have noted in many different places in this book, children's social and cognitive processes are not separate phenomena; they influence each other and should both be considere together in child study.

We have examined two major contexts in which children acquire social competence: the family and the peer group. Of course other institutions, such as school, affect children's social competence. We also outlined different ways in which social competence could be measured. Following the recommendation stressed throughout the book, we suggest using both psychometric and observational methodologies.

11

Children's Play

We dedicate a separate chapter to children's play because we think it represents the quintessential developmental activity. Play is what young children do, and in some ways play sets off childhood from later developmental periods. Indeed, some scholars in the area of animal behavior consider all activities that juveniles engage in play (see Fagen, 1981, 1998, for reviews)! Consequently, observations of children at play provide the investigator with insight into child competence in a number of areas (e.g., communication skills, role taking, cooperation, motor coordination). As noted in our chapter on development, however, play can be viewed as an imperfect version of mature behaviors that must be learned.

The notion that play is used in the assembly of skills and is disassembled when the skill is mastered has been labeled the *scaffolding* view of play (Bateson, 1981) and is consistent with the theories of Piaget and Vygotsky. For example, the role of pretend play would be an aid to children's learning adult societal roles.

On the other hand, when play is considered to be important to the niche of childhood and not an imperfect version of adult behavior it is considered *metamorphic* (Bateson, 1981). For example, pretend play during childhood relates to a child's sense of potency and self-efficacy during a period when he or she is often confronted with his inability to do things. This confidence motivates children to persevere at various tasks.

Second, play can be used as an instructional mode. Again, the distinction between scaffolding and metamorphic views of play is crucial to maintain. Play is often used in the former sense as a way of teaching skills and concepts. For example, pretend play is often used as a way in which to teach reading and writing (Christie, 1991; A. D. Pellegrini & Galda, 1993). Alternatively, play can be encouraged in school as a way in which children gain confidence and skill.

In this chapter children's play is defined and examined in terms of its role in applied settings, primarily school. Further, a number of methods for categorizing and analyzing children's play are outlined.

WHAT IS PLAY?

Play is most generally defined in terms of activity serving no immediate purpose, although as noted earlier, some consider all behavior exhibited by juveniles to be play. For example, an activity is considered play if it is not serious, is an exaggerated version of its functional equivalent, or where means of an activity are stressed over the ends. In this section, we explore definitions of play suggested by Rubin, Fein, and Vandenburg (1983). They defined play along three dimensions: as psychological disposition, according to contexts that elicit playful behaviors, and as observable behavior. These dimensions are summarized in Table 11.1.

Play as Disposition

The six dispositional criteria include: intrinsic motivation, attention to means, the "What can I do with this" disposition, nonliteral behaviors, flexibility, and active engagement. The intrinsic motivation criterion for play suggests that children play because they want to, not because of appetite drives, social demands, or rewards external to the play act per se. Vygotsky's theory provides

TABLE 11.1
Dimensions of Play

1. Play as disposition
   a. Intrinsic motivation
   b. Attention to means
   c. "What can I do with it?"
   d. Nonliteral
   e. Flexibility
   f. Active engagement
2. Play as context
   a. Familiar
   b. Free choice
   c. Stress-free
3. Play as observable behavior
   a. Functional
   b. Fymbolic
   c. Games with rules

some guidance as to what motivates children to play: The sense of mastery and potency in much of children's play, especially fantasy play, is a motivator.

It is difficult to observe intrinsic motivation, however, and this may partially responsible for the fact that neither children nor adults use it as a criterion to differentiate play from nonplay (P. K. Smith & Volstedt, 1985).

Attention to means is related to intrinsic motivation to the extent that the play behaviors are self-imposed and free from external sanctions; children are more concerned with the playful acts themselves than with the outcomes of those acts. To use an adult-oriented example here, swimming would be playful if the adult enjoyed the act of swimming. It would be less playful if it were done primarily to stay slim. The means over ends criterion, however, does presents an interesting problem: How can play simultaneously serve important functions and but not be concerned with ends, or function? It may be that play serves no immediate function but does serve a function deferred until adulthood. This view is consistent with the scaffolding metaphor of play.

The "What can I do with it?" disposition is prevalent. As such, play is person-directed, whereas exploration is stimulus-directed. Children must explore stimuli before they can play with them. That is, in order to play with something, we must first be familiar with the stimuli. Exploration serves this familiarization function. The path from exploration to play is evidenced both ontogenetically and microgenetically.

Ontogenetically, infants up to about $7^1/_2$ months explore objects. After that time play accounts for increasing proportions of time, until at about 15 months infants spend close to equal time in exploration and play. Thereafter, however, play displaces explorations (Belsky & Most, 1981).

Microgenetically, or the development within a specific task, we find that when presented with a new or novel toy or tasks, children explore that stimulus before they play with it (Rubin et al., 1983). From an assessment perspective this continuum is relevant: It is imperative that children be familiar with toys before we assess their ability to play with them. Very often the toys we use in assessment contexts are unfamiliar to certain groups of children. So as not to artificially suppress children's exhibition of competence we should take care to use familiar stimuli.

Nonliteral behaviors suggest that children use an "as if" disposition to simulate, or represent, other persons, activities, or objects in play. This criterion limits play to acts of pretense, or make-believe. However, pretense play might be considered the paradigm example of play in that children and adults alike use it as a defining attribute of play (P. K. Smith & Vollstedt, 1985).

The flexibility criterion differentiates play from games with externally defined rules. Play is rule-governed but the rules are constructed within the play event by players and the rules are subject to change during play episodes. For example, in playing house children have rules about the ways in which mothers and fathers behave. These rules, however, are defined by the children during play and are subject to change. Children often disagree about rules during play and renegotiate the rules. Games with rules, like checkers, on the other hand, have permanent, predetermined rules.

Play is characterized by children's active engagement with objects and other players. Players themselves choose the activities they participate in and then define the nature of their interaction in that activity. That is, they are not passive participants in activities to the extent that they redefine objects and roles. They do not play with these stimuli in ways specified by predetermined rules.

These play criteria should be used to categorize the degree to which children's activities are playful. Thus, behaviors meeting three criteria would be more playful than those meeting one or two (Krasnor & Pepler, 1980). As a result, play can be categorized as "more or less play," not dichotomously as "play or not play." Behaviors meeting all criteria might be categorized as "pure play," whereas behaviors with fewer components are "less purely play." Simply put, acts should not be categorized as "play" or "not play"; they should be rated along a continuum from "pure play" to "nonplay."

Play as Context

Play can also be defined according to contexts that typically evoke playful behavior (Rubin et al., 1983). Although this set of criteria confounds the situations in which play is observed with the behaviors themselves, context can be useful in determining if a behavior is playful or not. For example, a behavior observed on a playground is more likely to be play than one in a school study hall. Such "relational" criteria in defining play (Martin & Bateson, 1993) are, however, limited. Obviously, not everything on the playground is play; it might be aggression, for example.

Relational criteria can be useful, however, in determining those dimensions of contexts that support play. Familiar peers and play props that actively engage children are usually present in play-eliciting contexts. As was noted in the section on play as disposition, children must explore, or become familiar, with stimuli before they play with them. Further, children in play-eliciting contexts often are free to choose the activities in which they engage. Thus, adult intervention in play-eliciting contexts is minimum. If children are to engage actively with peers and materials they must be free from stress. Stress can be caused by hunger, fatigue, illness, and the presence of unfriendly adults, peers, or both.In short, play occurs in safe, comfortable contexts. For this reasons, the presence of play can be used as a gauge of the quality of an environment. Quality environments are those where children exhibit playful behaviors. Low-quality environments inhibit play.

Play as Observable Behavior

The behaviors comprising this definition are based on Piaget's (1962) observations of children's play. The observable categories of play according to this model are practice or functional play, symbolic play, and games with rules. Research has documented these play categories as hierarchic (A. D. Pellegrini, 1980; Rubin & Maioni, 1975). That is, they occur in this specified order. Indeed, these categories correspond to Piaget's sensorimotor, preoperational, and concrete operational forms of intelligence, respectively.

In this model of play as observable behavior, Piaget (1962) conceived of play primarily as assimilation; that is, in play, children incorporate stimuli into existent cognitive schema with minimal changes in those schema. Play behaviors are immature forms of their adult variants. Play helps children, through consolidation, to move toward operational intelligence. As such, play, as conceptualized by Piaget, does not lead development because children are minimally accommodating to external stimuli during play; play serves a consolidating role.

In practice play, children detach functional motor behaviors from the contexts in which they were developed by way of combinations, repetitions, and variations of these behaviors (e.g., reaching for and grasping of different objects).

In symbolic play, children practice using representational media (e.g., gestures or words) to designate real events, persons, or both. They are exercising their semiotic, or representational, skills in symbolic play. In games with rules, children practice obeying externally imposed rules. Such subordination to external rules assumes operational thought because children must subordinate their behavior to abstract, externally imposed rules.

In this chapter we use the play as observable behavior criteria as a method of analyzing children's play.

CATEGORIZING PLAY

In this chapter, Piaget's (1962) model of play as observable behavior is used as a way of categorizing cognitive aspects of play. In addition, we use an adaptation of Parten's (1932) social participation system to categorize social aspects of play. The model of categorizing play to be presented here is useful in ranking the relative maturity of different forms of play. Investigators can use the system to gauge children's social-cognitive status. The model to be presented in this section is most useful with preschool and kindergarten children to the extent that most of its categories (e.g., functional, constructive, and dramatic) are observed during those periods. For primary school children's play, another form tends to be observed: rough-and-tumble (R & T) play, which is discussed later in the chapter.

Piaget's observations of children's play formed the basis of a four-category system used by Smilansky (1968) and Rubin (Rubin & Maioni, 1975) to categorize cognitive aspects of children's play: practice, or functional, constructive, dramatic, and games with rules. These terms, you will remember, were defined in the play as observable behavior subsection. Although Piaget did not consider construction as play (because it was primarily accommodative; e.g., P. K. Smith, Takhvar, Gore, & Vollstedt, 1985), it is still useful as a way in which to look at children in classroom environments.

Children's playful behaviors can simultaneously be categorized according along a social dimension, as suggested by Parten (1932) and further developed by Rubin and his colleagues (e.g., Rubin, Maioni, & Hornung, 1976) as follows: unoccupied behavior, solitary play, parallel play, associative play, and cooperative play. Unoccupied behavior has children alone, not actively engaged. In solitary play children are actively involved with materials but they do not seek out other children. Parallel play has children engaged in an activity near other children but not interacting with them. Associative play, a form of social play, has children interacting with each other in a group for short periods of time; group composition, however, changes frequently in associative play. For example, three children may start off playing, but children frequently leave and rejoin other groups. Cooperative play involves children interacting with others in a common activity for a sustained period.

Observers of children's play have found it difficult to differentiate reliably between associative and cooperative interaction. To eliminate this reliability problem it is suggested that observers combine these two categories into one interactive category.

The cognitive and social categories should be used to complement each other. That is, they can be combined into a social–cognitive matrix wherein both the cognitive and social aspect of children's play can be simultaneously described (Rubin et al., 1976). This matrix is depicted in Table 11.2. Constructive play can be solitary, parallel, or interactive.

By categorizing both cognitive and social aspects of play simultaneously, the observer gains more information about the cognitive and social value of playful acts. For example, an observer utilizing only the cognitive criteria would categorize a child repeatedly playing Superman alone as dramatic play. As is seen in the section on correlates of play, preschoolers who engage primarily in dramatic play are usually more mature than children who engage primarily in functional and constructive play. Thus, an observer might conclude, mistakenly, that this child's play is relatively mature. These conclusions would be misleading, however, because the observer did not consider the social aspects of the child's behavior as well as the cognitive aspects. Mature preschoolers typically engage in cooperative not solitary-dramatic play (Rubin & Clark, 1982). Indeed, children who engage in solitary-dramatic play, as opposed to interac-

TABLE 11.2
Social–Cognitive Play Matrix

Child's name _____ Date _____ Context _____

Others present _____

	Functional	Constructive	Dramatic	Games–Rules
Solitary				
Parallel				
Interactive				

tive-dramatic play, are less advanced on other social-cognitive measures. However, certain types of solitary play, such as solitary-constructive, have been shown to be better predictors of social-cognitive performance than measures of interactive play (Rubin, 1982), thus the importance of considering both cognitive and social dimensions of play.

Psychometric Qualities of the Play Matrix

We advocated the use of this system to evaluate children's cognitive and social developmental status. If play is to be used as an instructional mode, it is incumbent on educators to show the efficacy of this method. More specifically, it should be documented how children's play relates to other, more traditional, measures of educational attainment. Only by systematic assessment can educators gauge the worth of children's play. A reliable and valid assessment form is needed for this documentation.

In this section we outline the psychometric qualities of the cognitive–social play matrix outlined in the preceding section. A reliable and valid assessment instrument is an important part of any assessment procedure. First we examine its reliability, then its validity.

As we noted in other chapters, an assessment instrument must be reliable in order to be valid. Because we are discussing an observational instrument, interrater reliability is an important attribute. By interrater reliability we mean the extent to which two or more people observing the same behaviors agree on what they see. For example, two people observing a child playing Batman with another child should agree on the child's behavior as dramatic interactive. Interrater agreement is typically expressed in terms of percentage of agreement or correlation coefficients scores between observers. For example, two observers each categorized 100 instances of the same child's play; their categorizations were the same for 95 and different for 5 of these behaviors. Therefore, the observers have a 95% (95/100) interrater reliability for that one set of observations.

High interrater (80%–100%) reliability scores are necessary before the measures can be considered valid. Simply put, two or more people must consistently agree on what they actually see before any statement can be made about what the behaviors mean. Researchers have consistently had high interrater agreement for the cognitive play categories in the matrix. The observers in Rubin's studies had 95% agreement for the cognitive categories (Rubin & Maioni, 1975; Rubin et al., 1976); the observers in the Pellegrini (1980) studies had 84% agreement.

Interrater agreement statistics for the social categories vary. Rubin et al. (1976) reported 95% agreement. Fein, Moorin, and Enslein (1982) noted the problem of observers being able to reliably differentiate associative from cooperative play. However, when the associative and cooperative categories are combined into the interactive play category, interrater agreement for the three categories (solitary, parallel, and interactive) is typically high—93% (Pellegrini, 1982a). As noted, for reasons of improved reliability we recommend using only those three categories.

High reliability alone, however, is no guarantee that the measurement will be valid. Validity is defined as the truthfulness of the measure: Are we measuring what we say we are measuring? Three types of validity—construct, concurrent, and predictive—are relevant to our discussion of using the social–cognitive matrix to assess the relations between children's play and educational attainment. Construct validity refers to an instrument's ability to measure psychological qualities. The construct validity of our matrix refers to the hierarchic structure of the play categories. More specifically, if the cognitive categories have construct validity, children consistently observed in the lower categories on the matrix should be at a lower level of cognitive development than children observed at higher levels. Similarly, younger, less developed children should be observed more frequently than older children in the lower categories.

Separate studies of the construct validity of the cognitive and social categories have been made. Generally, research supports the hierarchic structure of the cognitive categories functional, dramatic, and games, but questions the hierarchic structure of the social categories. For example, kindergartners' cognitive levels of play were found by Pellegrini (1980) to be hierarchic. In this observational study, kindergartners' free play was categorized according to Smilansky's (1968) cognitive categories. Children's performance on the Metropolitan Readiness Test (MRT) was used as a measure of their cognitive achievement. Children who most frequently engaged in dramatic play scored highest on the MRT; children who most frequently engaged in constructive play scored lower on the MRT than dramatic players but higher than functional players. These results support the notion that more sophisticated cognitive skills are required to engage in higher forms of cognitive play, as measured by the Smilansky categories.

The work of other researchers further supports the hierarchic structure of these cognitive categories. Rubin and his colleagues have shown that as children mature they more frequently engage in higher forms of cognitive play and less frequently engage in lower forms (see Rubin, Fein, & Vandenberg, 1983, for a summary). For example, functional play accounts for 53% of the free play of children between 14 and 30 months of age, whereas it accounts for only 14% of the free play of children 6 to 7 years of age. Similarly, at 3½ years of age constructive play comprises 40% of children's free play, whereas at 6 to 7 years of age it comprises 51% of free play. As noted earlier, however, P. K. Smith and his colleagues (P. K. Smith et al., 1985; P. K. Smith & Vollstedt, 1985) question the place of constructive activities in the play hierarchy. They noted, first, that Piaget (1962) viewed constructive play as primarily accommodative and, therefore, not play. Second, they reported that a number of studies have failed to show consistent age-related changes for preschool children's constructive play. They recommended that more research be conducted on this issue before we disregard the place of constructive activities in this play hierarchy. This brief discussion of the hierarchic nature of the cognitive categories indicates that the categories may have construct validity. Categorizations of the cognitive aspects of children's play to can be used to make inferences about cognitive status. We recommend, however, that observers use both cognitive and social criteria of play before making evaluations of children's cognitive status.

Parten (1932) originally suggested that the social categories were hierarchic. She stated that solitary and parallel play decreased between 2 and 4½ years of age, whereas group play increased. More recent research, however, indicates that solitary play alone is not an indicator of immaturity (Moore, Evertson, & Brophy, 1974; Rubin, 1982). For example, some children who frequently engage in solitary play may be doing educational and goal-directed activities during this time (Moore et al., 1974). Further, the difficulties involved in differentiating associative from cooperative play raises reliability problems with Parten's categories. As previously noted, a more reliable method of coding social interaction is to group associative and cooperative in an interactive play category. We recommend using the three aforementioned social categories: solitary, parallel, and interactive. This system does seem to have construct validity. This is, older preschoolers tend to engage in more social and less nonsocial play than younger preschoolers during free play (A. D. Pellegrini, 1982a).

Another problem with Parten's (1932) original model was her conception of parallel interaction; it was thought to be a behavior indicating a stage of children's social development. Research suggests that parallel play is not a stage (Bakeman & Brownlee, 1980). It has been suggested that children use parallel play as a strategy to enter a group. For example, if a child wants to join a group playing with blocks, he or she might start playing with blocks next to that group. In their way he or she can more readily initiate a response to social overtures.

The social–cognitive matrix categories also have concurrent validity. That is, they are significantly related to other measures of school performance. The strength of the relations between social-cognitive aspects of children's play and other performances measures (e.g., scores on reading achievement tests) determine the use of the matrix as a complementary form of assessment. More specifically, if children's play is significantly related to school performance measures, childrens play ratings can be used as a complementary form of assessment.

Finally, we are concerned with predictive validity, or the extent to which measures of play in this matrix accurately predict children's behavior. The longitudinal research that has been conducted suggests that predictive relations exist between kindergartners' play behavior (e.g., parallel-constructive) and first-grade sociometric status (Rubin & Daniels-Beirness,1983).

To conclude, the play matrix outlined earlier has strong psychometric properties while also being extremely usable.

Relations Between Play as Measured on the Play Matrix and School Performance

Aspects of children's play have been correlated with their performance on both cognitive and social measures. Rubin and Maioni (1975) found significant relations between preschoolers' cognitive play styles and their classification and spatial abilities. Preschoolers who engaged in functional play, an immature form of play for this age group, tended to do poorly on classification and spatial tasks. Children who engaged primarily in dramatic play, on the other hand, tended to do well on both classification and spatial tasks.

Pellegrini's (1980) observations of kindergartners' free play, as previously described, are consistent with the results of Rubin and Maioni (1975): Children who played at higher levels of the cognitive play continuum tended to score higher on measures of school-related achievement (i.e., reading readiness, school language, and word-writing fluency).

Rubin and Clark (1982) have utilized the social–cognitive matrix to further describe relations between play and other cognitive measures. In this study they were interested in the relations between nonsocial (solitary and parallel) play and one measure of cognitive performance: the number of simple and complex blocks constructions. Solitary-functional, parallel-constructive, and parallel-dramatic play tended to relate positively to the building of less complex blocks structures. Thus, it seems as though those children who engaged in solitary-functional and parallel play were cognitively less advanced than children who engaged in solitary-constructive play.

The importance of using both cognitive and social categories should be evident from the results discussed thus far. Using only the cognitive categories may mislead the observer to the extent that a particular form of cognitive play could be classified as more or less mature, depending on the social category in which it is embedded.

Children's social competence is also an important index of educational attainment. Indeed, in President Clinton's 1997 State of the Union address he stressed the role of values in education. Children in schools, he emphasized, should learn how to interact cooperatively with peers and adults and rely less on aggression to solve social problems. As such, educators should be concerned with children's social competence. Children's play, as measured by the matrix, is related to measures of social competence.

Rubin (1982; Rubin & Clark, 1982; Rubin & Daniels-Beirness,1983) examined the relations between preschoolers' play and different aspects of their social competence. He found that preschoolers engaging in solitary-functional or solitary-dramatic play also tended to be unpopular and rated as hyperactive and anxious-fearful, respectively, as rated on Behar and Stringfield's (1976) instrument. Parallel-dramatic play also related to children being rated as anxious, fearful, and hyperactive by their teachers.

These data continue to support the notion that preschoolers tending to engage in functional and parallel play may be at a lower level in terms of their general social competence. The relatively easy-to-use, but psychometrically powerful, observational instrument displayed in Table 11.3 should be used as a first step in the assessment of children. If children do seem to engage in functional and parallel play, further assessment may be needed. In addition, those working with children should be taught to use this observational system as an adjunct to their usual battery of criterion- and norm-referenced assessments. As we all know, the more measures of students' behavior we have, the more valid will be our conclusions.

Using the Matrix in Classrooms

We are advocating the use of the matrix as an adjunct to other forms of assessment. The extent to which an assessment instrument can be used in applied settings depends on both its technical and usability qualities. We recommend, first, that a number of blank copies of the matrix be run off. Then the teacher should set off time, say once a week, where he or she or an aid "scan" the classroom using a separate sheet for each child. (see chap. 6, on observational methods, for a more detailed description of scan sampling.) The separate observations for each child across the school year should be kept in a file and used for assessment and evaluation.

The instrument, unlike many other forms of assessment, is also usable. Teachers do not have to undergo extensive training in order to use the matrix reliably. In addition, the results of the assessment do not have to be sent to a publisher or to a psychologist to be scored or interpreted.

Preservice and in-service professionals can be trained to use this instrument reliably after only 2 hours of instruction. After discussing definitions and examples of each category, students should try to code videotapes of children interacting in different settings. The use of a coding sheet (such as the one depicted in Table 11.3) for each child in each distinct observation makes the task easier.

Children should be observed during free play time when they are free to interact with the peers and activities of their choice. The observer should decide on the time intervals at which to code the children's behavior. As noted earlier, the observer can scan a separate child every 5 seconds until the whole classroom is observed. This procedures could be repeated weekly.

Alternatively, the observer may choose to sample individual children's play in more depth, coding one child's behavior every 10 seconds or every minute during the whole free play period. At each time interval the observer should record on the matrix the social-cognitive aspect of play exhibited by the child. These recordings should occur at each time interval (e.g., every minute, for the whole free-play period). Only one child's behavior should be coded on one sheet for each observation; the observer may need 15 observation sheets to observe one child at 1-minute intervals for a 15-minute free-play period. After these preparatory conditions have been met the observation can begin.

The observer should place an X in the box describing the child's behavior at the specific observational time intervals; separate sheets should be used. The coding of content and number of other children present is important to the extent that these two factors can influence children's play behaviors (A. D. Pellegrini, 1984a). For example, art materials and puzzles typically elicit constructive-solitary play from children. Further, when children, are playing with blocks by

TABLE 11.3
A Case Study of Using the Play Matrix

Child's Name: Jack   Date: 10/22/98   Block Context
Others present: Frank, Sam

	Functional	Constructive	Dramatic	Games–Rules
Solitary				
Parallel				
Interactive			X	

Note. This is an example of one observation in a time sampling observation of play.

themselves, they will probably play constructively. However, when two or more children are present, they will probably engage in dramatic play. As such, context, in addition to developmental status, may influence children's social-cognitive behaviors. Thus, the observer should observe children in many different contexts before making conclusions about their social-cognitive status.

By way of warning, this matrix is most useful for observing preschool children during indoor play. It is less useful with older children and for outdoor play as much of what children do, such as chasing and play fighting, is not stressed in the matrix.

Further, the number of times we observe children is also an important factors. As we noted in an earlier chapter, the more observations, or samples, of behavior we have the more likely we will be able to describe the activity of interest. First, we recommend that a number of observations should be conducted within 1 day. Second, we should observe a child across a number of days.

ANALYZING PLAY ACROSS THE PERIOD OF CHILDHOOD

In this section we analyze in more depth those forms of play which are most common during the period of childhood, symbolic play and physically vigorous play.

Symbolic Play

Symbolic, or pretend, play is defined as non literal play, where one thing represents something else. Pretend, as noted earlier, can be either social or solitary and begins during the second year of life, often in the context of mother–child play. The play of securely, compared to insecurely, attached children with mother is more sophisticated. This basis in adult play may provide the base from which children play with peers. At around 3 years children are capable of sustaining pretend play with peers. Pretend peaks during the late preschool period, and then declines (Rubin et al., 1983). It accounts for about one third of children's free behavior at 5 years of age, although girls engage in pretense, particularly play following domestic themes, more frequently and at more sophisticated levels than boys (Rubin et al., 1983).

More specifically, in pretend play children have one thing represent another thing. For example, a broom can represent a horse. These representation often are part of a larger play theme enactment. For example, using a broom to represent a horse might be part of enacting a cowboy episode.

The ways in which children represent objects in play can be classified along two dimensions: object and ideational transformations. These two dimensions indicate the extent to which children's symbolic play transformations are dependent on objects (object transformations) or independent of objects (ideational transformations). For example, an object transformation might involve a child holding a baby doll and singing to it. An ideational transformation, on the other hand, might involve a child cradling an invisible baby in her or his arms and singing to it; no object is present. By 3 years of age children are quite facile in using ideation transformations in their play. McLoyd's (1980) categorization of object and ideational transformations, displayed in the following, should provide some concrete example into the dimensions of these categories. We have added to this scheme, breaking down further dimensions of roles, as outlined by Garvey (1990).

OBJECT AND IDEATIONAL TRANSFORMATIONS

Object Transformation (McLoyd, 1980)

1. Animation: Giving inanimate objects living attributes. For example, a child says about a stuffed animal "My doggie's going for a walk."
2. Reification: "Reifying an imaginary object which is functionally related to an existing object" (p. 1135); for example, a child pretends to drink out of an empty cup and says "This soda's good."
3. Attribution of object property: An object property is attributed to an existent or imaginary object that is functionally related to a real object. For example, a child makes a bang sound while firing a plastic gun.
4. Substitution: An existing object is given a new identity. For example, a child says about a block, "This is my car."

Ideational Transformations

5. Object realism: Pretends an imaginary object exists. The imaginary object, however, bears no resemblance to the signified object. For example, a child says, "I'm using this brush as the lawnmower to cut the grass."
6. Attribution of nonexistent object property: A nonexistent object is given a property. For example, a child says, "I'm taking my vitamin" as he takes a nonexistent pill.
7. Situation attribution: Pretends a make-believe situation exists. For example, "O.K., this is the doctor's office."
8. Role attribution: Portrays a fantasy role. For example, "I'll be the nurse.
8a. Types of roles played (Garvey, 1990):
    i. Functional roles are defined by actions played; they are animate but not necessarily human. For example, a child playing with a truck might play at being a driver.
    ii. Character roles can be stereotyped or fictional. Stereotypic roles relate, primarily, to occupation; for example, a cowboy. Fictional roles usually have proper names and appear on TV or in literature; for example, Batman.
    iii. Family roles are enactments of family members and usually occur in pairs. These roles can also coincide with functional roles. For example, a mother can serve the meal.

The role categories suggested by Garvey are not hierarchic. That is, one role does not seem to be more difficult to enact than another. Children do, however, tend to enact family roles most frequently and enact gender-appropriate roles. For example, boys play fathers, whereas girls play mothers. Within gender-appropriate roles, older children tend to play higher status roles (e.g., mother) whereas younger children play lower status roles (e.g., daughter; Garvey, 1977).

The way in which children weave individual play transformations into a coherent play episode also should be considered. Generally, very young children's play episodes are at the level of a single scheme, such as "This is my baby," and then break down. With age and increased linguistic and social skills, children's themes become integrated into longer, more cooperative themes (Wolf & Grollman, 1982).

Factors Effecting Symbolic Play.

As noted earlier, girls, compared to boys, are more facile in pretend players, as are securely attached, compared to insecurely attached, children. At a more macrosystem level, we find that factors such as the value placed on play by society and its institutions, such as school boards, has an obvious effect. Play is more frequent and more sophisticated in those settings where it is valued.

At the level of culture, we find few differences between the play of African American and European American children. Where differences do exist, they are often due to the unfamiliarity of the setting, props, or both, and when children are given opportunities to become familiar, differences are minimized (McLoyd, 1982).

At a more microlevel, the props that children play with affects the extent to which they will use object–ideational transformations and the level of theme integration. Generally, children's play follows the themes suggested by the toys with which they are playing. However, with props that do not have a clear definition, or functionally ambiguous props, such as pipe cleaners and Styrofoam shapes, preschoolers use more ideational than object transformation (A. D. Pellegrini, 1987a). The reason is straightforward. The props have no explicit function, so children do not depend on them for their make-believe play.

Functionally explicit props (e.g., dolls), on the other hand, tend to elicit more sustained fantasy themes (A. D. Pellegrini, 1987a). It may be that preschoolers' limited cognitive resources result in their inability to transfer an ambiguous prop (e.g., verbally redefine it) *and* weave that prop into a complex theme. With explicit props, the first step is done for them to the extent that the props do not need to be redefined.

Outcomes of Pretend Play.

Numerous benefits have been associated with pretend play. As noted earlier, many theories of play predict deferred, not immediate, benefits; however, most of the studies have only examined benefits during childhood. Further, many of the positive benefits associated with pretend, such as increased creativity and more creative solutions to problems were due to experimenter bias, not play (P. K. Smith, 1988). There is evidence, however, that preschool children's use of abstract play transformations relates to their subsequent ability to write individual words (Galda, A. D. Pellegrini, & Cox, 1989). Both individual word writing and symbolic representation are example of first-order symbolization (Vygotsky, 1978) where symbols represent concrete entities. Further, during social pretend, children talk about cognitive and linguistic processes, such as "Doctors can't say that." This ability to talk about language and thought is evidence of children's metacognitive and metalingustic abilities, which in turn are related to reading.

Physical Activity Play

As children move into primary school they are given fewer opportunities to play. What opportunities they are given are typically in the from of recess on the playground (A. D. Pellegrini & P. K. Smith, 1998). Play opportunities beyond preschool are usually limited, because educators think that they interfere with the primary business of schooling, learning the three Rs. As we noted earlier, this is a limited view of schooling in that even the President of the United States is stressing the role of social skills in schools. Play at recess across the school years may provide some of the few opportunities youngsters have to interact with peers. These opportunities are very important in children's social competence, as we discussed in chapter 10.

In this section of the chapter we describe the forms of play that children exhibit on the playground during recess as well as examining factors that affect them. Finally, we note some of the benefits associated with those forms of play.

Although preschool and kindergarten children's play can be captured rather well using the four-level scheme of functional, constructive, dramatic, and games, it does not account for most of what elementary school children do when they play. Play for this group of children typically occurs outdoors at recess. A significant portion of that play, especially for boys, is physically vigorous and can take the form of chase, rough-and-tumble play (R & T), and games. We suggest that R&T is the form of play that acts as a bridge between social pretend and games with rules.

Gross motor play is a basic form of physical activity and includes chase, run, jump, swing, and so forth. For children in the late preschool and early primary school periods, this form of behavior accounts for 15 to 20% of their free-play behavior (McGrew, 1972a; P. K. Smith & Connolly, 1980).

Also about this time play is becoming much more social. R&T is that form of physical activity play which has social dimensions. The term R & T was first used in behavioral science by Harlow (1962; Harlow & Harlow, 1962) to describe the playful, quasi-agonistic behaviors of rhesus monkeys. Since that time a group of human ethologists, lead by Blurton Jones (1972b, 1976) and P. K. Smith (P. K. Smith & Connolly, 1980) have provided extensive behavior and structural descriptions of the category. R & T is characterized by the following behaviors: run, jump, flee, wrestle, and open hand beat. Structurally, R & T involves children engaging in reciprocal role taking (Fagen, 1981; A. Humphreys & P. K. Smith, 1984). For example, in chase, children typically alternate between the chaser and chased, and in play fighting, aggressor victim roles are alternated. Regarding the functional or consequential criterion, children remain together at the conclusion of R & T bouts, often engaging in other forms of social play like cooperative games, (A. D. Pellegrini, 1988). Ecologically, R & T tends to occur out of doors, on soft, grassy surfaces (A. Humphreys & P. K. Smith, 1984, A. D. Pellegrini, 1989a). Importantly, R & T and aggression are distinct behaviors for most children; the exception being aggressive boys (A. D. Pellegrini, 1988, 1995).

Like other forms of play, R & T follows in inverted U-development function: Accounting for 5% of preschool free-play behavior, increasing to around 10 to 13% at 7 years of age and declining to about 5% again for 11-year-olds (A. D. Pellegrini & P. K. Smith, 1998). Boys engage in R & T more frequently than girls (e.g., A. D. Pellegrini, 1989a; A. D. Pellegrini & P. K. Smith, 1998; Whiting & Edwards, 1973).

R & T is a controversial category because of its frequent confusion with aggression. Close examination, however, illustrates clear distinctions between R & T and aggression. Behaviorally, aggression is composed of the following behaviors (which are independent of R & T in most children): fixate, frown, hit (closed hand), push, task-and-grab. These behaviors, unlike play, are stable through childhood (Olweus, 1979). Structurally, aggression is characterized by unilateral, not reciprocal roles: Aggressors remain aggressors and victims; victims further try to separate themselves from aggressors after an aggressive behavior. Ecologically, aggression tends to occur in the context of property disputes (A. Humphreys & P. K. Smith, 1984). Unlike R & T, no specific playground location seems to elicit aggression (A. D. Pellegrini, 1989a). Like R & T, boys, more than girls, tend to exhibit aggressive behaviors.

Another reason for the controversial nature of R & T lies in the different types of children who engage in it. Research suggests that sociometrically defined popular and rejected elementary school children engage in R & T is qualitatively different and serves different functions for these two groups of children (A. D. Pellegrini, 1988, 1989b). Whereas for popular children R & T leads directly into games and continued cooperation, for rejected children it leads to aggression.

During the period of adolescence, frequency of R & T declines (A. D. Pellegrini, 1995). Most boys spend their free time on the playground in more sedentary activities, often in groups that include both boys and girls. These adolescents, it seems, are becoming interested in heterosexual relationships. Those adolescent boys who still engage in R & T tend not to spend their time in groups that are integrated with boys and girls together. Boys who initiate R & T typically do it as a way in which to bully a weaker student and it typically ends with the tougher boy hurting the weaker boy. In short, R & T during adolescence, unlike childhood, is an aggressive category.

To conclude this section, we can state that R & T and aggression may be distinct categories *only* for popular children; they seem to be interrelated for rejected children and for adolescents. This finding, in addition to the conflict of R & T and aggression, are probably responsible for R & T being considered an antisocial social behavior.

Factors Effecting Physical Activity Play.   As we noted earlier boys' play is more vigorous than girls'. Furthermore, it tends to occur in spacious areas, like playgrounds and on soft surfaces, like grass. If we look at school scheduling level variables, we also find that children's play on the playground is more vigorous after they have been confined to sedentary work for longer compared to shorter periods of time (A. D. Pellegrini, Huberty, & Jones, 1995; P. K. Smith & Hagan, 1980).

Outcomes of Physical Activity Play.   We begin at the most general level. Regarding chase and gross-motor forms of play, it is probably the case that these forms of activity relate to children's muscle and skeletal growth. The movements associated with these forms of exercise increase muscle strength and differentiation and bone density (A. D. Pellegrini & P. K. Smith, 1998).

Regarding the role of vigorous play breaks, or recesses, in the course of the school day we found that breaks from schoolwork, not physical play per se, increased children's attention to seat work (A. D. Pellegrini, 1995). This is consistent with work in Japanese schools which has shown that students' performance in schoolwork can be maximized if they are given frequent breaks (every 50–60 minutes) during the course of the school day.

Regarding the specific benefits associated with R & T, that specific groups of children assign different meanings to R & T behaviors has implications for possible functions of R & T. Functional examinations of play have generally been concerned with motor, cognitive, or social skills training (Martin & Caro, 1985). We address only the possibility of R & T serving a social skills training function. We can examine the extent to which it serves an antisocial, aggressive function or a prosocial function by examining the probability of aggressive or cooperative acts, respectively, immediately following R & T bouts. For popular children R & T moved into cooperative games at a greater than chance probability. For rejected children, on the other hand, it went to aggression in 1:4.

We also examined the relation between R & T and social problem solving. In the play context, because of its safe, nonexploitative nature, children experiment with different social roles. Consequently, individual social routines and strategies are broken down, recombined, and generalized. Our research supports this claim, but only for popular, not rejected, children (A. D. Pellegrini, 1988, 1989a). The relation between R & T and social problem solving for popular children may have been due to their exchanging R & T roles, such as offender/defender. Such exchange is one way of preventing playmates' boredom and thus ensuring sustained play (Aldis, 1975). Further, role reversals provide children, usually those in submissive roles, with opportunities to rest during R & T. These rest periods may be another strategy to ensure sustained play. Using these varied strategies to sustain play is similar to what children were asked to do on the social-problem-solving tasks: provide a variety of ways to initiate and sustain play.

CONCLUSION

In this chapter we suggested that children's play is an important part of childhood and one that is vital to their school experience. We outlined ways in which children's play can be categorized and studied. In our discussion of these categorization schemes we stressed how these various aspects of play related to children's general social-cognitive competence. Given the relations between play and other aspects of development, analyses of children's play provide valid insights into children's social-cognitive competence. We should be cautious, however, about the role of play in development.

Finally, researchers in the area of children's play must be cautious of the "play ethos" (P. K. Smith, 1988); that is, the notion that play is all good. We know that play is related to something for some people; we should thus proceed with caution. Indeed, some of the problems in this area, particularly as they are applied to education, are the results of oversimplifying complex problems, like the role of play in development and education.

Bibliography

Adair, J., Sharp, D., & Huynh, C. (1989). Hawthorne control procedures in educational experiments: A reconsideration of their use and effectiveness. *Review of Educational Research, 59*, 215–228.

Ainsworth, M. (1971). *Infancy in Uganda.* Baltimore: Johns Hopkins University Press.

Ainsworth, M., & Bell, S. C. (1970). Attachment, exploration and separation: Illustrated by the behavior of one-year-olds in a strange situation. *Child Development, 41*, 49–67.

Aldis, O. (1975). *Play fighting.* New York: Academic Press.

Altman, J. (1974). Observational study of behavior: Sampling methods. *Behavior, 49*, 227–265.

Anderson, D. R., & Collins, P. A. (1988). *The impact on children's education: Television's influence on cognitive development.* Washington, DC: Office of Educational Research and Improvement, U.S. Department of Education.

Anderson, J. (1972). Attachment behavior out of doors. In N. Blurton Jones (Ed.), *Ethological studies in human behavior* (pp. 175–255). London: Cambridge University Press.

Anderson, S., & Messick, S. (1974). Social competency in your children. *Develop mental Psychology, 10*, 282–293.

Anglin, J. M. (1993). Vocabulary development: A morphological analysis. *Monographs of the Society for Research in Child Development, 58* (Serial No. 10).

Arend, R., Gove, F., & Sroufe, L. A. (1979). Continuity of individual adaptation from infancy to kindergarten: A predictive study of ego-resiliency and curiosity in preschoolers. *Child Development, 50*, 950–959.

Ashcraft, M. H. (1990). Strategic processing in children's mental arithmetic: A review and proposal. In D. F. Bjorklund (Ed.), *Children's strategies: Contemporary views of cognitive development* (pp. 185–211). Hillsdale, NJ: Lawrence Erlbaum Associates.

Aslin, R. N., Jusczyk, P. W., & Pisoni, D. B. (1998). Speech and auditory processing during infancy. In D. Kuhn & R. S. Siegler (Eds.), *Cognitive, language, and perceptual development* (Vol. 2, pp. 147–198). New York: Wiley.

Atkinson, R. C., & Shiffrin, R. M. (1971). The control of short-term memory. *Scientific American, 225*, 82–90.

Azmitia, M. (1988). Peer interaction and problem-solving: When are two heads better than one? *Child Development, 59*, 87–96.

Azmitia, M. (1992). Expertise, private speech, and the development of self-regulation. In R. M. Diaz & L. E. Berk (Eds.), *Private speech: From social interaction to self-regulation* (pp. 101–122). Hillsdale, NJ: Lawrence Erlbaum Associates.

Baillargeon, R. (1987). Object permanence in 3- and 4-month-old infants. *Developmental Psychology, 23*, 655–664.

Bakeman, R., & Brownlee, J. (1980). The strategies of parallel play. *Child Development, 51*, 873–878.

Bakeman, R., & Gottman, J. (1986). *Observing interaction: An introduction to sequential analysis.* New York: Cambridge University Press.

Baker, E. L., O'Neil, S., & Linn, R. L. (1993). Policy and validity for performance-based assessment. *American Psychologist, 48*, 1210–1218.

Ball, S. J., & Bogatz, G. A. (1970). *The first year of Sesame Street: An evaluation.* Princeton, NJ: Educational Testing Service.

Bandura, A. (1977). *Social learning theory.* Englewood Cliffs, NJ: Prentice-Hall.

Bandura, A. (1986). *Social foundations of thought and action: A social cognitive theory.* Englewood Cliffs, NJ: Prentice-Hall.

Bandura, A. (1989a). Regulation of cognitive processes through perceived self-efficacy. *Developmental Psychology, 25*, 729–735.

Bandura, A. (1989b). Social cognitive theory. In R. Vasta (Ed.), *Annals of child development* (Vol. 6, pp. 1–160). Greenwich, CT: JAI.

Bandura, A., & Walters, R. H. (1963). *Social learning theory and personality development.* New York: Holt, Rinehart & Winston.

Barker, R. (1968). *Ecological psychology.* Stanford, CA: Stanford University Press.

Barker, R., & Gump, P. (1964). *Big school, small school: High school size and student behavior.* Stanford, CA: Stanford University Press.

Barker, R., & Wright, H. (1955). *Midwest and its children.* New York: Harper & Row.

Barnett, M., King, L., & Howard, J. (1979). Inducing affect about self or other: Effects on generosity in children. *Developmental Psychology, 15*, 164–167.

Bates, E., Marcham, V., Thal, D., Fenson, L., Dale, P., Reznicik, J. S., Reilly, J., & Hartung, J. (1994). Developmental and stylistic variation in the composition of early vocabulary. *Journal of Child Language, 21*, 85–124.

Bateson, P. P. G. (1978). How does behavior develop? In P. P. G. Batson & P. Klopfer (Eds.), *Growing points in ethology* (Vol. 3, pp. 55–66). New York: Cambridge University Press.

Bateson, P. P. G. (1981). Discontinuities in development and changes in the organization of play in cats. In K. Immelman, G. Barlow, L. Petrinovich, & M. Main (Eds.), *Behavioral development* (pp. 281'). New York: Cambridge University Press.

Bauer, P. J. (1992). Memory for gender-consistent and gender-inconsistent event sequences by twenty-five-month-old children. *Child Development, 64*, 285–297.

Bauer, P. J. (1995). Recalling past events: From infancy to early childhood. *Annals of Child Development, 11*, 25–71.

Baugh, J. (1983). *Black street speech: Its history, structure, and survival.* New York: Academic Press.

Baumrind, D. (1967). Child care practices anteceding three patterns of preschool behavior. *Genetic Psychology Monographs, 75*, 43–88.

Baumrind, D. (1971). Current patterns of parental authority. *Developmental Psychology Monographs, 4*(1), 2.

Baumrind, D. (1972). An exploratory study of socialization effects on black children: Some black–white comparisons. *Child Development, 43*, 261–267.

Baumrind, D. (1980). New directions in socialization research. *American Psychologist, 35*, 631–661.

Behar, L., & Stringfield, S. (1976). A behavioral rating scale for preschool children. *Developmental Psychology, 10*, 601–610.

Behrend, D. A. Rosengren, K., & Perlmutter, M. (1989). A new look at children's private speech: The effects of age, task difficulty, and parent presence. *International Journal of Behavioral Development, 12*, 305–320.

Bellugi, U. (1967). *The acquisition of negation.* Unpublished doctoral dissertation, Harvard University, Cambridge, MA.

Belsky, J., & Most, R. K. (1981). From exploration to play. *Developmental Psychology, 17*, 630–639.

Ben-Zeev, S. (1977). The influence of bilingualism on cognitive strategy and cognitive development. *Child Development, 48*, 1009–1018.

Berenbaum, S. A., & Hines, M. (1992). Early androgens are related to childhood sex-typed toy preferences. *Psychological Science, 3*, 203–206.

Berk, L. E. (1992). Children's private speech: An overview of theory and the status of research. In R. M. Diaz & L. E. Berk (Eds.), *Private speech: From social interaction to self-regulation* (pp. 17–53). Hillsdale, NJ: Lawrence Erlbaum Associates.

Berk, L. E., & Spuhl, S. T. (1995). Maternal intervention, private speech, and task performance in preschool children. *Early Childhood Research Quarterly, 10*, 145–169.

Berko, J. (1958). The child's learning of English morphology. *Word, 14*, 150–177.

Berko Gleason, J. (Ed.). (1997). *The development of language* (4th edition). Boston: Allyn & Bacon.

Bernstein, B. (1971). *Class codes and control* (Vol. 1). London: Routledge & Kegan Paul.

Berndt, T., Hawkins, J., & Hoyle, S. (1986). Changes in friendship during a school year. *Child Development, 57*, 1284–1297.

Bickerton, D. (1990). *Language and species.* Chicago: University of Chicago Press.

Bigelow, B. (1977). Children's friendship expectations. *Child Development, 48*, 246–253.

Bjorklund, B. R., & Bjorklund, D. F. (1990). *Parents book of discipline.* New York: Ballatine.

Bjorklund, D. F. (1986a). Look at me! *Parents' Magazine, 61*, 8.

Bjorklund, D. F. (1986b). What children remember. *Parents' Magazine, 61*, 6.

Bjorklund, D. F. (1987). How age changes in knowledge base contribute to the development of children's memory: An interpretive review. *Developmental Review, 7*, 93–130.

Bjorklund, D. F. (Ed.). (1990). *Children's strategies: Contemporary review of cognitive development.* Hillsdale, NJ: Lawrence Erlbaum Associates.

Bjorklund, D. F. (1995). *Children's thinking: Developmental function and individual differences* (2nd ed.). Pacific Grove, CA: Brooks/Cole.

Bjorklund, D. F. (1997). The role of immaturity in human development. *Psychological Bulletin, 122*, 153–169.

Bjorklund, D. F., & Bjorklund, B. R. (1992). *Looking at children: An introduction to child development.* Pacific Grove, CA: Brooks/Cole.

Bjorklund, D. F., & Coyle, T. R. (1995). Utilization deficiencies in the development of memory strategies. In F. E. Weinert & W. Schneider (Eds.), *Memory performance and competencies: Issues in growth and development* (pp. 161–180). Hillsdale, NJ: Lawrence Erlbaum Associates.

Bjorklund, D. F., Coyle, T. R., & Gaultney, J. F. (1992). Developmental differences in the acquisition of an organizational strategy: Evidence for the utilization deficiency hypothesis. *Journal of Experimental Child Psychology, 54*, 434–448.

Bjorklund, D. F., Gaultney, J. F., & Green, B. L. (1993). "I watch therefore I can do": The development of meta-imitation over the preschool years and the advantage of optimism in one's imitative skills. In R. Pasnak & M. L. Howe (Eds.), *Emerging themes in cognitive development* (Vol. 2, pp. 79–102). New York: Springer-Verlag.

Bjorklund, D. F., & Green, B. L. (1992). The adaptive nature of cognitive immaturity. *American Psychologist, 47*, 46–54.

Bjorklund, D. F., & Harnishfeger, K. K. (1987). Developmental differences in the mental effort requirements for the use of an organizational strategy in free recall. *Journal of Experimental Child Psychology, 44*, 109–125.

Bjorklund, D. F., & Harnishfeger, K. K. (1990). Children's strategies: Their definition and origins. In D. F. Bjorklund (Ed.), *Children's strategies: Contemporary views of cognitive development* (pp. 309–323). Hillsdale, NJ: Lawrence Erlbaum Associates.

Bjorklund, D. F., & Miller, P. H. (Eds.). (1997). New themes in strategy development. *Developmental Review, 17,* 407–410.

Bjorklund, D. F., Miller, P. H., Coyle, T. R., & Slawinski, J. L. (1997). Instructing children to use memory strategies: Evidence of utilization deficiencies in memory training studies. *Developmental Review, 17,* 411–442.

Bjorklund, D. F., & Muir, J. E. (1988). Children's development of free recall memory: Remembering on their own. In R. Vasta (Ed.), *Annals of child development* (Vol. 5, pp. 79–123). Greenwich, CT: JAI.

Bjorklund, D. F., Muir-Broaddus, J. E., & Schneider, W. (1990). The role of knowledge in the development of strategies. In D. F. Bjorklund (Ed.), *Children's strategies: Contemporary views of cognitive development* (pp. 25–95). Hillsdale, NJ: Lawrence Erlbaum Associates.

Bjorklund, D. F., & Reubens, A. (1997). [Collaborative learning of simple addition strategies between young children and their mothers in the context of a game]. Unpublished raw data, Florida Atlantic University, Boca Raton.

Block, J. (1977). *Lives through time.* Berkeley, CA: Bancroft.

Block, J., Block, J. H., & Keyes, S. (1988). Longitudinally foretelling drug usage in adolescence: Early childhood personality and environmental precursors. *Child Development, 59,* 336–355.

Bloom, B. (Ed.). (1956). *Taxonomy of educational objectives—Handbook 1: Cognitive domain.* New York: McKay.

Bloom, L. (1998). Language acquisition in development contexts. In D. Kuhn & R. S. Siegler (Eds.), *Cognitive, langauge, and perceptual development* (pp. 309–370). New York: Wiley.

Bloom, L., Hood, L., & Lightbown, P. (1974). Imitation in language development: If, when and why. *Cognitive Psychology, 6,* 380–420.

Blount, B. (1972). Aspects of socialization among the Luo of Kenya. *Language in Society, 1,* 235–248.

Blount, B. (1984). Mother infant interaction: Features and function of parental speech in English and Spanis. In A. Pellegrini & T. Yawkey (Eds.), *The development of oral and written language in social contexts* (pp.3–30). Norwood, NJ: Ablex.

Blurton Jones, N. (1972a). Categories of child–child interaction. In N. Blurton Jones (Ed.), *Ethological studies of child behavior* (pp. 97–129). London: Cambridge University Press.

Blurton Jones, N. (1972b). Characteristics of ethological studies of human behavior. In N. Blurton Jones (Ed.), *Ethological studies of child behavior* (pp. 3–33). London: Cambridge University Press.

Blurton Jones, N. (1976). Rough-and-tumble play among nursery school children. In J. Bruner, A. Jolly, & K. Sylva (Eds.), *Play—Its role in development and evolution* (pp. 352–363). New York: Basic Books.

Borke, H. (1975). Piaget's mountains revisited: Changes in the egocentric landscape. *Developmental Psychology, 11,* 240–243.

Boulton, M., & Smith, P. K. (1989). Issues in the study of children's rough-and-tumble play. In M. Bloch & A. Pellegrini (Eds.), *The ecological context of children's play* (pp. 57–83). Norwood, NJ: Ablex.

Bower, T. G. R. (1982). *Development in infancy.* San Francisco: W. H. Freeman.

Bowlby, J. (1951). *Maternal care and mental health.* Geneva: World Health Organization.

Bowlby, J. (1969). *Attachment and loss* (Vol. 1–Attachment). New York: Basic Books.

Bracht, G., & Glass, G. (1968). The external validity of experiments. *American Educational Research Journal, 5,* 437–474.

Brainerd, C. J. (1977). Cognitive development and concept learning: An interpretive review. *Psychological Bulletin, 84,* 919–939.

Brainerd, C. J. (1978). *Piaget's theory of intelligence.* Englewood Cliffs, NJ: Prentice-Hall.

Brainerd, C. J., & Allen, T. W. (1971). Training and generalization of density conversation: Effects of feedback and consecutive similar stimuli. *Child Development, 42*, 693–704.

Brandt, R. S. (Ed.). (1991). *Cooperating learning and the collaborative school.* Alexandria, VA: Association for Supervision and Curriculum Development.

Bretherton, I., & Waters, E. (Eds.). (1985). Growing points of attachment theory and research. *Monographs for the Society for Research in Child Development, 50*(1–2), 209.

Brim, O. (1975). Macro-structural influences in child development and the need for childhood social interactions. *American Journal of Orthopsychiatry, 45*, 516–524.

Brody, G., Stoneman, Z., & Wheatley, P. (1984). Peer pressure in the presence and absence of observers. *Child Development, 55*, 425–428.

Bronfenbrenner, U. (1979). *The ecology of human development.* Cambridge, MA: Harvard University Press.

Bronfenbrenner, U., & Crouter, A. (1983). The evolution of environmental models in developmental research. In W. Kessen (Ed.), *Handbook of child psychology* (Vol. 1, pp.357–414). New York: Wiley.

Bronson, W. C. (1981). *Toddlers' behaviors with agemates: Issues of interaction, cognition, and affect.* Norwood, NJ: Ablex.

Brown, A. L., & Scott, M. S. (1971). Recognition memory for pictures in preschool children. *Journal of Experimental Child Psychology, 11*, 401–412.

Brown, A. L., & Smiley, S. S. (1978). The development of strategies for studying texts. *Child Development, 49*, 1076–1088.

Brown, R. (1973). *A first language: The early stages.* Cambridge, MA: Harvard University Press.

Brown, R., & Fraser, C. (1963). The acquisition of syntax. In C. N. Cofer & B. Musgrave (Eds.), *Verbal behavior and learning: Problems and process* (pp. 158–196). New York: McGraw-Hill.

Bruner, J. S. (1972). The nature and uses of immaturity. *American Psychologist, 27*, 687–708.

Bruner, J. S. (1980). *Under five in Britain.* London: Methuen.

Bruner, J. S. (1983). *Child's talk: Learning to use language.* New York: Norton.

Bruner, J. S. (1986). *Actual minds, possible words.* Cambridge, MA: Harvard University Press.

Bruner, J. S., & Sherwood, V. (1976). Peekaboo and the learning of role structures. In J. Bruner, A. Jolly, & K. Sylva (Eds.), *Plays—Its role in development and evolution* (pp. 277–285). New York: Basic Books.

Bukowski, W., & Hoza, B. (1989). Popularity and friendship. In T. Berndt & G. Ladd (Eds.), *Peer relationships in child development* (pp. 15–45). New York: Wiley.

Burghardt, G. M. (1977). Amending Tinbergen: A fifth aim for ethology. In R. W. Mitchell & N. S. Thompson (Eds.), *Anthropomorphism, anecdotes, and animals* (pp. 254–276). Albany: State University of New York Press.

Butterfield, E. C., & Siperstein, G. N. (1972). Influence of contingent auditory stimulation on non-nutritional suckle. In J. F. Bosma (Ed.), *Third symposium on oral sensation and perceptions: The mouth of the infant* (p..313–334). Springfield, IL: Thomas.

Byrd, D. M., & Gholson, B. (1985). Reading, memory, and metacognition. *Journal of Educational Psychology, 77*, 428–436.

Campbell, D., & Stanley, J. (1963). *Experimental and quasi-experimental designs for research.* Chicago: Rand McNally.

Campos, J. J., Barrett, K. C., Lamb, M., Goldsmith, H., & Sternberg, C. (1983). Socioemotional development. In M. Haith & J. Campos (Eds.), *Handbook of child psychology* (Vol. 2, pp. 783–916). New York: Wiley.

Carey, S. (1977). The child as a word learner. In M. Halle, J. Bresnan, & G. A. Miller (Eds.), *Linguistic theory and psychological reality* (pp. 264–293). Cambridge, MA: MIT Press.

Case, R. (1985). *Intellectual development: Birth to adulthood.* New York: Academic Press.

Case, R., Kurland, M., & Goldberg, J. (1982). Operational efficiency and the growth of short-term memory span. *Journal of Experimental Child Psychology, 33*, 386–404.

Cassell, W. S., & Bjorklund, D. F. (1995). Developmental patterns of eyewitness memory and suggestibility: An ecologically based short-term longitudinal study. *Law & Human Behavior, 19*, 507–532.

Cassell, W. S., Roebers, C. E. M., & Bjorklund, D. F. (1996). Developmental patterns of eyewitness responses to increasingly suggestive questions. *Journal of Experimental Child Psychology, 61*, 116–133.

Cassidy, J. (1988). Child–mother attachment and the self in six-year-olds. *Child Development, 59*, 121–134.

Ceci, S. J. (1996). *On intelligence: A bioecological treatise on intellectual development* (expanded ed.). Cambridge, MA: Harvard University Press.

Ceci, S. J., & Bruck, M. (1993). Suggestibility of the child witness: A historical review and synthesis. *Psychological Bulletin, 113*, 403–439.

Ceci, S. J., & Bruck, M. (1995). *Jeopardy in the courtroom: A scientific analysis of children's testimony*. Washington, DC: American Psychological Association.

Ceci, S. J., Crotteau-Huffman, M., Smith, E., & Loftus, E. W. (1994). Repeatedly thinking about non- events. *Consciousness & Cognition, 3*, 388–407.

Ceci, S. J., Loftus, E. F., Leichtman, M., & Bruck, M. (1994). The role of source misattributions in the creation of false beliefs among preschoolers. *International Journal of Clinical Experimental Hypnosis, 62*, 304–320.

Ceci, S. J., Ross, D. F., & Toglia, M. D. (1987). Suggestibility of children's memory: Psychological implications. *Journal of Experimental Psychology: General, 116*, 38–49.

Chandler, M., Fritz, A. S., & Hala, S. (1989). Small-scale deceit: Deception as a member of two-, three-, and four-year-olds' early theories of mood. *Child Development, 60*, 1263–1277.

Charlesworth, R., & Hartup, W. (1967). Positive social reinforcement in the nursery school peer group. *Child Development, 38*, 993–1002.

Charlesworth, W. R. (1978). Ethology: Its relevance for the study of human adaptation. In G. P. Sachett (Ed.), *Observing behavior* (Vol. 1, pp. 7–32). Baltimore: University Park Press.

Cheyne, D., & Seyfarth, R. (1990). *How monkeys see the world*. Chicago: University of Chicago Press.

Chi, M. T. H. (1978). Knowledge structure and memory development. In R. Siegler (Ed.), *Children's thinking: What develops?* (pp. 73–96). Hillsdale, NJ: Lawrence Erlbaum Associates.

Chomsky, N. (1959). A review of Skinner's *Verbal behavior*. *Language, 35*, 26–58.

Christie, J. F. (Ed.). (1991). *Play and early literacy development*. Albany: State University of New York Press.

Cicourel, A. (1973). *Cognitive sociology*. New York: Penguin.

Circus: A comprehensive program of assessment services for primary children. (1975). Princeton, NJ: Educational Testing Service.

Coates, D. L., & Lewis, M. (1984). Early mother–infant interaction and infant cognitive status as predictors of school performance and cognitive behavior in six-year-olds. *Child Development, 55*, 1219–1230.

Cohn, D. A. (1990). Child–mother attachment of six-year-olds and social competence at school. *Child Development, 61*, 152–162.

Coie, J., & Kupersmidt, J. (1983). A behavioral analysis of emerging social status in boys' groups. *Child Development, 54*, 1400–1416.

Cole, M. (1988). Cross-cultural research in the sociohistorical tradition. *Human Development, 31*, 137–157.

Connell, J., & Serbin, L. (1977). Behaviorally-based masculine- and feminine-activity preference scales for preschoolers: Correlates with other classroom behaviors and cognitive tests. *Child Development, 48*, 1411–1416.

Connolly, K., & Dalgleish, M. (1989). The emergence of a tool using skill in infancy. *Developmental Psychology, 25*, 849–912.

Connolly, K., & Elliott, J. (1972). The evolution and ontogeny of hand functions. In N. Blurton Jones (Ed.), *Ethological child behaviour* (pp. 329–384). London: Cambridge University Press.

Cook, T. D., Appelton, H., Conner, R. F., Schaffer, A., Tabkin, G., & Weber, J. S. (1975). Sesame Street *revisted*. New York: Russell Sage Foundation.

Cooper, R. P., & Aslin, R. N. (1990). Preference for infant-directed speech in the first month after birth. *Child Development, 61*, 1584–1595.

Cooper, R. P., & Aslin, R. N. (1994). Developmental differences in infant attention to the spectral properties of infant-directed speech. *Child Development, 65*, 1663–1677.

Coopersmith, S. (1967). *The antecedents of self-esteem*. New York: W. H. Freeman.

Cowan, N., & Davidson, G. (1984). Salient childhood memories. *Journal of Genetic Psychology, 145*, 101–107.

Coyle, T. R., & Bjorklund, D. F. (1997). Age differences in, and consequences of, multiple- and variable strategy use on a multitrial sort-recall task. *Developmental Psychology, 33*, 372–380.

Cozby, P. C., Worden, P. E., & Kee, D. W. (1989). *Research methods in human development*. Mountain View, CA: Mayfield.

Crowley, K., & Siegler, R. S. (1993). Flexible strategy use in young children's tic-tac-toe. *Cognitive Science, 17*, 531–561.

Cummings, E. M. (1980). Caregiver stability and day care. *Developmental Psychology, 16*, 31–37.

Curtiss, S. (1977). *Genie: A psycholinguistic study of a modern day "wild child."* New York: Academic Press.

Daehler, M. W., & Bukatko, D. (1977). Recognition memory for pictures in very young children: Evidence from attentional preferences using a continuous presentation procedure. *Child Development, 48*, 693–696.

DeCasper, A. J., & Fifer, W. P. (1980). Of human bonding: Newborns prefer their mother's voice. *Science, 208*, 1174–1776.

DeCasper, A. J., & Spence, M. J. (1986). Prenatal maternal speech influences newborns' perception of speech sounds. *Infant Behavior and Development, 9*, 133–150.

Delpit, L. D. (1990). Language diversity and learning. In S. Hynds & D. L. Rubin (Eds.), *Perspectives on talk and learning* (pp. 247–266). Urbana, IL: National Council of Teachers of English.

Dempster, F. N. (1985). Short-term memory development in childhood and adolescence. In C. J. Brainerd & M. Pressley (Eds.), *Basic processes in memory development: Progress in cognitive development research* (pp. 209–248). New York: Springer.

Denins, W. (1973). *Children of the Croche*. New York: Appleton-Century-Crofts.

DeStefano, J. (1972). Social variation in language: Implications for teaching reading to Black ghetto children. In J. A. Figurel (Ed.), *Better reading in urban schools* (pp. 18–24). Newark, DE: International Reading Association.

de Villiers, P. A., & de Villiers, J. G. (1979). *Early language*. Cambridge, MA: Harvard University Press.

Dewey, J. (1938). *Experience and education*. New York: Collier.

Diamond, A. (1985). Development of the ability to use recall to guide action as indicated by infants' performance on A-B. *Child Development, 56*, 868–883.

Diaz, R. M. (1983). Thought and two languages: The impact of bilingualism on cognitive development. *Review of Research in Education, 10*, 23–54.

Dobson, J. (1970). *Dare to discipline*. Toronto: Bantam.

Dodge, K., Petit, G., McClaskey, C. L., & Brown, M. (1986). Social compentent children. *Monographs of the Society for Research in Child Development, 51*(Serial No. 213).

Dodson, F. (1977). *How to discipline with love*. New York: Signet.

Dollard, J., Doob, L. W., Miller, N. E., Mowrer, O. H., & Sears, R. R. (1939). *Frustration and aggression*. New Haven, CT: Yale University Press.

Donald, M. (1991). *Origins of the modern mind: Three stages in the evolution of culture and cognition*. Cambridge, MA: Harvard University Press.

Dunn, J. (1988). *The beginnings of social understanding*. Cambridge, MA: Harvard University Press.

Edwards, C. P., & Whiting, B. B. (1988). *Children of different worlds*. Cambridge, MA: Harvard University Press.

Egeland, B., & Sroufe, L. (1981). Attachment and early maltreatment. *Child Development, 52*, 44–52.

Eilers, R. E., Gavin, W. J., & Wilson, W. R. (1979). Lingustic experience and phonemic perception in infancy: A cross-linguistic study. *Child Development, 50*, 14–18.

Eimas, P. D., Siqueland, E. R., Jusczyk, P., & Vigorito, J. (1971). Speech perception in infants. *Science, 71*, 303–306.

Einstein, A. (1933). *On the method of theoretical physics*. New York: Oxford University Press.

Eisenberg, N. (1983). Sex-types toy choices: What do they signify. In M. Liss (Ed.), *Social and cognitive skills* (pp. 45–70). New York: Academic Press.

Ellis, S., & Rogoff, B. (1986). Problem solving in children's management of instruction. In E. Mueller & C. Cooper (Eds.), *Process and outcome in peer relationships* (pp. 301–325). Orlando, FL: Academic Press.

Endsley, R., & Bradbard, M. (1981). *Quality daycare*. Englewood Cliffs, NJ: Prentice-Hall.

Erickson, F. (1986). Qualitative methods in research on teaching. In M. Wittrock (Ed.), *Handbook on research in teaching* (pp. 119–161). New York: Macmillan.

Evans, E. (1982). Curriculum models in early childhood education. In B. Spodek (Ed.), *Handbook of research in early childhood education* (pp. 107–134). New York: The Free Press.

Evans, M. A. (1985). Self-initated speech repairs: A reflection of communicative monitoring in young children. *Developmental Psychology, 21*, 365–371.

Fabes, R. A., Fultz, J., Eisenberg, N., May-Plumlee, T., & Christopher, F. S. (1989). Effects of rewards on children's prosocial motivation: A socialization study. *Developmental Psychology, 25*, 509–515.

Fagen, R. (1981). *Animal play behavior*. New York: Oxford University Press.

Fagen, R. (1984). Play and behavioral flexibility. In P. K. Smith (Ed.), *Play in animals and humans* (pp. 159–174). London: Basil Blackwell.

Fagot, B. I., Leinbach, M. D., & Hagan, R. (1986). Gender labeling and the adoption of sex-typed behaviors. *Developmental Psychology, 22*, 440–443.

Fantuzzo, J. W., Sutton-Smith, B., Coolahan, K. C., Manz, P., Canning, S., & Debnam, D. (1995). Assessment of play interaction behaviors in low income children: Penn Interactive Play Scale. *Early Childhood Research Quarterly, 10*, 105–120.

Farrar, M. J., & Goodman, G. S. (1992). Developmental changes in event memory. *Child Development, 63*, 173–187.

Fassnacht, G. (1982). *Theory and practice of observing behavior*. New York: Academic Press.

Fein, G., Moorin, E., & Enslein, J. (1982). Pretense and peer behavior: An intersectional analysis. *Human Development, 25*, 392–406.

Feldhaufer, H., Midgley, C., & Eccles, J. (1988). Student, teacher, and observer perceptions of the classroom environment before and after the transition to junior high school. *Journal of Early Adolescence, 8*, 133–156.

Fernald, A. (1992). Human maternal vocalizations to infants as biologically relevant signals: An evolutionary perspective. In J. H. Barkow, L. Cosmides, & J. Tooby (Eds.), *The adaptive mind: Evolutionary psychology and the generation of culture* (pp. 391–428). New York: Oxford University Press.

Field, D. (1987). A review of preschool conversation training: An analysis of analyses. *Developmental Review, 7*, 210–251.

Field, T. (1979). Games parents play with normal and high-risk infants. *Child Psychiatry and Human Development, 10*, 41–48.

Fillmore, L. (1979). Individual differences in second language acquistion. In C. Fillmore, D. Kempler, & W. Wang (Eds.), *Individual differences in language ability and language behavior*. New York: Academic Press.

Fitzgerald, H. E., & Brackbill, Y. (1976). Classical conditioning in infancy: Development and constraints. *Psychological Bulletin, 83*, 353–376.

Fivush, R., & Hamond, N. R. (1990). Autobiographical memory across the preschool years: Toward reconceptualizing childhood amnesia. In R. Fivush & J. A. Hudson (Eds.), *Knowing and remembering in young children* (pp. 223–248). Cambridge,England: Cambridge University Press.

Flavell, J. H. (1970). Developmental studies of mediated memory. In H. W. Reese & L. P. Lipsitt (Eds.), *Advances in child development and child behavior* (Vol. 5, pp. 182–211). New York: Academic Press.

Flavell, J. H. (1978). Metacognitive development. In J. M. Scandura & C. J. Brainerd (Eds.), *Structural/process theories of complex human behavior* (pp. 213–224). Alphen a. d. Rijn, The Netherlands: Sythoff and Noordhoff.

Flavell, J. H., Green, F. L., Flavell, E. R., & Grossman, J. B. (1997). The development of children's knowledge about inner speech. *Developmental Psychology, 68*, 39–47.

Flavell, J. H., & Miller, P. H. (1998). Social cognition. In D. Kuhn & R. S. Siegler (Eds.), *Cognitive, language, and perceptual development* (Vol. 2, pp. 851–899). New York: Wiley.

Flavell, J. H., & Wellman, H. M. (1977). Metamemory. In R. V. Kail, Jr. & J. W. Hagen (Eds.), *Perspectives on the development of memory and cognition* (pp. 3–33). Hillsdale, NJ: Lawrence Erlbaum Associates.

Forman, G., & Kuscher, D. (1977). *The child's construction of knowledge.* Monterey, CA: Brooks/Cole.

Friedrich, L. K., & Stein, A. H. (1973). Aggressive and prosocial television programs and the natural behavior of preschool children. *Monographs of the society for Research in Child Development, 38* (Serial No. 151).

Gage, N. (1989). The paradigm wars and their aftermath. *Educational Researcher, 18*, 4–10.

Gage, N., & Needels, M. (1989). Process–product research on teaching: A review of criticisms. *Elementary School Journal, 89*, 253–300.

Gagne, R. (1978). *The conditions of learning.* New York: Holt, Rinehart & Winston.

Galda, L. (1981). Literature as the center of the curriculum. *The Advocate, 1*, 38-44.

Galda, L. (1984). Narrative competence. In A. Pellegrini & T. Yawkey (Eds.), *The development of oral and written language in social contexts* (pp. 105–118). Norwood, NJ: Ablex.

Galda, L., & Pellegrini, A. D. (Eds.). (1985). *Play, language, and story: The development of children's literate behavior.* Norwood, NJ: Ablex.

Galda, L., Pellegrini, A. D., & Cox, S. (1989). A short-term longitudinal study of preschoolers' emergent literacy. *Research in the Teaching of English, 23*, 292–309.

Garbarino, J. (1989). An ecological perspective on the role of play in child development. In M. Bloch & A. D. Pellegrini (Eds.), *The ecological context of children's play* (pp. 16–34). Norwood, NJ: Ablex.

Gardner, H. (1993, April). *Teaching for understanding.* Paper presented at the Teachers' Cognition Workshop, Tel Aviv, Israel.

Gardner, R. C., & Lambert, W. E. (1972). *Attitudes and motivation in second-langauge learning.* Rowley, MA: Newbury House.

Garfinkle, H. (1967). *Studies in ethomethodology.* Englewood Cliffs, NJ: Prentice-Hall.

Garvey, C. (1990). *Play.* Cambridge, MA: Harvard University Press.

Gauvain, M., & Rogoff, B. (1989). Collaborative problem solving and children's planning skills. *Developmental Psychology, 25*, 139–151.

Gazzaniga, M. S. (1985). *The social brain: Discovering the networks of the mind.* New York: Basic Books.

Geary, D. C. (1994). *Children's mathematical development: Research and practical applications.* Washington, DC: American Psychological Association.

Gelman, R. (1969). Conservation acqusition: A problem of learning to attend to relevant attributes. *Journal of Experimental Child Psychology, 7*, 167–187.

Gelman, R., & Williams, E. M. (1998). Enabling constraints for cognitive development and learning. In D. Kuhn & R. S. Siegler (Eds.), *Cognitive, language, and perceptual development* (Vol. 2, pp. 575–630). New York: Wiley.

Gjerde, P. (1988). Parental concordance on child rearing and the interactive emphases of parents: Sex differentiated relationships during the preschool years. *Developmental Psychology, 24,* 700–706.

Goodlad, J. (1984). *A place called school.* New York: McGraw-Hill.

Goodman, G. S., & Reed, R. S. (1986). Age differences in eyewitness testimony. *Law and Human Behavior, 19,* 317–332.

Goodwin, W. L., & Goodwin, L. D. (1997). Using standardized measures for evaluating young children's learning. In B. Spodek & O. Saracho (Eds.), *Issues in early childhood education assessment and evaluation* (pp. 92–107). New York: Teachers College Press.

Gopnik, A., & Astington, J. W. (1988). Children's understanding of representational change and its relation to the understanding of false belief and the appearance–reality distinction. *Child Development, 59,* 26–37.

Gopnik, A., & Slaughter, V. (1991). Young children's understanding of changes in their mental states. *Child Development, 62,* 98–110.

Gottlieb, G. (1983). The psychobiological approach to developmental issues. In J. J. Campos & M. Haith (Eds.), *Handbook of child psychology: Infancy and developmental psychobiology* (Vol. 2, pp. 1–26). New York: Wiley.

Gottman, J., & Roy, A. (1990). *Sequential analyses.* New York: Cambridge University Press.

Grice, H. P. (1975). Logic and conversation. In P. Cole & J. Morgan (Eds.), *Speech acts: Syntax and semantics* (Vol. 3, pp. 41–58). New York: Academic Press.

Grieser, D., & Kuhl, P. K. (1989). Categorization of speech by infants: Support for speech-sound protoypes. *Developmental Psychology, 25,* 577–588.

Groen, G. J., & Parkman, J. M. (1972). A chronometric analysis of simple addition. *Psychological Review, 79,* 329–343.

Gump, P. (1989). Ecological psychology and issues of play. In M. Bloch & A. D. Pellegrini (Eds.), *The ecological contexts of children's play* (pp.35–56). Norwood, NJ: Ablex.

Guttentag, R. E. (1984). The mental effort requirement of cumulative rehearsal: A developmental study. *Journal of Experimental Child Psychology, 37,* 92–106.

Gzesh, S. M., & Surber, C. F. (1985). Visual perspective-taking skills in children. *Child Development, 56,* 1204–1213.

Hala, S., Chandler, M., & Fritz, A. S. (1991). Fledgling theories of mind: Deception as a marker of three-year-olds' understanding of false belief. *Child Development, 62,* 83–97.

Hall, G. S. (1916). *Adolescence.* New York: Appleton.

Hallinan, M. (1981). Recent advances in sociometry. In S. Asher & J. Gottman (Eds.), *The development of children's friendships* (pp. 91–115). New York: Cambridge University Press.

Harkness, S., & Super, C. (1993). The developmental niche: Implications for children's literacy development. In L. Eldering & P. Leseman (Eds.), *Early intervention and culture* (pp. 115–129). New York: UNESCO Publications.

Harlow, H. (1962). The heterosexual affection system in monkeys. *American Psychologist, 17,* 1–9.

Harlow, H., & Harlow, M. (1962). Social deprivation in monkeys. *Scientific American, 207(5),* 136.

Harnishfeger, K. K., & Bjorklund, D. F. (1990). Children's strategies: A brief history. In D. F. Bjorklund (Ed.), *Children's strategies: Contemporary views of cognitive development* (pp. 1–22). Hillsdale, NJ: Lawrence Erlbaum Associates.

Hartup, W. (1983). Peer relations. In E. M. Hetherington (Ed.), *Handbook of child psychology* (Vol. 4, pp. 103–196). New York: Wiley.

Hartup, W. (1989). Social relationships and their developmental significance. *American Psychologist, 44,* 120–126.

Hartup, W. (1996). The company they keep: Friendships and their developmental significance. *Child Development, 67,* 1–13.

Hasher, L., & Zacks, R. T. (1979). Automatic and effortful processes in memory. *Journal of Experimental Psychology: General, 108,* 356–388.

Haskett, G. J. (1971). Modification of peer preferences of first-grade children. *Developmental Psychology, 4,* 429–433.

Hayes, D. (1978). Cognitive bases for liking and disliking among preschool children. *Child Development, 49,* 906–909.

Hazen, N. L., & Durrett, M. E. (1982). Relationship of security of attachment to exploration and cognitive mapping abilities in 2-year-olds. *Developmental Psychology, 18,* 751–759.

Heath, S. B. (1983). *Ways with words.* New York: Cambridge University Press.

Heath, S. B. (1985). Play, language, and literacy. In L. Galda & A. D. Pellegrini (Eds.), *Play, language, and story: The development of children's literate behavior* (pp. 147–166). Norwood, NJ: Ablex.

Heath, S. B. (1989). Oral and literate traditions among Black Americans living in poverty. *American Psychologist, 44,* 367–373.

Hetherington, C., Cox, M., & Cox, R. (1978). The aftermath of divorce. In J. Stevens & M. Mathews (Eds.), *Mother–child, father–child relations* (pp. 119–125). Washington, DC: National Association for the Education of Young Children.

Hetherington, E., & Parke, R. (1979). *Child psychology.* New York: McGraw-Hill.

Hinde, R. (1959). Unitary drives. *Animal Behavior, 7,* 130–141.

Hinde, R. (1983). Ethology and child development. In J. J. Campos & M. H. Haith (Eds.), *Handbook of child psychology: Infancy and developmental psychology* (Vol. 2, pp. 27–94). New York: Wiley.

Hinde, R. (1987). *Individuals, relationships, and culture.* New York: Cambridge University Press.

Hirsh-Pasek, K., & Golinkoff, R. M. (1991). Language comprehension: A new look at the same old themes. In N. A. Krasnegor, D. R. Rumbaugh, R. L. Schiefelbusch, & M. Studdert-Kennedy (Eds.), *Biological and behavioral determinants of language development* (pp. 301–320). Hillsdale, NJ: Lawrence Erlbaum Associates.

Hirsh-Pasek, K., Golinkoff, R. M., & Naigles, L. (1996). Young children's use of syntactic frames to derive meaning. In K. Hirsh-Pasek & R. M. Golinkoff (Eds.), *The origins of grammar: Evidence from early language comprehension* (pp. 123–159). Cambridge, MA: MIT Press.

Hocke, E., & DeMeis, D. (1990). Depression in mothers of infants: The role of maternal employment. *Developmental Psychology, 26,* 285–291.

Hoff-Ginsberg, E. (1997). *Language development.* Pacific Grove, CA: Brooks/Cole.

Hogrefe, G. J., Wimmer, H., & Perner, J. (1986). Ignorance versus false belief: A developmental lag in attribution of epistemic states. *Child Development, 57,* 567–582.

Hopkins, K. D., & Stanley, J. C. (1981). *Educational and psychological measurement and valuation.* Englewood Cliffs, NJ: Prentice-Hall.

Howe, M. L., & Courage, M. L. (1993). On resolving the enigma of infantile amnesia. *Psychological Bulletin, 113,* 305–326.

Howes, C. (1992). *The collaborative construction of pretend.* Albany: State University of New York Press.

Hudson, J. A. (1990). The emergence of autobiographical memory in mother–child conversation. In R. Fivush & J. A. Hudson (Eds.), *Knowing and remembering in young children* (pp. 166–196). Cambridge, England: Cambridge University Press.

Humphreys, A., & Smith, P. K. (1984). Rough-and-tumble play in preschool on a playground. In P. K. Smith (Ed.), *Play in anmials and humans* (pp. 270–291). London: Blackwell.

Humphreys, A., & Smith, P. K. (1987). Rough-and-tumble play, friendship and dominance in school children: Evidence for continuity and change with age. *Child Development, 58,* 201–212.

Humphreys, L. G. (1980). Me thinks they do protest too much. *Intelligence, 4,* 179–183.

Humphreys, L. G., & Parsons, C. K. (1979). Piagetian tasks measure intelligence and intelligence tests assess cognitive development. *Intelligence, 3*, 369–382.

Humphreys, L. G., Rich, S. A., & Davey, T. C. (1985). A Piagetian test of general intelligence. *Developmental Psychology, 21*, 872–877.

Hutt, C. (1979). Exploration and play. In B. Sutton-Smith (Ed.), *Play and learning* (pp. 251–298). New York: Plenum.

Hymes, D. (1970). Competence and performance in linguistic theory. In R. Huxley & E. Ingram (Eds.), *Language acquisition* (pp. 3–24). New York: Academic Press.

Hymes, D. (1972). Models of interaction of language and social life. In J. Gumperz & D. Hymes (Eds.), *Directions in socio-linguistics* (pp. 8–28). New York: Holt, Rinehart & Winston.

Ingram, D. (1989). *First language acquisition: Method, description, and explanation.* London: Cambridge University Press.

Inhelder, B., & Piaget, J. (1958). *The growth of logical thinking from childhood to adolescence.* New York: Basic Books.

Irvine, J. T. (1978). Wolof "magical thinking": Culture and conservation revisited. *Journal of Cross-Cultural Psychology, 9*, 300–310.

Itard, J. M. G. (1962). *The wild boy of Aveyron* (G. Humphrey & M. Humphrey, trans.). New York: Appleton-Century-Crofts. (Original work published in 1908)

Jacobs, E. (1988). Clarifying qualitative research: A focus on traditions. *Educational Researcher, 17*, 22–24.

Jakobson, R. (1968). *Child language, aphasia and phonological universals.* The Hague: Mouton.

Jensen, A. R. (1980). *Bias in mental testing.* New York: The Free Press.

Johnson, D. W., & Johnson, R. T. (1987). *Learning together and alone: Cooperative, competitive, and individualistic learning* (2nd ed.). Englewood Cliffs, NJ: Prentice-Hall.

Johnson, D. W., & Johnson, R. T. (1989). *Cooperation and competition: Theory and research.* Edina, MN: Interaction.

Johnson, J., & Ershler, J. (1981). Developmental trends in preschool play as a function of classroom program and child gender. *Child Development, 52*, 994–1004.

Johnson, J. S., & Newport, E. L. (1989). Critical period effects in second language learning: The influence of maturational state on the acquisition of English as a second language. *Cognitive Psychology, 21*, 60–99.

Johnson, M. (1935). The effect of behavior of variation in the amount of play equipment. *Child Development, 6*, 56–68.

Johnson, R. (1962). A study of children's moral judgments. *Child Development, 33*, 327–354.

Jones, I., & Pellegrini, A. D. (1996). First graders' computer assisted writing: Metacognitive and linguistic effects. *American Educational Research Journal, 33*, 691–718.

Jones, N. B. (Ed.). (1974). *Ethological studies in child behavior.* New York: Cambridge University Press.

Kagan, J. (1969). Inadequate evidence and illogical conclusions: Environment, heredity, and intelligence. *Harvard Educational Review, 39*, 126–129.

Kagan, J. (1971). *Change and continuity in infancy.* New York: Wiley.

Kagan, J. (1980). Perspectives on continuity. In O. Brim & J. Kagan (Eds.), *Constancy and change across the life span* (pp. 26–74). Cambridge, MA: Harvard University Press.

Kagan, J. (1988). *Unstable ideas.* Cambridge, MA: Harvard University Press.

Kail, R. (1993). The role of a global mechanism in developmental change in speed of processing. In M. L. Howe & R. Pasnak (Eds.), *Emerging themes in cognitive development.* New York: Springer-Verlag.

Kail, R. V., & Salthouse, T. A. (1994). Processing speed as a mental capacity. *Acta Psychologica, 86*, 199–225.

Kamii, C., & DeVries, R. (1978). *Physical knowledge in preschool education.* Englewood Cliffs, NJ: Prentice-Hall.

Karzon, R. G. (1985). Discrimination of polysyllabic sequences by one- to four-month-old infants. *Journal of Experimental Child Psychology, 39*, 326–342.

Katz, S., Lautenschlager, G. J., Blackburn, A. B., & Harris, F. H. (1990). Answering reading comprehension questions without passages on the SAT. *Psychological Science, 1*, 122–127.

Kaufman, A. S., & Kaufman, N. L. (1972). Test built from Piaget's and Gesell's tasks as predictors of first-grade achievement. *Child Development, 43*, 521–535.

Keating, D. P. (1975). Precocious cognitive development at the level of formal operations. *Child Development, 46*, 276–280.

Kee, D. W., & Davies, L. (1988). Mental effort and elaboration: A developmental analysis. *Contemporary Educational Psychology, 13*, 221–228.

Kee, D. W., & Davies, L. (1990). Mental effort and elaboration: Effects of accessibility and construction. *Journal of Experimental Child Psychology, 49*, 264–274.

Kerlinger, F. (1973). *Foundations of behavioral research.* New York: Holt, Rinehart & Winston.

Kerlinger, F. (1980). *Behavioral research: A conceptual approach.* New York: Holt, Rinehart & Winston.

Kingma, J. (1984). Traditional intelligence, Piagetian tasks, and initial arithmetic in kindergarten and primary school grade one. *Journal of Genetic Psychology, 145*, 49–60.

Kohlberg, L., & Mayer, R. (1972). Development as the aim of education. *Harvard Educational Review, 42*, 449–496.

Kohlberg, L., Yaeger, J., & Hjertholm, E. (1968). Private speech: Four studies and a review of theories. *Child Development, 39*, 691–736.

Kohler, W. (1925). *The mentality of apes.* New York: Harcourt Brace.

Kramer, J. A., Hill, K. T., & Cohen, L. B. (1975). Infants' development of object permanence: A refined methodology and new evidence for Piaget's hypothesized ordinality. *Child Development, 46*, 149–155.

Krasnor, L., & Pepler, D. (1980). The study of children's play: Some future directions. In K. Rubin (Ed.), *Child's play* (pp. 85–96). San Francisco: Jossey-Bass.

Krasnor, L., & Rubin, K. (1981). The assessment of social problem solving in young children. In T. Marlussi, C. Glass, & M. Genest (Eds.), *Cognitive assessment* (pp. 452–476). New York: Guilford.

Kuhl, P. K. (1987). Perception of speech and sound in early infancy. In P. Salapatek & L. Cohen (Eds.), *Handbook of infant perception* (pp. 275–382). New York: Academic Press.

Kuhl, P. K., Andruski, J. E., Christovich, I. A., Christovich, L. A., Kozhevnikova, E. V., Ryskina, V. L., Stolyarova, E. I., Sundberg, U., & Lacerda, F. (1997). Cross-language analysis of phonetic units in language addressed to infants. *Science, 277*, 684–686.

Kuhn, D., Langer, J., Kohlberg, L., & Haan, N. S. (1977). The development of formal operations in logical and moral judgment. *Genetic Psychology Monographs, 95*, 97–188.

Laboratory of Comparative Human Cognition. (1983). Culture and cognitive development. In W. Kessen (Ed.), *History, theory, and methods* (Vol. 1, pp. 295–356). New York: Wiley.

Labov, W. (1972). *Language identity.* Philadelphia: University of Pennsylvania Press.

Ladd, G., & Price, J. (1987). Predicting childrens' social and school adjustment following the transition from preschool to kindergarten. *Child Development, 58*, 1168–1189.

LaFreniere, P. J., & Sroufe, L. A. (1985). Profiles of peer competence in the prescchol: Interrelations between measures, influence of social ecology, and relation to attachment history. *Developmental Psychology, 21*, 56–69.

Lamb, M. (1978). *Social and personality development.* New York: Holt, Rinehart & Winson.

Lancy, D. F. (1993). *Qualitative research in education.* New York: Longman.

Lancy, D. F. (1996). *Playing on the mother ground: Cultural routines for children's development.* New York: Guilford.

Lasky, R. E., Syrdal-Lasky, A., & Klein, R. E. (1975). VOT discrimination by four to six and a half month old infants from Spanish environments. *Journal of Experimental Child Psychology, 20*, 215–225.

Lawton, J., & Fowler, N. (1989). A description of teacher and child language in two preschool programs. *Early Childhood Research Quarterly, 4*, 407–432.

Lazar, I., & Darlington, R. (1982). Lasting effects of early education. *Monographs of the Society for Research in Child Development, 47*, 2–3.

Lenneberg, E. (1966). *The biological foundations of language*. New York: Wiley.

Lepper, M. R., Greene, D., & Nisbett, R. E. (1973). Undermining children's intrinsic interest with extrinsice rewards: A test of the overjustification hypothesis. *Journal of Personality and Social Psychology, 28*, 129–137.

Lever, J. (1976). Sex differences in the games children play. *Social Problems, 23*, 470–487.

Levin, I., & Druyan, S. (1993). When sociocognitive transaction among peers fails: The case of misconceptions in science. *Child Development, 64*, 1571–1591.

Lewin, K. (1954). Behavior and development as a function of the total situation. In L. Carmichael (Ed.), *Manual of child psychology* (pp. 918–970). New York: Wiley.

Lewis, M., Feiring, C., McGuffog, C., & Jaskir, J. (1984). Predicting psychopathology in six-year-olds from early social relations. *Child Development, 55*, 123–136.

Lewis, M., Young, G., Brooks, J., & Michalson, L. (1975). The beginning of friendship. In M. Lewis & L. Rosenblum (Eds.), *Friendship and peer relations* (pp. 27–66). New York: Wiley.

Lieberman, P. (1967). *Intonations, perceptions, and language*. Cambridge, MA: MIT Press.

Liebert, R. M., & Sprafkin, J. (1988). *The early window: Effects of television on children and youth* (3rd ed.). New York: Pergamon.

Lintz, L. M., Fitzgerald, H. E., & Brackbill, Y. (1967). Conditioning the eyeblink responses to sound in infants. *Psychonomic Science, 7*, 405–406.

Little, A. H., Lipsitt, L. P., & Rovee-Collier, C. (1984). Classical conditioning and retention of the infant's eyelid response: Effects of age and interstimulus interval. *Journal of Experimental Child Psychology, 37*, 512–524.

Locke, J. L. (1983). *Phonological acquisition and chance*. New York: Academic Press.

Locke, J. L. (1993). *The child's path to spoken language*. Cambridge, MA: Harvard University Press.

Locke, J. L. (1994). Phases in the child's development of language. *American Scientist, 82*, 436–445.

Lunzar, F. A., Dolan, T., & Wilkinson, J. E. (1976). The effectiveness of measures of operativity, language and short-term memory in the prediction of reading and mathematical understanding. *British Journal of Educational Psychology, 46*, 295–306.

Maccoby, E. (1988). Gender as a social category. *Developmental Psychology, 24*, 755–765.

Maccoby, E., & Jacklin, C. N. (1987). Gender segregation in childhood. In H. W. Rose (Ed.), *Advances in child development and behavior* (Vol. 20, pp. 239–287). New York: Academic Press.

Maccoby, E., & Martin, J. (1983). Socialization in the context of the family: Parent–child interaction. In M. Hetherington (Ed.), *Handbook of child psychology* (Vol. 4, pp. 1–102). New York: Wiley.

Maccoby, E., & Masters, J. (1970). Attachment and dependency. In P. H. Mussen (Ed.), *Carmichael's manual of child psychology* (Vol. 2, pp. 73–158). New York: Wiley.

Maccoby, E., & Zellner, M. (1970). *Experiments in primary education: Aspects of Project Follow-Through*. New York: Harcourt, Brace, & Jovanovich.

Macfarlane, A. (1975, April). *Olfaction in the development of social preferences in the human neonate*. Paper presented at the CIBA Foundation Symposium 33: Parent–Infant Interaction, Amsterdam.

Mahler, M., Pine, F., & Bergman, A. (1975). *The psychological birth of the human infant*. New York: Basic Books.

Mandler, J. (1997). Representation. In D. Kuhn & R. S. Siegler (Eds.), *Cognition, perception, and language*. New York: Wiley.

Maratsos, M. (1998). The acquisition of grammar. In D. Kuhn & R. S. Siegler (Eds.), *Cognitive, language, and perceptional development* (pp. 421–466). New York: Wiley.

Marcus, G. F. (1995). Children's overregulation of English plurals: A quantitative analysis. *Journal of Child Language, 22*, 447–460.

Marcus, G. F., Pinker, S., Ullman, M., Hollander, M., Rosen, T. J., & Xu, F. (1992). Overregulations in language acquisition. *Monographs of the Society for Research in Child Development, 57* (Serial No. 228).

Marean, G. C., Werner, L. A., & Kuhl, P. K. (1992). Vowel categorization by very young infants. *Developmental Psychology, 28*, 396–405.

Martin, P., & Bateson, P. (1993). *Measuring behavior*. London: Cambridge University Press.

Martin, P., & Caro, T. (1985). On the functions of play and its role in behavioral development. In J. Rosenblatt, C. Beer, M. C. Busnel, & P. Slater (Eds.), *Advances in the study of behavior* (Vol. 15, pp. 59–103). New York: Academic Press.

Matas, L., Arend, R. A., & Sroufe, L. A. (1978). Continuity of adaptation in the second year: The relationship between quality of attachment and later competence. *Child Development, 49*, 547–556.

McCall, R. B. (1980). *Fundamental statistics for psychology*. New York: Holt, Rinehart & Winston.

McCall, R. B. (1977). Challenges to a science of developmental psychology. *Child Development, 48*, 333–344.

McCall, R. B., Appelbaum, M. I., & Hogarty, P. S. (1973). Developmental changes in mental performance. *Monographs of the Society for Research in Child Development, 38* (Serial No. 150).

McCall, R. B., Eichorn, D. H., & Hogarty, P. S. (1977). Transitions in early mental development. *Monographs of the Society for Research in Child Development, 42* (Serial No. 171).

McCandless, B., & Marshall, H. (1957). A picture-sociometric technique for preschool children and its relation to teacher judgments of friendship. *Child Development, 28*, 139–148.

McGrew, W. (1972a). *An ethological study of children's behavior*. New York: Academic Press.

McGrew, W. (1972b). Aspects of social development in nursery school children with emphasis on introduction to the group. In N. Blurton Jones (Ed.), *Ethological studies of child behavior* (pp. 129–156). London: Cambridge University Press.

McLoyd, V. (1980). Verbally expressed modes of transformation in the fantasy and play of black preschool children. *Child Development, 51*, 1133–1139.

McLoyd, V. (1982). Social class differences in social dramatic play: A critique. *Developmental Review, 2*, 1–30.

Mead, G. (1934). *Mind, self, and society*. Chicago: University of Chicago Press.

Mead, M. (1928). *Coming of age in Samoa*. New York: Morrow.

Mead, M. (1930). *Growing up in New Guinea*. New York: Morrow.

Mead, M. (1954). Research on primitive children. In L. Carmichael (Ed.), *Manual of child psychology* (pp. 735–780). New York: Wiley.

Medawar, P. (1976). Does ethology throw any light on human behavior? In P. P. G. Bateson & R. A. Hinde (Eds.), *Growing points in ethology* (pp. 497–506). London: Cambridge University Press.

Mehan, H. (1978). Structuring school structure. *Harvard Educational Review, 48*, 32–64.

Mehan, H. (1979). *Learning lessons*. Cambridge, MA: Harvard University Press.

Melmed, P. J. (1971). Black English phonology: The question of reading interference. *Monographs of the Language-Behavior Research Laboratory, 1*.

Meltzoff, A. N. (1988). Infant imitation after a 1-week delay: Long-term memory for novel acts and multiple stimuli. *Developmental Psychology, 24*, 470–476.

Meltzoff, A. N. (1995). What infant memory tells us about infantile amnesia: Long-term recall and deferred imitation. *Journal of Experimental Child Psychology, 59*, 497–515.

Messick, S. (1994). The interplay of evidence and consequences in the validation of performance assessment. *Educational Researcher, 23*(2), 13–23.

Messick, S. (1995). Validity of psychological assessment. *American Psychologist, 50*, 741–749.

Miller, N. E., & Dollard, J. (1941). *Social learning and imitation*. New Haven, CT: Yale University Press.

Miller, P. A., & Weiss, M. C. (1981). Children's attention allocation, understanding of attention, and performance on the incidental learning task. *Child Development, 57,* 1183–1190.

Miller, P. H. (1990). The development of strategies of selective attention. In D. F. Bjorklund (Ed.), *Children's strategies: Contemporary views of cognitive development* (pp. 157–184). Hillsdale, NJ: Lawrence Erlbaum Associates.

Miller, P. H. (1994). Individual differences in children's strategic behavior: Utilization deficiencies. *Learning and Individual Differences, 6,* 285–307.

Miller, P. H., & Seier, W. L. (1994). Strategy utilization deficiencies in children: When, where and why. In H. W. Reese (Ed.), *Advances in child development and behavior* (Vol. 25, pp. 107–156). New York: Academic Press.

Miller-Jones, D. (1989). Culture and testing. *American Psychologist, 44,* 360–366.

Minuchin, P., & Shapiro, E. (1983). The school as a context for social development. In E. M. Hetherington (Ed.), *Handbook of child psychology* (Vol. 4, pp. 197–274). New York: Wiley.

Money, J., & Ehrhardt, A. A. (1972). *Man and woman, boy and girl.* Baltimore: Johns Hopkins University Press.

Montepare, J. M., & McArthur, L. B. (1986). The influence of facial characteristics on children's age perceptions. *Journal of Experimental Child Psychology, 42,* 303–314.

Moore, B., Underwood, B., & Rosenham, D. (1973). Affect and altruism. *Developmental Psychology, 8,* 99–104.

Moore, B. S., & Eisenberg, N. (1984). The development of altruism. In G. J. Whitehurst (Ed.), *Annals of Child Development* (Vol. 1, pp. 107–174). Greenwich, CT: JAI.

Moore, N., Evertson, C., & Brophy, J. (1974). Solitary play: Some functional reconsideration. *Developmental Psychology, 10,* 830–834.

Moreno, J. (1951). *Sociometry, experimental method, and the science of society.* Beacon, NY: Beacon House.

Mowrer, O. (1960). *Learning theory and symbolic processes.* New York: Wiley.

Moss, E. (1992). Shifting conceptions of validity in educational measurement. *Review of Educational Researcher, 62,* 229–258.

Mueller, E. (1972). The maintenance of verbal exchanges between young children. *Child Development, 43,* 930–938.

Mueller, E., & Brenner, J. (1977). The origins of social skills and interaction among play group toddlers. *Child Development, 48,* 854–861.

Mueller, E., & Lucas, T. (1977). A developmental analysis of peer interaction among toddlers. In M. Lewis & L. Rosenblum (Eds.), *Friendship and peer relations.* New York: Wiley.

Mueller, E., & Rich, A. (1976). Clustering and socially-directed behaviors in a play-group of 1-year-old boys. *Journal of Child Psychology and Psychiatry, 17,* 315–322.

National Association for the Education of Young Children. (1988). NAEYC position statement on developmentally appropriate practice in the primary grades, serving 5- through 8-year-olds. *Young Children, 43*(2), 64–84.

National Association for the Education of Young Children. (1992). *Developmentally appropriate practice in early childhood programs serving infants, toddlers, younger preschoolers.* Washington, DC: Author.

Neil, A. S. (1960). *Summerhill.* New York: Hart.

Neill, S. (1976). Aggressive and non-aggressive fighting in twelve- to thirteen-year-old pre-adolescent boys. *Journal of Child Psychology and Psychiatry, 17,* 213–220.

Nelson, J., & Aboud, F. E. (1985). The resolution of social conflict between friends. *Child Development, 56,* 1009–1017.

Nelson, K. (1974). Variations in children's concepts by age and category. *Child Development, 45,* 577–584.

Nelson, K. (1993). The psychological and social origins of autobiographical memory. *Psychological Science, 4,* 7–14.

Nelson, K. (1996). *Language in cognitive development: The emergence of the mediated mind.* New York: Cambridge University Press.

Nelson, K., & Gruendel, J. (1979). At morning it's lunchtime: A scriptal view of children's dialogue. *Discourse Processes, 2,* 73–94.

Newcomb, A., Brady, J., & Hartup, W. (1979). Friendship and incentive condition as determinants of children's task-oriented behavior. *Child Development, 50,* 878–881.

Newport, E. L. (1990). Maturational constraints on language learning. *Cognitive Science, 14,* 11–28.

Ogbu, J. (1974). *The next generation: An ethnography of education in an urban neighborhood.* New York: Academic Press.

Ogbu, J. (1988). Culture, development, and education. In A. D. Pellegrini (Ed.), *Psychological bases for early education* (pp. 245–274). Chichester: Wiley.

Olweus, D. (1979). Stability and aggressive reaction patterns in males: A review. *Psychological Bulletin, 86,* 852–875.

Olweus, D. (1980). Familial and temperamental determinants of aggressive behavior in adolescent boys: A causal analysis. *Developmental Psychology, 16,* 644–660.

Ornstein, P. A., Gordon, B. N., & Larus, D. M. (1992). Children's memory for a personally experienced event: Implications for testimony. *Applied Developmental Psychology, 6,* 49–60.

Oyama, S. (1976). A sensitive period in the acquisition of a nonnative phonological system. *Journal of Psycholinguistic Research, 5,* 261–285.

Park, K. A., & Water, E. (1989). Security of attachment and preschool friendships. *Child Development, 60,* 1079–1081.

Parker, J., & Asher, S. (1987). Peer relations and later personal adjustment: Are low-accepted children at-risk? *Psychological Bulletin, 102,* 357–389.

Parten, M. (1932). Social participation among preschool children. *Journal of Abnormal and Social Psychology, 27,* 243–269.

Pastor, D. (1981). The quality of mother–infant attachment and its relationship to toddler's initial sociability with peers. *Developmental Psychology, 17,* 326–335.

Patterson, G. (1986). Performance models for anti-social boys. *American Psychologist, 41,* 432–444.

Patterson, G., DeBarsyshe, B., & Ramsey, E. (1989). A developmental perspective on antisocial behavior. *American Psychologist, 44,* 329–335.

Peal, E., & Lambert, W. E. (1962). The relation of bilingualism to intelligence. *Psychological Monographs, 76,* (Serial No. 546).

Pellegrini, A. D. (1980). The relationship between preschoolers' play and achievement in prereading, language, and writing. *Psychology in the Schools, 17,* 530–535.

Pellegrini, A. D. (1982a). Development of preschoolers' social-cognitive play behaviors. *Perceptual and Motor Skills, 5,* 1109–1110.

Pellegrini, A. D. (1982b). Explorations in preschoolers' construction of cohesive text in two play contexts. *Discourse Processes, 5,* 101–108.

Pellegrini, A. D. (1983). The sociolinguistic context of the preschool. *Journal of Applied Developmental Psychology, 4,* 397–405.

Pellegrini, A. D. (1984a). The effect of classroom play centers on preschoolers' functional uses of language. In A. D. Pellegrini & T. Yawkey (Eds.), *The development of oral and written language in social context* (pp. 129–144). Norwood, NJ: Ablex.

Pellegrini, A. D. (1984b). Identifying causal elements in the thematic-fantasy play paradigm. *American Educational Research Journal, 21,* 691–702.

Pellegrini, A. D. (1984c). The social-cognitive ecology of preschool classrooms. *International Journal of Behavioral Development, 7,* 321–332.

Pellegrini, A. D. (1985). The relations between symbolic play and and literate behavior: A review and critique of the empirical literature. *Review of Educational Research, 55,* 207–221.

Pellegrini, A. D. (1987a). The effects of play context on the development of young children's verbalized fantasy. *Semiotica, 65,* 285–293.

Pellegrini, A. D. (1987b). Rough-and-tumble play: Developmental and education significance. *Educational Psychologist, 22,* 23–43.

Pellegrini, A. D. (1988). Elementary school children's rough-and-tumble play and social competence. *Developmental Psychology, 24*, 802–806.

Pellegrini, A. D. (1989a). Elementary school children's rough-and-tumble play. *Early Childhood Research Quarterly, 4*, 245–260.

Pellegrini, A. D. (1989b). What is a category? The care of rough-and-tumble play. *Ethology and Sociobiology, 10*, 331–341.

Pellegrini, A. D. (1992). Ethological studies of the categorization of children's social behavior: A review. *Early Education and Development, 3*, 284–297.

Pellegrini, A. D. (1995). *School recess and playground behavior.* Albany: State University of New York Press.

Pellegrini, A. D. (1996). *Observing children in their natural worlds: A methodological primer.* Mahwah, NJ: Lawrence Erlbaum Associates.

Pellegrini, A. D., & Bjorklund, D. F. (1996). The place of recess in school: Issues in the role of recess in children's education and development: An introduction to the theme issue. *Journal of Research in Childhood Education, 11*, 5–13.

Pellegrini, A. D., & Bjorklund, D. F. (1997). The role of recess in children's cognitive performance. *Educational Psychologist, 32*, 35–40.

Pellegrini, A. D., & Galda, L. (1982). The effects of thematic-fantasy play training on the development of children's story comprehension. *American Educational Research Journal, 19*, 443–455.

Pellegrini, A. D., & Galda, L. (1993). Ten years after: A reexamination of the symbolic play and literacy research. *Reading Research Quarterly, 28*, 163–175.

Pellegrini, A. D., Galda, L., & Flor, D. (1997). Relationships, individual differences, and children's use of literate language. *British Journal of Educational Psychology, 67*, 139–152.

Pellegrini, A. D., Galda, L., & Rubin, D. (1984). Context in text: The development of oral and written language in two genres. *Child Development, 55*, 1549–1555.

Pellegrini, A. D., & Horvat, M. (1995). A developmental contextual critique of attention deficit hyperactivity disorder. *Educational Researcher, 24*, 13–19.

Pellegrini, A. D., & Perlmutter, J. (1989). Classroom contextual effects on children's play. *Developmental Psychology, 25*, 289–296.

Pellegrini, A. D., Perlmutter, J., Galda, L., & Brody, G. (1990). Joint reading between Black Head Start children and their mothers. *Child Development, 61*, 441–453.

Pellegrini, A. D., & Smith, P. K. (1998). Physical activity play: The nature and function of a neglected aspect of play. *Child Development, 69*, 577–598.

Pellegrini, D. S., Masten, A., Garmezy, N., & Ferrarese, M. (1987). Correlations of social competence in middle childhood. *Journal of Child Psychology and Psychiatry, 28*, 699–714.

Perner, J. (1991). *Understanding the representational mind.* Cambridge, MA: MIT Press.

Perner, J., Leekam, S., & Wimmer, H. (1987). The three-year-olds' difficulty with false belief: The case for a conceptual deficit. *British Journal of Developmental Psychology, 5*, 125–137.

Pettit, G. S., Dodge, K. A., & Brown, M. M. (1988). Early family experience, social problem solving patterns, and children's social competence. *Child Development, 59*, 107–120.

Phyffe-Perkins, E. (1980). Children's behavior in preschool settings: A review of research concerning the influence of the physical environment. In L. Katz (Ed.), *Current topics in early childhood education* (pp. 91–126). Norwood, NJ: Ablex.

Piaget, J. (1930). *The child's conception of physical causality.* London: Routledge & Kegan Paul.

Piaget, J. (1952). *The origins of intelligence in children.* New York: Norton.

Piaget, J. (1954). *The construction of reality in the child.* New York: Basic Books.

Piaget, J. (1955). *The language and thought of the child.* New York: World.

Piaget, J. (1962). *Play, dreams, and imitations.* New York: Norton.

Piaget, J. (1965a). *The child's conception of number.* New York: Norton.

Piaget, J. (1965b). *The moral development of the child.* New York: The Free Press.

Piaget, J. (1967). Genesis and structure in the psychology of intelligence. In J. Piaget (Ed.), *Sic psychological studies* (pp. 143–158). New York: Vintage.

Piaget, J. (1969). *The child's conception of the world.* Totowa, NJ: Littlefield & Adams.

Piaget, J. (1970). Piaget's theory. In P. Mussen (Ed.), *Carmichael's manual of child psychology* (Vol. 1, pp. 703–732). New York: Wiley.

Piaget, J. (1972). Intellectual evolutions from adolescence to adulthood. *Human Development, 15,* 1–12.

Piaget, J. (1977). The role of action in the development of thinking. In W. F. Overton & J. M. Gallagher (Eds.), *Knowledge and development* (pp. 17–42). New York: Plenum Press.

Piaget, J. (1983). Piaget's theory. In J. H. Flavell & E. M. Markman (Eds.), *Cognitive development* (pp. 103–128). New York: Wiley.

Piaget, J., & Inhelder, B. (1967). *The child's conception of space.* New York: Norton.

Piaget, J., & Inhelder, B. (1969). *The psychology of the child.* New York: Basic Books.

Pinker, S. (1994). *The language instinct: How the mind creates language.* New York: Morrow.

Plumert, J. M. (1995). Relations between children's overestimation of their physical abilities and accident proneness. *Developmental Psychology, 31,* 866–876.

Poole, D. A., & White, L. T. (1991). Effects of question repetition on the eyewitness testimony of children and adults. *Developmental Psychology, 27,* 975–986.

Prugh, D., Staub, E., Sands, H., Kirschbaum, R., & Lenihan, E. (1953). A study of the emotional reactions of children in families to hospitalization and illness. *American Journal of Orthopsychiatry, 23,* 70–106.

Radkye-Yarrow, M., Zahn-Waxler, C., & Chapman, N. (1983). Children's prosocial dispositions and behavior. In E. Hetherington (Ed.), *Handbook of child psychology* (Vol. 4, pp. 469–546). New York: Wiley.

Recht, D. R., & Leslie, L. (1988). Effect of prior knowledge on good and poor reader's memory for text. *Journal of Educational Psychology, 80,* 16–20.

Reese, H. W. (1962). Verbal mediation as a function of age level. *Psychological Bulletin, 59,* 502–509.

Renshaw, P. (1981). The roots of current peer interaction research: A historical analysis of the 1930s. In S. Asher & J. Gootman (Eds.), *The development of children's friendships* (pp. 1–28). New York: Cambridge University Press.

Resnick, L. (1987). Learning in and out of school. *Educational Researcher, 16,* 13–20.

Reynolds, G. S. (1968). *A primer of operant conditioning.* Glenview, IL: Scott Foresman.

Rice, M. L. (1989). Children's language acquisition. *American Psychologist, 44,* 149–156.

Rice, M. L., Huston, A. C., Truglio, R., & Wright, J. (1990). Words from "Sesame Street": Learning vocabulary while viewing. *Developmental Psychology, 26,* 421–428.

Rist, R. (1970). Student social class and teacher expectations. *Harvard Educational Review, 39,* 411–415.

Rogoff, B. (1990). *Apprenticeship in thinking: Cognitive development in social context.* New York: Oxford University Press.

Rogoff, B. (1998). Cognition as a collaborative process. In D. Kuhn & R. S. Siegler (Eds.), *Cognition language, and perceptual development* (Vol. 2, pp. 679–744). New York: Wiley.

Rogoff, B., & Morelli, G. (1989). Perspectives on children's development from cultural psychology. *American Psychologist, 44,* 343–348.

Rondal, J. A., Ghiotto, M., Bredart, S., & Bachelet, J. F. (1987). Age-relation, reliability, and grammatical validity of measures of utterance length. *Journal of Child Language, 14,* 433–446.

Rosemond, J. K. (1981). *Parent power.* New York: Pocket.

Ross, H. S., & Lollis, S. P. (1989). A social relations analysis of the peer relationships. *Child Development, 60,* 1082–1091.

Rubenstein, J., & Howes, C. (1976). The effects of peers on toddler interaction with mothers and toys. *Child Development, 47,* 597–605.

Rubin, K. (1982). Nonsocial play in preschoolers: Necessary evil. *Child Development, 53,* 651–657.

Rubin, K., & Clark, L. (1982, April). *Preschool teachers' ratings of behavioral problems: Observational, sociometric, and social cognitive*. Paper presented at the annual meeting of the American Educational Research Association, New York.

Rubin, K., & Daniels-Beirness, T. (1983). Concurrent and predictive correlates of sociometric status in kindergarten and first grade. *Merrill–Palmer Quarterly, 29*, 337–351.

Rubin, K., Fein, G., & Vandenberg, B. (1983). *Play*. In E. M. Hetherington (Ed.), *Handbook of child psychology* (Vol. 4, pp. 693–774). New York: Wiley.

Rubin, K., & Maioni, T. (1975). Play preference and its relationship to ecogentrism, popularity, and classification skills in preschoolers. *Merrill–Palmer Quarterly, 21*, 171–179.

Rubin, K., Maioni, T., & Hornung, M. (1976). Free play behaviors in middle- and lower-class preschoolers: Parten and Piaget revisited. *Child Development, 47*, 414–419.

Rubin, K., Watson, R., & Jambor, T. (1978). Free-play behaviors in preschool and kindergarten children. *Child Development, 49*, 534–536.

Rutter, M. (1985). Family and school influences. In A. R. Nicol (Ed.), *Longitudinal studies of child psychology and psychiatry* (pp. 357–403). London: Wiley.

Rutter, M., Maughan, B., Mortimore, P., & Ouston, J. (1979). *Fifteen thousand hours*. Cambridge, MA: Harvard University Press.

Sabin, E. J., Clemmer, E. J., O'Connell, D. C., & Kowal, S. (1979). A pausological approach to speech development. In A. W. Siegman & S. Feldstein (Eds.), *Of speech and time: Temporal speech patterns in interpersonal contexts* (pp. 35–55). Hillsdale, NJ: Lawrence Erlbaum Associates.

Sachs, J. (1977). The adaptive significance of linguistic input to prelinguistic infants. In C. E. Snow & C. A. Ferguson (Eds.), *Talking to children: Language input and acquisition* (pp. 51–61). Cambridge, England: Cambridge University Press.

Sackett, G., Gluck, J., & Ruppertral, G. (1978). Introduction. In G. Sackett (Ed.), *Observing behavior* (Vol. 11, pp. 1–14)). Baltimore: University Park Press.

Sackett, G., Sameroff, A., Cairns, R., & Suomi, S. (1981). Continuity in behavioral development: Theoretical and empirical issues. In K. Immelmann, G. Barlow, L. Petrinovich, & M. Main (Eds.), *Behavioral development* (pp. 23–57). New York: Cambridge University Press.

Saltz, E., Dixon, D., & Johnson, J. (1977). Training disadvantaged preschoolers on various fantasy activities: Effects on cognitive functioning and impulse control. *Child Development, 48*, 367–380.

Samalin, N. (1987). *Loving your child is not enough: Positive discipline that works*. New York: Viking.

Sattler, J. M. (1988). *Assessment of children*. San Diego: Author.

Savage-Rumbaugh, E. S., Murphy, J., Sevcik, R. A., Brakke, K. E., Williams, S. L., & Rumbaugh, D. M. (1993). Language acquisition in ape and child. *Monographs of the Society for Research in Child Development, 58* (Serial No. 233).

Saxe, G., Guberman, S., & Gearhart, M. (1987). Social processes in early number development. *Monographs of the Society for Research in Child Development, 52* (Serial No. 216).

Scarr, S., Phillips, D., & McCartney, K. (1990). Facts, fantasies and the future of child care in the United States. *Psychological Science, 1*, 26–35.

Schneider, W. (1985). Developmental trends in the metamemory–memory behavior relationship: An integrated review. In D. L. Forrest-Pressley, G. E. MacKinnon, & T. G. Waller (Eds.), *Cognitive, metacognition, and human performance* (pp. 57–109). New York: Academic Press.

Schneider, W. (1991, April). *Performance prediction in young children: Effects of skill, metacognition, and wishful thinking*. Paper presented at the annual meeting of the Society for Research in Child Development, Seattle, WA.

Schneider, W., & Bjorklund, D. F. (1998). Memory. In D. Kuhn & R. S. Siegler (Eds.), *Cognitive, language, and perceptual development* (pp. 467–521). New York: Wiley.

Schneider, W., Bjorklund, D. F., & Maier-Brückner, W. (1996). The effects of expertise and IQ on children's memory: When knowledge is and when it is not enough. *International Journal of Behavioral Development, 19*, 773–796.

Schneider, W., Korkel, J., & Weinert, F. E. (1989). Domain-specific knowledge and memory performance: A comparison of high- and low-aptitude children. *Journal of Educational Psychology, 81*, 306–312.

Schneider, W., Korkel, J., & Weinert, F. E. (1990). Expert knowledge, general abilities, and text processing. In W. Schneider & F. E. Weinert (Eds.), *Interactions among aptitude, strategies, and knowledge in cognitive performance* (pp. 235–251). New York: Springer-Verlag.

Schumann, J. (1993). Some problems with falsification: An illustration from SLA research. *Applied Linguistics, 14*, 295–306.

Schwartz, J. (1972). Effects of peer familiarity on the behavior of preschoolers in a novel situation. *Journal of Personality and Social Psychology, 24*, 1276–1284.

Sears, R., Maccoby, E., & Levin, H. (1957). *Patterns of child rearing*. Evanston, IL: Row & Peterson.

Shaffer, D. R. (1993). *Social and personal development* (3rd ed.). Pacific Grove, CA: Brooks/Cole.

Shantz, C. (1987). Conflicts between children. *Child Development, 58*, 283–305.

Sheingold, K., & Tenney, Y. (1982). Memory for a salient childhood event. In U. Neisser (Ed.), *Memory observed: Remembering in natural contexts* (pp. 201–212). San Francisco: W. H. Freeman.

Shelton, W., Stevens, S., & Tucker, W. (1960). *The varieties of human physique*. New York: Harper.

Shiffrin, R. M., & Schneider, W. (1977). Controlled and automatic human information processing: II. Perceptual learning, automatic attending, and a general theory. *Psychological Review, 84*, 129–190.

Siegler, R. S. (1988). Individual differences in strategy choices: Good student, not-so-good students, and perfectionists. *Child Development, 59*, 833–851.

Siegler, R. S. (1996). *Emerging minds: The process of change in children's thinking*. New York: Oxford University Press.

Siegler, R. S., & Jenkins, E. (1989). *How children discover strategies*. Hillsdale, NJ: Lawrence Erlbaum Associates.

Siegler, R. S., Robinson, M., Liebert, D. E., & Liebert, R. M. (1973). Inhelder and Piaget's pendulum problem: Teaching preadolescents to act as scientists. *Developmental Psychology, 9*, 97–101.

Sigel, I. (1965). Developmental considerations of the nursery school experience. In P. Neubauer (Ed.), *Concepts of development in early childhood education* (pp. 84–111). Springfield, IL: Thomas.

Singer, J. L. (1980). The power and limitations of television: A cognitive affective analysis. In P. H. Tannenbaum & R. Abeles (Eds.), *The entertainment functions of television*. London: Academic Press.

Skeels, H., M., & Dye, H. B. (1939). A study of the effects of differential stimulation on mentally retarded children. *Program of the American Association of Mental Deficiency, 44*, 114–136.

Skinner, B. F. (1957). *Verbal behavior*. New York: Appleton-Century-Crofts.

Slavin, R. E. (1990). *Cooperative learning: Theory, research, and practice*. Boston: Allyn & Bacon.

Slobin, D. I. (1970). Universals of grammatical development in children. In G. B. Flores, J. Arcais, & W. J. M. Levelt (Eds.), *Advances in psycholinguistics*. Amsterdam: North-Holland.

Smilansky, S. (1968). *The effects of sociodrama play on disadvantaged preschool children*. New York: Wiley.

Smith, M. (1926). An investigation of the development of the sentence and the extent of vocabulary in young children. *University of Iowa Studies in Child Welfare, 3*(5).

Smith, P. K. (1976). Ethological methods. In B. Foss (Ed.), *New perspectives in child development* (pp. 87–137). London: Penguin.

Smith, P. K. (1982). Does play matter? Functions and evolutionary aspects of animal and human play. *The Behavioral and Brain Scienes, 5*, 139–184.

Smith, P. K. (1985). The reliability and validity of one/zero sampling: Misconceived criticisms and unacknowledged assumptions. *British Educational Research Journal, 11*, 215–220.

Smith, P. K. (1988). The play ethos. In A. D. Pellegrini (Ed.) *Psychological bases for early education* (pp. 207–226). Chichester: Wiley.

Smith, P. K., & Connolly, K. (1972). Patterns of play and social interaction in preschool children. In N. Blurton Jones (Ed.), *Ethological studies in child behavior* (pp. 64–96). New York: Cambridge University Press.

Smith, P. K., & Connolly, K. (1980). *The ecology of preschool behavior.* New York: Cambridge University Press.

Smith, P. K., & Hagan, T. (1980). Effects of deprivation on exercise play in nursery school children. *Animal Behavior, 28*, 922–928.

Smith, P. K., & Sluckin, A. (1979). Ethology, ethogeny etics, emics, biology, and culture: On the limitations of dichotomies. *European Journal of Social Psychology, 9*, 397–415.

Smith, P. K., Takhvar, M., Gore, N., & Vollstedt, R. (1985). Play in young children: Problems of definition, categorization, and measurement. *Early Child Development and Care, 19*, 37–54.

Smith, P. K., & Vollstedt, R. (1985). Defining play: An empirical study of the relationship between play and various play criteria. *Child Development, 56*, 1042–1050.

Snow, C. E., & Ferguson, C. A. (Eds.). (1977). *Talking to children: Language input and acquisition.* Cambridge, England: Cambridge University Press.

Snyderman, M., & Rothman, S. (1987). Survey of expert opinion on intelligence and aptitude testing. *American Psychologist, 42*, 137–144.

Socha, T. J., & Socha, D. M. (1994). Children's task-group communication. In L. R. Frey (Ed.), *Group communication in context: Studies of natural groups* (pp. 227–246). Hillsdale, NJ: Lawrence Erlbaum Associates.

Spear, N. E. (1984). Ecologically determined dispositions control the ontogeny of learning and memory. In R. V. Kail, Jr., & N. E. Spear (Eds.), *Comparative perspectives on the development of memory* (pp. 325–358). Hillsdale, NJ: Lawrence Erlbaum Associates.

Spelke, E. S. (1991). Physical knowledge in infancy: Reflection on Piaget's theory. In S. Carey & R. Gelman (Ed.), *Epigenesis of mind: Essays in biology and knowledge* (pp. 133–169). Hillsdale, NJ: Lawrence Erlbaum Associates.

Spelke, E. S., & Newport, E. (1998). Nativism, empiricism, and the development of knowledge. In R. M. Lerner (Ed.), *Cognitive, language, and perceptual development* (pp. 275–340). New York: Wiley.

Spitz, R. A. (1946). Hospitalism. *Psychoanalytical Study of the Child, 2*, 113–117.

Spitz, R. A. (1965). *The first year of life.* New York: International Universities Press.

Spivak, G., & Shure, M. (1974). *Social adjustment of young children.* San Francisco: Jossey-Bass.

Sroufe, L. (1979). The coherence of individual development: Early care, attachment and subsequent developmental issues. *American Psychologist, 34*, 834–841.

Sroufe, L., & Fleeson, J. (1986). Attachment and the construction of relationships. In W. Hartup & Z. Rubin (Eds.), *Relationships and development* . Hillsdale, NJ: Lawrence Erlbaum Associates.

Stahl, S., & Miller, P. (1989). Whole language and language experience approaches for beginning reading: A quantitative research synthesis. *Review of Educational Research, 59*, 87–116.

Staat, A. (1971). Linguistic-mentalistic theory versus an explanatory S-R learning theory of language development. In D. Slobin (Ed.), *The ontogenesis of grammar* (pp. 103–152). New York: Academic Press.

Stark, R. (1979). Prespeech segmental feature development. In P. Fletcher & M. Garman (Eds.), *Language acquisition.* New York: Cambridge University Press.

Stebbin, L., St. Pierre, R., Proper, E., Anderson, R., & Gerva, T. (1976). *Education as experimentation: A planned variation model* (Vol. 4-A). Cambridge, MA: Abt.

Steinberg, L., Dornbusch, S. M., & Brown, B. B. (1992). Ethnic differences in adolescent achievement. *American Psychologist, 47*, 723–729.

Steinberg, L., Elmen, J. D., & Mounts, N. J. (1989). Authoritative parenting, psychosocial maturity and academic success in adolescents. *Child Development, 60,* 1424–1436.

Steinberg, L., Mounts, N. S., Lamborn, S. D., & Dornbusch, S. M. (1991). Authoritative parenting and adolescent adjustment across varied ecological niches. *Journal of Research in Adolescence, 1,* 19–36.

Stipek, D. (1984). Young children's performance expectations: Logical analysis or wishful thinking? In J. G. Nicholls (Ed.), *Advances in motivation and achievement: The development of achievement motivation* (Vol. 3, pp. 33–56). Greenwich, CT: JAI.

Stipek, D., & Daniels, D. (1988). Declining perceptions of competence: A consequence of changes in the child or the educational environment? *Journal of Educational Psychology, 80,* 352–356.

Stoel-Gammon, C., & Menn, L. (1997). Phonological development: Learning sounds and sound patterns. In J. Berko Gleason (Ed.), *The development of language* (pp. 69–121). Boston, MA: Allyn & Bacon.

Stone, C. A., & Day, M. C. (1978). Levels of availability of a formal operational strategy. *Child Development, 49,* 1054–1065.

Stone, L. (1976). *Family and fortune: Studies in aristocratic finance in the 16th and 17th centuries.* Oxford, England: Claredon.

Strayer, J. (1980). A naturalistic study of empathetic behaviors and their relation to affective states and perspective taking skills in preschool children. *Child Development, 51,* 815–822.

Sullivan, K., & Winner, E. (1993). Three-year-olds' understanding of mental states: The influence of trickery. *Journal of Experimental Child Psychology, 56,* 135–148.

Suomi, S. J., & Harlow, H. F. (1972). Social rehabilitation of isolate-reared monkeys. *Developmental Psychobiology, 6,* 487–496.

Super, C. M. (1976). Environmental effects on motor development: The case of "African infant precocity." *Developmental Medicine and Child Neurology, 18,* 561–567.

Super, C. M., & Harkness, S. (1986). The developmental niche. *International Journal of Behavioral Development, 9,* 545–569.

Thelen, E., & Ulrich, B. D. (1991). Hidden skills. *Monographs of the Society for Research in Child Development, 56*(1, Serial No. 223).

Thompson, J. R., & Chapman, R. S. (1977). Who is "Daddy" revisited? The status of two-year-olds' overextended words in use and comprehension. *Journal of Child Language, 4,* 359–375.

Tinbergen, N. (1963). On aims and methods of ethology. *Zietschrift fur Tierpsychologil, 20,* 410–433.

Tonkova-Yompol'skaya, R. V. (1969). Development of speech intonation in infants during the first two years of life. *Soviet Psychology, 7,* 48–54.

Trehub, S. E., Trainor, L. J., & Unyk, A. M. (1993). Music and speech processing in the first year of life. In H. W. Reese (Ed.), *Advances in child development and behavior* (Vol. 24, pp. 2–35). San Diego, CA: Academic Press.

Tudge, J. R. H. (1992). Processes and consequences of peer collaboration: A Vygotskian analysis. *Child Development, 63,* 1364–1379.

Umbel, V. M., Pearson, B. Z., Fernandez, S. C., & Oller, D. K. (1992). Measuring bilingual children's receptive vocabularies. *Child Development, 63,* 1012–1020.

Underwood, B., Froming, W., & Moore, B. (1977). Mood, attention, and altruism: A search for mediating variables. *Developmental Psychology, 13,* 541–542.

Uzgiris, I. C., & Hunt, J. McV. (1975). *Assessment infancy: Original scales of psychological development.* Urbana: University of Illinois Press.

Vandell, D. L. (1980). Sociability with peers and mother during the first year. *Developmental Psychology, 16,* 355–361.

Vandell, D. L., Henderson, V. K., & Wilson, K. S. (1988). A longitudinal study of children with day-care experiences of varying quality. *Child Development, 59,* 1286–1292.

Vygotsky, L. S. (1962). *Thought and language.* Cambridge: MIT Press. (Original work published 1934)

Vygotsky, L. S. (1967). Play and its role in the mental development of the child. *Soviet Psychology, 12,* 62–76.

Vygotsky, L. S. (1978). *Mind in society.* Cambridge, MA: Harvard University Press.

Wachs, T. D. (1985, March). *Measurement of the environment in the study of the organism environment interaction.* Paper presented at the biennial meeting of the Society for the Study of Child Development, Seattle, WA.

Walker, C. H. (1987). Relative importance of domain knowledge and overall aptitude in acquisition of domain-related information. *Cognition and Instruction, 4,* 25–42.

Walsh, D. J., Tobin, J. J., & Graue, M. E. (1993). The interpretive voice: Qualitative research in early childhood education. In B. Spodek (Ed.), *Handbook of research in early childhood education* (pp. 464–476). New York: Macmillan.

Warren, A. R., & McCloskey, L. A. (1997). Language in social contexts. In J. Berko-Gleason (Ed.), *The development of language* (pp. 210–258). Boston: Allyn & Bacon.

Waters, E., & Sroufe, L. (1983). Social competence as a developmental construct. *Developmental Review, 3,* 79–97.

Watson, J. B., & Raynor, R. A. (1920). Conditional emotional reactions. *Journal of Experimental Psychology, 3,* 1–14.

Wechsler, D. (1974). *Manual for the Wechsler Intelligence Scale for Children–Revised.* New York: Psychological Corporation.

Wellman, H. M. (1977). Tip of the tongue and feeling of knowing experiences: A developmental study of memory monitoring. *Child Development, 48,* 13–21.

Wellman, H. M. (1988). The early development of memory strategies. In F. Weinert & M. Perlmutter (Eds.), *Memory development: Univeral changes and individual differences* (pp. 3–29). Hillsdale, NJ: Lawrence Erlbaum Associates.

Wellman, H. M. (1990). *The child's theory of mind.* Cambridge, MA: MIT Press.

Werker, J. F., Gilbert, J. H. V., Humphrey, K., & Tees, R. C. (1981). Developmental aspects of cross-language speech perception. *Child Development, 52,* 349–355.

Werner, E. (1988). A cross-cultural perspective on infancy. *Journal of Cross-Cultural Psychology, 19,* 96–113.

Wertsch, J. V. (1985). *Vygotsky and the social formation of mind.* Cambridge, MA: Harvard University Press.

Wertsch, J. V., & Tulviste, P. (1992). L. S. Vygotsky and contemporary developmental psychology. *Developmental Psychology, 28,* 548–557.

Whalen, C. (1983). Hyperactivity, learning problems, and attention deficit disorder. In T. Ollenick & M. Hersen (Eds.), *Handbook of child psychology* (pp. 151–199). New York: Plenum.

White, B., & Watts, J. (1973). *Experience and environment.* Englewood Cliffs, NJ: Prentice-Hall.

White, S. H., & Pillemer, D. B. (1979). Childhood amnesia and the development of a socially accessible memory system. In J. F. Kihlstrom & F. J. Evans (Eds.), *Functional disorders of memory* (pp. 29–73). Hillsdale, NJ: Lawrence Erlbaum Associates.

Whitehurst, G. J., & Sonnenschein, S. (1985). The development of communication: A functional analysis. In G. J. Whitehurst (Ed.), *Annals of child development* (Vol. 2, pp. 1–48). Greenwich, CT: JAI.

Whitting, B., & Edwards, C. (1973). A cross-cultural analysis of sex-differences in the behavior of children age three through 11. *Journal of Social Psychology, 91,* 171–188.

Wilcox, J., & Webster, E. (1980). Early discourse behavior: An analysis of children's responses to listener feedback. *Child Development, 51,* 1120–1125.

Wilcox, K. (1982). Ethnography as a methodology and its application to the study of schooling: A review. In G. Spinder (Ed.), *Doing the ethnography of schooling* (pp. 456–488). New York: Holt, Rinehart & Winston.

Willatts, P. (1990). Development of problem-solving strategies in infancy. In D. F. Bjorklund (Ed.), *Children's strategies: Contemporary views of cognitive development* (pp. 23–66). Hillsdale, NJ: Lawrence Erlbaum Associates.

Williams, E. (1965). An ecological orientation in psychology. *Merrill–Palmer Quarterly, 11*, 317–343.

Wilson, M. (1989). Child development in the context of the Black extended family. *American Psychologist, 44*, 380–385.

Wimmer, H., & Perner, J. (1983). Beliefs about beliefs: Representation and constraining function of wrong beliefs in young children's understanding of deception. *Cognition, 13*, 103–128.

Witelson, S. F. (1987). Neurobiological aspects of language in children. *Child Development, 58*, 653–688.

Wolcott, H. F. (1982). Mirrors, models, and monitors: Educator adaptations of the ethnographic innovation. In G. Spinder (Ed.), *Doing the ethnography of schooling* (pp. 68–95). New York: Holt, Rinehart & Winston.

Wolf, D., & Grollman, S. (1982). Ways of playing. In D. Pepler & K. Rubin (Eds.), *The play of children* (pp. 46–63). Basel, Switzerland: Karger.

Wood, D., Bruner, J. S., & Ross, G. (1976). The role of tutoring in problem-solving. *Journal of Child Psychology and Psychiatry, 17*, 89–100.

Wright, M. (1980). Measuring the social competence of preschool children. *Canadian Journal of Behavioral Science, 12*, 17–32.

Yussen, S. R., & Levy, V. M., Jr. (1975). Developmental changes in predicting one's own span of short-term memory. *Journal of Experimental Child Psychology, 19*, 502–508.

Zigler, E., & Trickett, P. (1978). I.Q., social competence, and evaluation of early childhood intervention programs. *American Psychologist, 33*, 789–798.

Author Index

Subject Index